we the media

# we the media

## GRASSROOTS JOURNALISM
## BY THE PEOPLE, FOR THE PEOPLE

## DAN GILLMOR

O'REILLY®

BEIJING · CAMBRIDGE · FARNHAM · KÖLN · PARIS · SEBASTOPOL · TAIPEI · TOKYO

## We the Media
by Dan Gillmor

Published by O'Reilly Media, Inc., 1005 Gravenstein Highway North, Sebastopol, CA 95472.

O'Reilly Media books may be purchased for educational, business, or sales promotional use. Online editions are also available for most titles (*safari.oreilly.com*). For more information, contact our corporate/institutional sales department: (800) 998-9938 or *corporate@oreilly.com*.

| | |
|---|---|
| **Editor:** | Allen Noren |
| **Production Editor:** | Mary Brady |
| **Cover Designer:** | Emma Colby |
| **Interior Designer:** | Melanie Wang |

**Printing History:**

| | |
|---|---|
| July 2004: | First Edition. |

ISBN: 0-596-00733-7
[C]

# Contents

*Freedom of the press is limited to those who own one.*

—A. J. Liebling

*If you don't like the news...go out and make some of your own.*

—Wes "Scoop" Nisker

# Introduction

We freeze some moments in time. Every culture has its frozen moments, events so important and personal that they transcend the normal flow of news.

Americans of a certain age, for example, know precisely where they were and what they were doing when they learned that President Franklin D. Roosevelt died. Another generation has absolute clarity of John F. Kennedy's assassination. And no one who was older than a baby on September 11, 2001, will ever forget hearing about, or seeing, airplanes exploding into skyscrapers.

In 1945, people gathered around radios for the immediate news, and stayed with the radio to hear more about their fallen leader and about the man who took his place. Newspapers printed extra editions and filled their columns with detail for days and weeks afterward. Magazines stepped back from the breaking news and offered perspective.

Something similar happened in 1963, but with a newer medium. The immediate news of Kennedy's death came for most via television; I'm old enough to remember that heartbreaking moment when Walter Cronkite put on his horn-rimmed glasses to glance at a message from Dallas and then, blinking back tears, told his viewers that their leader was gone. As in the earlier time, newspapers and magazines pulled out all the stops to add detail and context.

September 11, 2001, followed a similarly grim pattern. We watched—again and again—the awful events. Consumers of news learned the *what* about the attacks, thanks to the television networks that showed the horror so graphically. Then we learned some of the *how* and *why* as print publications and thoughtful broadcasters worked to bring depth to events that defied mere words. Journalists did some of their finest work and made me proud to be one of them.

But something else, something profound, was happening this time around: news was being produced by regular people who had something to say and show, and not solely by the "official" news organizations that had traditionally decided how the first draft of history would look. This time, the first draft of history was being written, in part, by the former audience. It was possible—it was inevitable—because of new publishing tools available on the Internet.

Another kind of reporting emerged during those appalling hours and days. Via emails, mailing lists, chat groups, personal web journals—all nonstandard news sources—we received valuable context that the major American media couldn't, or wouldn't, provide.

We were witnessing—and in many cases were part of—the future of news.

Six months later came another demonstration of tomorrow's journalism. The stakes were far lower this time, merely a moment of discomfort for a powerful executive. On March 26, 2002, poor Joe Nacchio got a first-hand taste of the future; and this time, in a small way, I helped set the table.

Actually, Nacchio was rolling in wealth that day, when he appeared at PC Forum, an exclusive executive conference in suburban Phoenix. He was also, it seemed, swimming in self-pity.

In those days Nacchio was the chief executive of regional telephone giant Qwest, a near-monopoly in its multistate marketplace. At the PC Forum gathering that particular day, he was complaining about difficulties in raising capital. Imagine: whining about the rigors of running a monopoly, especially when Nacchio's own management moves had contributed to some of the difficulties he was facing.

I was in the audience, reporting in something close to real time by publishing frequent conference updates to my weblog, an online journal of short web postings, via a wireless link the conference had set up for attendees. So was another journalist weblogger, Doc Searls, senior editor of Linux Journal, a software magazine.

Little did we know that the morning's events would turn into a mini-legend in the business community. Little did I know that the experience would expand my understanding of how thoroughly the craft of journalism was changing.

One of my posts noted Nacchio's whining, observing that he'd gotten seriously richer while his company was losing much of its market value—another example of CEOs raking in the riches while shareholders, employees, and communities got the shaft. Seconds later I received an email from Buzz Bruggeman, a lawyer in Florida, who was following my weblog and Searls's from his office in Orlando. "Ain't America great?" Bruggeman wrote sarcastically, attaching a hyperlink to a Yahoo! Finance web page showing that Nacchio had cashed in more than $200 million in stock while his company's stock price was heading downhill. This information struck me as relevant to what I was writing, and I immediately dropped this juicy tidbit into my weblog, with a cyber-tip of the hat to Bruggeman. ("Thanks, Buzz, for the link," I wrote parenthetically.) Doc Searls did likewise.

"Around that point, the audience turned hostile," wrote Esther Dyson, whose company, Edventure Holdings, held the conference.[1] Did Doc and I play a role? Apparently. Many people in the luxury hotel ballroom—perhaps half of the executives, financiers, entrepreneurs, and journalists—were also online that morning. And at least some of them were amusing themselves by following what Doc and I were writing. During the remainder of Nacchio's session, there was a perceptible chill toward the man. Dyson, an investor and author, said later she was certain that our weblogs helped create that chill.[2] She called the blogging "a second conference occurring around, through, and across the first."

Why am I telling this story? This was not an earth-shaking event, after all. For me, however, it was a tipping point.

Consider the sequence of news flow: a feedback loop that started in an Arizona conference session, zipped to Orlando, came back to Arizona and ultimately went global. In a world of satellite communications and fiber optics, real-time journalism is routine; but now we journalists had added the expertise of the audience.

Those forces had lessons for everyone involved, including the "newsmaker"—Nacchio—who had to deal with new pressures on the always edgy, sometimes adversarial relationship between journalists and the people we cover. Nacchio didn't lose his job because we poked at his arrogance; he lost it, in the end, because he did an inadequate job as CEO. But he got a tiny, if unwelcome, taste of journalism's future that morning.

The person in our little story who tasted journalism's future most profoundly, I believe, was neither the professional reporter nor the newsmaker, but Bruggeman. In an earlier time, before technology had collided so violently with journalism, he'd been a member of an audience. Now, he'd received news about an event without waiting for the traditional coverage to arrive via newspapers or magazines, or even web sites. And now he'd become part of the journalistic process himself—a citizen reporter whose knowledge and quick thinking helped inform my own journalism in a timely way.

Bruggeman was no longer just a consumer. He was a producer. He was making the news.

This book is about journalism's transformation from a 20th century mass-media structure to something profoundly more grassroots and democratic. It's a story, first, of evolutionary change. Humans have always told each other stories, and each new era of progress has led to an expansion of storytelling.

This is also a story of a modern revolution, however, because technology has given us a communications toolkit that allows anyone to become a journalist at little cost and, in theory, with global reach. Nothing like this has ever been remotely possible before.

In the 20th century, making the news was almost entirely the province of journalists; the people we covered, or "news-makers"; and the legions of public relations and marketing people who manipulated everyone. The economics of publishing and broadcasting created large, arrogant institutions—call it Big Media, though even small-town newspapers and broadcasters exhibit some of the phenomenon's worst symptoms.

Big Media, in any event, treated the news as a lecture. We told you what the news was. You bought it, or you didn't. You might write us a letter; we might print it. (If we were television and you complained, we ignored you entirely unless the com-plaint arrived on a libel lawyer's letterhead.) Or you cancelled your subscription or stopped watching our shows. It was a world that bred complacency and arrogance on our part. It was a gravy train while it lasted, but it was unsustainable.

Tomorrow's news reporting and production will be more of a conversation, or a seminar. The lines will blur between pro-ducers and consumers, changing the role of both in ways we're only beginning to grasp now. The communication network itself will be a medium for everyone's voice, not just the few who can afford to buy multimillion-dollar printing presses, launch satel-lites, or win the government's permission to squat on the public's airwaves.

This evolution—from journalism as lecture to journalism as a conversation or seminar—will force the various communities of interest to adapt. Everyone, from journalists to the people we cover to our sources and the former audience, must change their ways. The alternative is just more of the same.

We can't afford more of the same. We can't afford to treat the news solely as a commodity, largely controlled by big insti-tutions. We can't afford, as a society, to limit our choices. We can't even afford it financially, because Wall Street's demands on Big Media are dumbing down the product itself.

There are three major constituencies in a world where anyone can make the news. Once largely distinct, they're now blurring into each other.

*Journalists*

We will learn we are part of something new, that our readers/listeners/viewers are becoming part of the process. I take it for granted, for example, that my readers know more than I do—and this is a liberating, not threatening, fact of journalistic life. Every reporter on every beat should embrace this. We will use the tools of grassroots journalism or be consigned to history. Our core values, including accuracy and fairness, will remain important, and we'll still be gatekeepers in some ways, but our ability to shape larger conversations—and to provide context—will be at least as important as our ability to gather facts and report them.

*Newsmakers*

The rich and powerful are discovering new vulnerabilities, as Nacchio learned. Moreover, when anyone can be a journalist, many talented people will try—and they'll find things the professionals miss. Politicians and business people are learning this every day. But newsmakers also have new ways to get out their message, using the same technologies the grassroots adopts. Howard Dean's presidential campaign failed, but his methods will be studied and emulated because of the way his campaign used new tools to engage his supporters in a conversation. The people at the edges of the communications and social networks can be a newsmaker's harshest, most effective critics. But they can also be the most fervent and valuable allies, offering ideas to each other and to the newsmaker as well.

*The former audience*

Once mere consumers of news, the audience is learning how to get a better, timelier report. It's also learning how to join the process of journalism, helping to create a massive conversation and, in some cases, doing a better job than the professionals. For example, Glenn Reynolds, a.k.a. "Instapundit," is not just one of the most popular webloggers; he has amassed considerable influence in the process. Some grassroots journalists will become professionals. In the end, we'll have more voices and more options.

I've been in professional journalism for almost 25 years. I'm grateful for the opportunities I've had, and the position I hold. I respect and admire my colleagues, and believe that Big Media does a superb job in many cases. But I'm absolutely certain that the journalism industry's modern structure has fostered a dangerous conservatism—from a business sense more than a political sense, though both are apparent—that threatens our future. Our resistance to change, some of it caused by financial concerns, has wounded the journalism we practice and has made us nearly blind to tomorrow's realities.

Our worst enemy may be ourselves. Corporate journalism, which dominates today, is squeezing quality to boost profits in the short term. Perversely, such tactics are ultimately likely to undermine us.

Big Media enjoys high margins. Daily newspapers in typically quasi-monopoly markets make 25–30 percent or more in good years. Local TV stations can boast margins north of 50 percent. For Wall Street, however, no margin is sufficiently rich, and next year's profits must be higher still. This has led to a hollowing-out syndrome: newspaper publishers and broadcasting station managers have realized they can cut the amount and quality of journalism, at least for a while, in order to raise profits. In case after case, the demands of Wall Street and the greed of investors have subsumed the "public trust" part of journalism. I don't believe the First Amendment, which gives journalists valuable leeway to inquire and publish, was designed with corporate profits in mind. While we haven't become a wholly cynical business yet, the trend is scary.

Consolidation makes it even more worrisome. Media companies are merging to create ever larger information and entertainment conglomerates. In too many cases, serious journalism—and the public trust—continue to be victims. All of this leaves a journalistic opening, and new journalists—especially citizen journalists—are filling the gap.

Meanwhile, even as greed and consolidation take their toll, those historically high margins are under attack. Newspapers, for example, have two main revenue streams. The smaller by far comes from circulation: readers who pay to have the paper delivered at home or buy it from a newsstand. The larger is advertising, from employment classifieds to retail display ads, and every one of those ad revenue streams is under attack from competitors like eBay and craigslist, which can happily live on lower margins (or, as in the case of eBay, the world's largest classified-advertising site, establish a new monopoly) and don't care at all about journalism.

In the long term, I can easily imagine an unraveling of the business model that has rewarded me so well, and—despite the effect of excessive greed in too many executive suites—has managed to serve the public respectably in vital ways. Who will do big investigative projects, backed by deep pockets and the ability to pay expensive lawyers when powerful interests try to punish those who exposed them, if the business model collapses? Who would have exposed the Watergate crimes in the absence of powerful publishers, especially *The Washington Post*'s Katharine Graham, who had the financial and moral fortitude to stand up to Richard Nixon and his henchmen. At a more prosaic level, who will serve, for better or worse, as a principal voice of a community or region? Flawed as we may be in the business of journalism, anarchy in news is not my idea of a solution.

A world of news anarchy would be one in which the big, credible voices of today were undermined by a combination of forces, including the financial ones I just described. There would be no business model to support the institutional journalism that, for all its problems, does perform a public service. Credibility matters. People need, and want, trusted sources—and those sources have been, for the most part, serious journalists. Instead of journalism organizations with the critical mass to fight the good fights, we may be left with the equivalent of countless pamphleteers and people shouting from soapboxes. We need something better.

Happily, the anarchy scenario doesn't strike me as probable, in part because there will always be a demand for credible news and context. Also possible, though I hope equally unlikely, is a world of information lockdown. The forces of central control are not sitting quietly in the face of challenges to their authority.

In this scenario, we could witness an unholy alliance between the entertainment industry—what I call the "copyright cartel"—and government. Governments are very uneasy about the free flow of information, and allow it only to a point. Legal clampdowns and technological measures to prevent copyright infringement could bring a day when we need permission to publish, or when publishing from the edge feels too risky. The cartel has targeted some of the essential innovations of tomorrow's news, such as the peer-to-peer file sharing that does make infringement easier but also gives citizen journalists one of the only affordable ways to distribute what they create. Governments insist on the right to track everything we do, but more and more politicians and bureaucrats shut off access to what the public needs to know—information that increasingly surfaces through the efforts of nontraditional media.

In short, we cannot just assume that self-publishing from the edges of our networks—the grassroots journalism we need so desperately—will survive, much less thrive. We will need to defend it, with the same vigor we defend other liberties.

Instead of a news anarchy or lockdown, I seek a balance that simultaneously preserves the best of today's system and encourages tomorrow's emergent, self-assembling journalism. In the following pages, I hope to make the case that it's not just necessary, and perhaps inevitable, but also eminently workable for all of us.

It won't be immediately workable for the people who already get so little attention from Big Media. Today, citizen journalism is mostly the province of what my friend and former newspaper editor Tom Stites calls "a rather narrow and very privileged slice of the polity—those who are educated enough to take part in the wired conversation, who have the technical skills, and who are affluent enough to have the time and equipment." These are the very same people we're leaving behind in our Brave New Economy. They are everyday people, buffeted by change, and outside the conversation. To our discredit, we have not listened to them as well as we should.

The rise of the citizen journalist will help us listen. The ability of anyone to make the news will give new voice to people who've felt voiceless—and whose words we need to hear. They are showing all of us—citizen, journalist, newsmaker—new ways of talking, of learning.

In the end, they may help spark a renaissance of the notion, now threatened, of a truly informed citizenry. Self-government demands no less, and we'll all benefit if we do it right.

Let's have this conversation, for everyone's sake.

# Chapter 1

# From Tom Paine to Blogs and Beyond

We may have noticed the new era of journalism more clearly after the events of September 11, but it wasn't invented on that awful day. It did not emerge fully formed or from a vacuum. What follows doesn't pretend to be a history of journalism. Rather, these are observations, including some personal experiences that help illustrate the evolution of what we so brazenly call "new media."

At the risk of seeming to slight the contributions from other nations, I will focus mostly on the American experience. America, born in vocal dissent, did something essential early on. The U.S. Constitution's First Amendment has many facets, including its protection of the right of protest and practice of religion, but freedom of speech is the most fundamental part of a free society. Thomas Jefferson famously said that if given the choice of newspapers or government, he'd take the newspapers. Journalism was that important to society, he insisted, though as president, attacked by the press of his day, he came to loathe what he'd praised.

Personal journalism is also not a new invention. People have been stirring the pot since before the nation's founding; one of the most prominent in America's early history was Ben Franklin, whose *Pennsylvania Gazette* was civic-minded and occasionally controversial.

There were also the pamphleteers who, before the First Amendment was enshrined into law and guaranteed a free press, published their writings at great personal risk. Few Americans can appreciate this today, but journalists are still dying elsewhere in the world for what they write and broadcast.

One early pamphleteer, Thomas Paine, inspired many with his powerful writings about rebellion, liberty, and government in the late 18th century. He was not the first to take pen to paper in hopes of pointing out what he called common sense, nor in trying to persuade people of the common sense of his ideas. Even more important, perhaps, were the (at the time) anonymous authors of the Federalist Papers. Their work, analyzing the proposed Constitution and arguing the fundamental questions of how the new Republic might work, has reverberated through history. Without them, the Constitution might never have been approved by the states. The Federalist Papers were essentially a powerful conversation that helped make a nation.

There have been several media revolutions in U.S. history, each accompanied by technological and political change. One of the most crucial, Bruce Bimber notes in his book, *Information and American Democracy*,[3] was the completion of the final parts, in the early to middle 1800s, of what was then the most dependable and comprehensive postal system in the world. This unprecedented exercise in governmental assistance should be seen, Bimber argues, as "a kind of Manhattan project of communication" that helped fuel the rise of the first truly mass medium, newspapers. The news, including newspapers, was cheaply and reliably distributed through the mail.[4]

For most of American history, newspapers dominated the production and dissemination of what people widely thought of as news. The telegraph—a revolutionary tool from the day in 1844 when Samuel Morse's partner Alfred Vail dispatched the message "What hath God wrought?" from Baltimore to Washington D.C.—sped up the collection and transmission of the news. Local papers could now gather and print news of distant events.[5]

Newspapers flourished throughout the 19th century. The best were aggressive and timely, and ultimately served their readers well. Many, however, had little concern for what we now call objectivity. Papers had points of view, reflecting the politics of their backers and owners.

Newspapers have provoked public opinion for as long as they've been around. "Yellow journalism" achieved perhaps its ugliest prominence when early media barons such as Joseph Pulitzer and William Randolph Hearst abused their considerable powers. Hearst, in particular, is notorious for helping to spark the Spanish-American War in 1898 by inflaming public opinion.

As the Gilded Age's excesses began to tear at the very fabric of American society, a new kind of journalist, the muckraker, emerged at the end of the 19th century. More than most journalists of the era, muckrakers performed the public service function of journalism by exposing a variety of outrages, including the anticompetitive predations of the robber barons and cruel conditions in workplaces. Lincoln Steffens (*The Shame of the Cities*), Ida Tarbell (*History of the Standard Oil Company*), Jacob Riis (*How the Other Half Lives*), and Upton Sinclair (*The Jungle*) were among the daring journalists and novelists who shone daylight into some dark corners of society. They helped set the stage for the Progressive Era, and set a standard for the investigative journalists of the new century.

Personal journalism didn't die with the muckrakers. Throughout the 20th century, the world was blessed with individuals who found ways to work outside the mainstream of the moment. One of my journalistic heroes is I.F. Stone, whose weekly newsletter was required reading for a generation of Washington insiders. As Victor Navasky wrote in the July 21, 2003 issue of *The Nation*, Stone eschewed the party circuit in favor of old-fashioned reporting:

> His method: To scour and devour public documents, bury himself in The Congressional Record, study obscure Congressional committee hearings, debates and reports, all the time prospecting for news nuggets (which would appear as boxed paragraphs in his paper), contradictions in the official line,

examples of bureaucratic and political mendacity, documentation of incursions on civil rights and liberties. He lived in the public domain.[6]

A generation of journalists learned from Stone's techniques. If we're lucky, his methods will never go out of fashion.


## THE CORPORATE ERA

But in the 20th century, the big business of journalism—the corporatization of journalism—was also emerging as a force in society. This inevitable transition had its positive and negative aspects.

I say "inevitable" for several reasons. First, industries consolidate. This is in the nature of capitalism. Second, successful family enterprises rarely stayed in the hands of their founders' families; inheritance taxes forced some sales and breakups, and bickering among siblings and cousins who inherited valuable properties led to others. Third, the rules of American capitalism have been tweaked in recent decades to favor the big over the small.

As noted in the *Introduction*, however, the creation of Big Media is something of an historical artifact. It stems from a time when A.J. Liebling's famous admonition, that freedom of the press was for those people who owned a press, reflected financial reality. The economics of newspaper publishing favored bigness, and local monopolies came about because, in most communities, readers would support only one daily newspaper of any size.[7]

Broadcasting has played a key role in the transition to consolidation. Radio, then television, lured readers and advertisers away from newspapers,[8] contributing to the consolidation of the newspaper industry. But the broadcasters were simultaneously turning into the biggest of Big Media. As they grew, they brought the power of broadcasting to bear on the news, to great effect. Edward R. Murrow's reports on CBS, most notably his coverage of the wretched lives of farm workers and the evil politics of Joe McCarthy, were proud moments in journalism.

The news hegemony of the networks and big newspapers reached a peak in the 1960s and 1970s. Journalists helped bring down a law-breaking president. An anchorman, Walter Cronkite, was considered the most trusted person in America. Yet this was an era when news divisions of the major networks lost money but were nevertheless seen as the crown jewels for their prestige, fulfilling a longstanding (and now all but discarded) mandate to perform a public service function in their communities. The networks were sold to companies such as General Electric and Loews Corp., which saw only the bottom line. News divisions were required to be profit centers.

While network news may have been expensive to produce, local stations had it easier. But while the network news shows still retained some sense of responsibility, most local stations made no pretense of serving the public trust, preferring instead to lure viewers with violence and entertainment, two sure ratings boosters. It was an irresistible combination for resource-starved news directors: cheaper than serious reporting, and compelling video. "If it bleeds, it leads" became the all-too-true mantra for the local news reports, and it has stayed that way, with puerile celebrity "journalism" now added to the mix.

America has suffered from this simplistic view of news. Even in the 1990s, when crime rates were plummeting, local TV persisted in giving viewers the impression that crime was never a bigger problem. This was irresponsible because, among other things, it helped feed a tough-on-crime atmosphere that has stripped away crucial civil liberties—including most of our Fourth Amendment protection against unreasonable searches and seizures—and kept other serious issues off the air.

As the pace of life has quickened, our collective attention span has shortened. I suppose it's asking too much of commercial TV news to occasionally use the public airwaves to actually inform the public, but the push for profits has crowded out depth. The situation is made worse by the fact that most of us don't stop long enough to consider what we've been told, much less seek out context, thereby allowing ourselves to be shallow and to be led by people who take advantage of it. A shallow citizenry can be turned into a dangerous mob more easily than an informed one.

At the same time, big changes were occurring in TV journalism, and big newspaper companies were swallowing small papers around the nation. As noted, this didn't always reduce quality. In fact, the craft of newspaper journalism has never been better in some respects; investigative reporting by the best organizations continues to make me proud. And while some corporate owners—Gannett in particular—have tended to turn independent papers into cookie-cutter models of corporate journalism, sometimes they've actually improved on the original. But it's no coincidence that three of the best American newspapers, *The New York Times*, *The Wall Street Journal*, and *The Washington Post*, have an ownership structure—voting control by families and/or small groups of committed investors—that lets them take the long view no matter what Wall Street demands in the short term. Nor should it surprise anyone that these organizations are making some of the most innovative use of the Internet as they expand their horizons in the digital age.

It was cable, a technology that originally expanded broadcast television's reach in the analog age, which turned television inside out. Originally designed to get broadcast signals into hard-to-reach mountain valleys, cable grew into a power center in its own right when system owners realized that the big money was in more densely populated areas. Cable systems were monopolies in the communities they served, and they used the money in part to bring more channel capacity onto their systems.

The cable channel that changed the news business forever, of course, was Ted Turner's Cable News Network (CNN). We've forgotten what a daring experiment this was, given its subsequent success. At the time it was launched on June 1, 1980, many in the media business considered CNN little more than a bizarre corporate ego trip. As it turned out, CNN punched a hole in a dam that was already beginning to crumble from within.

Even if cable was bringing more choices, however, it was still a central point of control for the owner of the cables. Cable companies decided which package of channels to offer. Oh, sure, customers had a choice: yes or no. As we'll see in Chapter 11, cable is becoming part of a broadband duopoly that could threaten information choice in the future.

## FROM OUTSIDE IN

During this time of centralization and corporate ownership, the forces of change were gathering at the edges. Some forces were technological, such as the microprocessor that led straight to the personal computer, and a federally funded data-networking experiment called the ARPANET, the precursor to the Internet. Some were political and/or judicial, such as Supreme Court decisions that forced AT&T to let third parties plug their own phones into Ma Bell's network, and another that made it legal for purchasers of home videotape machines to record TV broadcasts for subsequent viewing.

Personal choice, assisted by the power of personal technology, was in the wind.

I got my first personal computer in the late 1970s. In the early 1980s, when I first became a journalist, I bought one of the earliest portable personal computers, an Osborne, and used it to write and electronically transmit news stories to publications such as *The New York Times* and *The Boston Globe*, for which I was freelancing from Vermont. I was enthralled by this fabulous tool that allowed me, a lone reporter in what were considered the boondocks, to report the news in a timely and efficient manner.

The commercial online world was in its infancy in those days, and I couldn't resist experimenting with it. My initial epiphany about the power of cyberspace came in 1985. I'd been using a word processor called XyWrite, the PC program of choice for serious writers in those days. It ran fast on the era's slow computers, and had an internal programming language, called XPL, that was both relatively easy to learn and incredibly capable. One day I found myself stymied by an XPL problem. I posted a short message on a word-processing forum on Compu-Serve, the era's most successful commercial online service. A day later, I logged on again and was greeted with solutions to my little problem from people in several U.S. cities and, incredibly, Australia.[9]

I was amazed. I'd tapped the network, asking for help. I'd been educated. This, I knew implicitly, was a big deal.

Of course, I didn't fully get it. I spent the 1986–87 academic year on a fellowship at the University of Michigan, which in those days was at the heart of the Internet—then still a university, government, and research network of networks—without managing to notice the Internet. John Markoff of *The New York Times*, the first major newspaper reporter to understand the Net's value, had it pretty much to himself in those days as a journalist, and got scoop after scoop as a result. One way he acquired information was by reading the Internet's public message boards. Collectively called Usenet, they were and still are a grab bag of "newsgroups" on which anyone with Net access can post comments. Usenet was, and remains, a useful resource.[10]

CompuServe wasn't the only way to get online in the 1980s. Other choices included electronic bulletin boards, known as BBS. They turned into technological cul-de-sacs, but had great value at the time. You'd dial into a local BBS via a modem on your computer, read and write messages, download files, and get what amounted to a local version of the Internet and systems such as CompuServe. You'd find a variety of topics on all of these systems, ranging from aviation to technology to politics, whatever struck the fancy of the people who used them.

Fringe politics found their way onto the bulletin boards early on. I was a reporter for the *Kansas City Times* in the mid-1980s and spent the better part of a year chasing groups such as the Posse Commitatus around the Farm Belt. This and other virulently antiestablishment organizations found ready ears amid a rural economic depression that made it easier to recruit farmers and other small-town people who felt they were victims of banks and governments. I found my way onto several online boards operated by radical groups; I never got very deep into the systems because the people running them understood the basics of security. Law-enforcement officials and others who watched the activities of the radicals told me at the time that the BBS was one of the radical right's most effective tools.[11]

## RANSOM-NOTE MEDIA

Personal technology wasn't just about going online. It was about the creation of media in new and, crucially, less expensive ways. For example, musicians were early beneficiaries of computer technology.[12] But it was desktop publishing where the potential for journalism became clearest.

A series of inventions in the mid-1980s brought the medium into its new era. Suddenly, with an Apple Macintosh and a laser printer, one could easily and cheaply create and lay out a publication. Big publishing didn't disappear—it adapted by using the technology to lower costs—but the entry level moved down to small groups and even individuals, a stunning liberation from the past.

There was one drawback of having so much power and flexibility in the hands of nonprofessionals. In the early days of desktop publishing, people tended to use too many different fonts on a page, a style that was likened, all too accurately, to ransom notes. But the typographical mishmash was a small price to pay for all those new voices.

Big Media was still getting bigger in this period, but it wasn't noticing the profound demographic changes that had been reshaping the nation for decades. Newsrooms, never mind coverage, scarcely reflected the diversity. Desktop publishing and its progeny created an opening for many new players to enter, not least of which was the ethnic press.

Big Media has tried to adapt. Newsrooms are becoming more diverse. Major media companies have launched or bought popular ethnic publications and broadcasters. But independent ethnic media has continued to grow in size, quality, and credibility: grassroots journalism ascendant.[13]

## OUT LOUD AND OUTRAGEOUS

Meanwhile, talk radio was also becoming a force, though not an entirely new one by any means. Radio has featured talk programs throughout its history, and call-in shows date back as far as 1945. Opinionated hosts, mostly from the political right, such as Father Coughlin, fulminated about government, taxes, cultural breakdowns, and a variety of issues they and their listeners were convinced hadn't received sufficient attention from the mainstream media. These hosts were as much entertainers as commentators, and their shows drew listeners in droves.

But modern talk radio had another crucial feature: the participation of the audience. People—regular people—were invited to have their say on the radio. Before that, regular people had no immediate or certain outlet for their own stories and views short of letters to the editor in newspapers. Now they could be part of the program, adding the weight of their own beliefs to the host's.

The people making this news were in the audience. Howard Kurtz, media writer for *The Washington Post*, believes that talk radio predated, and in many ways anticipated, the weblog phenomenon. Both mediums, he told me, reach out to and connect with "a bunch of people who are turned off by the mainstream media." Kurtz now writes a blog-like online column[14] for the *Post* in addition to his regular stories and column.

Talk radio wasn't, and isn't, just about political anger, even if politics and other issues of the day are the normal fodder. The genre has also become a broader sounding board. Doctors offer advice (including TV's fictional "Frasier Crane"), computer gurus advise non-geeks on what to buy, and lawyers listen to bizarre legal woes.

Talk radio gave me another mini-epiphany about the future of news. In the mid-1990s, not long after I moved to California, a mild but distinct earthquake rattled my house one day. I listened as a local talk station, junking its scheduled topics, took calls from around the San Francisco Bay Area, and got on-the-spot reports from everyday citizens in their homes and offices.

## THE WEB ERA EMERGENT

As the 1990s arrived, personal computers were becoming far more ubiquitous. Relatively few people were online, except perhaps on corporate networks connecting office PCs; college campuses; bulletin boards; or still-early, pre-web commercial services such as CompuServe and America Online. But another series of breakthroughs was about to move us into a networked world.

In 1991, Tim Berners-Lee created the hypertext technology that became the World Wide Web. He wrote software to serve, or dish out, information from connected computers, and a "client" program that was, in effect, the first browser. He also sparked the development of Hypertext Markup Language, or HTML, which allowed anyone with a modest amount of knowledge to publish documents as web pages that could be easily linked to other pages anywhere in the world. Why was this so vital? We could now move from one site and document to another with the click of a mouse or keyboard stroke. Berners-Lee had connected the global collection of documents the Net had already created, but he wanted to take the notion a step further: to write onto this web, not just read from it.

But there's something Berners-Lee purposely *didn't* do. He didn't patent his invention. Instead, he gave the world an open and extensible foundation on which new innovation could be built.

The next breakthrough was Mosaic, one of the early graphical web browsers to run on popular desktop operating systems. These browsers were a basis for the commercial Internet. The browser, and the relative ease of creating web pages, sparked some path-breaking experiments in what we now recognize as personal journalism. Let's note one of the best and earliest examples.

Justin Hall was a sophomore at Swarthmore College in 1993 when he heard about the Web. He coded some pages by hand in HTML. His "Justin's Links from the Underground"[15] may well have been the first serious weblog, long before specialized weblog software tools became available. The first visitor to Hall's site from outside the university came in 1994. He explained his motivations in an email:

> Why did I do it? The urge to share of oneself, to join a great global knowledge sharing party. The chance to participate in something cool. A deep geek archivist's urge to experiment with documenting and archiving personal media and experience. In college I realized that Proust and Joyce would have loved the web, and they likely would have tried a similar experiment—they wrote in hypertext, about human lives.
>
> It was journalism, but I was mostly reporting on me. In the early days, I wrote about the web, on the web, because few

other people were doing so. Once search engines and link directories emerged, I didn't need to catalog everything online. So I enjoyed having a tool to map my thoughts and experiences, and a chance to connect those thoughts and experiences to the rest of the electrified English-speaking world!

What had happened? Communications had completed a transformation. The printing press and broadcasting are a one-to-many medium. The telephone is one-to-one. Now we had a medium that was anything we wanted it to be: one-to-one, one-to-many, and many-to-many. Just about anyone could own a digital printing press, and have worldwide distribution.[16]

None of this would have surprised Marshall McLuhan. Indeed, his seminal works, especially *Understanding Media: The Extensions of Man*[17] and *The Medium is the Message*,[18] presaged so much of what has occurred. As he observed in the introduction to *Understanding Media*:

> After three thousand years of explosion, by means of fragmentary and mechanical technologies, the Western world is imploding. During the mechanical ages we had extended our bodies in space. Today, after more than a century of electric technology, we have extended our central nervous system itself in a global embrace, abolishing both space and time as far as our planet is concerned. Rapidly, we approach the final phase of the extensions of man—the technological simulation of consciousness, when the creative process of knowing will be collectively and corporately extended to the whole of human society, much as we have already extended our senses and our nerves by the various media.

Nor would it have come as a shock to Alvin Toffler, who explained in *The Third Wave*[19] how manufacturing technology had driven a wedge between producers and customers. Mass manufacturing drove down the unit cost of production but at the cost of something vital: a human connection with the buyer. Information technology, he said, would lead—among many other things—to mass customization, disintermediation (elimination of middlemen), and media convergence.

Perhaps no document of its time was more prescient about the Web's potential than the *Cluetrain Manifesto*,[20] which first appeared on the Web in April 1999. It was alternately pretentious and profound, with considerably more of the latter quality. Extending the ideas of McLuhan and many others, the four authors—Rick Levine, Christopher Locke, Doc Searls, and David Weinberger—struck home with me and a host of other readers who knew innately that the Net was powerful but weren't sure how to define precisely why.

"A powerful global conversation has begun," they wrote. "Through the Internet, people are discovering and inventing new ways to share relevant knowledge with blinding speed. As a direct result, markets are getting smarter—and getting smarter faster than most companies."

They explained why the Net is changing the very nature of business. "Markets are conversations," proclaimed their first of 95 theses with elegant simplicity.

Journalism is also a conversation, I realized. *Cluetrain* and its antecedents have become a foundation for my evolving view of the trade.

## WRITING THE WEB

The scene was now set for the rise of a new kind of news. But some final pieces had yet to be put in place. One was technological: giving everyday people the tools they needed to join this emerging conversation. Another was cultural: the realization that putting the tools of creation into millions of hands could lead to an unprecedented community. Adam Smith, in a sense, was creating a collective.

The toolmakers did, and continue to do, their part. And with the neat irony that has a habit of appearing in this transformation, a programmer's annoyance with journalists had everything to do with one of the most important developments.

Dave Winer had written and sold an outlining tool called "More," a Macintosh application.[21] He was a committed and knowledgeable Mac developer, but in the early 1990s, he found himself more and more annoyed by a trade press that, in his view, was getting the story all wrong.

At the time, Microsoft Windows was becoming more popular, and the hype machine was pronouncing Apple to be a troubled and, perhaps, terminally wounded company. Troubled, yes. But when the computer journalists persisted in saying, in effect, "Apple is dead, and there's no Macintosh software development anymore," Winer was furious. He decided to go around the established media, and with the rise of the Internet, he had a medium.

He published an email newsletter called "DaveNet." It was biting, opinionated, and provocative, and it reached many influential people in the tech industry. They paid attention. Winer's critiques could be abrasive, but he had a long record of accomplishments and deep insight.

Winer never really persuaded the trade press to give the Mac the ink it deserved. For its part, Apple made strategic mistakes that alienated software developers and helped marginalize the platform. And Windows, with the backing of Microsoft's roughhouse business tactics that turned into outright lawbreaking, became dominant.

But Winer realized he was onto something. He'd found journalism wanting, and he bypassed it. Then he expanded on what he'd started. Like Justin Hall, he created a newsy page in what later became known as the blog format—most recent material at the top.

In the late 1990s, Winer and his team at UserLand Software[22] rewrote an application called Frontier. One collection of new functions was given the name *Manila*, and it was one of the first programs that made it easy for novices to create their own blogs. My first blog was created on the beta version of Manila. Winer has suggested that traditional journalism will wither in the face of what he helped spawn. I disagree, but his contributions to the craft's future have been pivotal.

## OPEN SOURCING THE NEWS

The development of the personal computer may have empowered the individual, but there were distinct limits. One was software code itself. Proprietary programs were like black boxes. We could see what they did, but not how they worked.

This situation struck Richard Stallman, among others, as wrong. In January 1984, Stallman quit his post at the Massachusetts Institute of Technology's Artificial Intelligence Lab. He formally launched a project to create a free operating system and desktop software based on the Unix operating system that ran on many university computers.[23] Stallman's ideas ultimately became the foundation for Linux, the open source operating system that brought fame to Linus Torvalds.[24]

The goal of Stallman's work, then and now, was to ensure that users of computers always had free software programs for the most basic and important tasks. Free, in this case, was more about freedom than about cost. Stallman and others in this movement thought that the programming instructions—the source code—of free software had to be open for inspection and modification by anyone. In the late 1990s, as Linux was gaining traction in the marketplace, and as many free software applications and operating systems were available, the movement got another name: open source, describing the open availability of the source code.[25]

Open source software projects are a digital version of a small-town tradition: the barn raising. But open source projects can involve people from around the world. Most will never meet except online. Guided by project leaders—Torvalds in the case of Linux—they contribute bits and pieces of what becomes a whole package. Open source software, in many cases, is as good as or better than the commercial variety. And these programs are at the heart of the Internet's most basic functions: open source software powers most of the web server computers that dish out information to our browsers.

When the code is open for inspection, it's safer to use because people can find and fill the security holes. Bugs, the annoying flaws that cause program crashes and other unexpected behavior, can be found and fixed more easily, too.[26]

What does this have to do with tomorrow's journalism? Plenty.

Yochai Benkler, a Yale University law professor who has written extensively on the open source phenomenon, has made a strong case that this emergent style of organization applies much more widely than software. In a 2002 essay, "Coase's Penguin,"[27] he said the free software style could work better than the traditional capitalist structure of firms and markets in some circumstances. In particular, he said that it "has systematic advantages over markets and managerial hierarchies when the object of production is information or culture, and where the physical capital necessary for that production—computers and communications capabilities—is widely distributed instead of concentrated."

He could have been describing journalism. In his essay, and in the course of several long conversations we've had in the past several years, Benkler has made the case that several of the building blocks are already in place to augment Big Media, if not substitute it outright, with open source techniques.

He told me that bloggers and operators of independent news sites already do a respectable job of scanning for and sorting news for people who want it. The editorial function has been adopted not just by bloggers, but by a host of new kinds of online news operations. Some peer-reviewed news sites, such as the collaborative Kuro5hin,[28] which describes itself as "technology and culture, from the trenches," are doing interesting journalism by any standard, with readers contributing the essays and deciding which stories make it to the top of the page.

According to Benkler, only in the area of investigative journalism does Big Media retain an advantage over open source journalism. This is due to the resources Big Media can throw at an investigation. In Chapter 9, I will argue that even here, the grassroots are making serious progress.

In my own small sphere, I'm convinced that this already applies. If my readers know more than I do (which I know they do), I can include them in the process of making my journalism better. While there are elements of open source here, I'm not describing an entirely transparent process. But new forms of journalistic tools, such as the Wiki (which I'll discuss in the next chapter), are entirely transparent from the outset. More are coming.

An open source philosophy may produce better journalism at the outset, but that's just the start of a wider phenomenon. In the conversational mode of journalism I suggested in the *Introduction*, the first article may be only the beginning of the conversation in which we all enlighten each other. We can correct our mistakes. We can add new facts and context.[29]

If we can raise a barn together, we can do journalism together. We already are.

## TERROR TURNS JOURNALISM'S CORNER

By the turn of the new century, the key building blocks of emergent, grassroots journalism were in place. The Web was already a place where established news organizations and newcomers were plying an old trade in updated ways, but the tools were making it easier for anyone to participate. We needed a catalyst to show how far we'd come. On September 11, 2001, we got that catalyst in a terrible way.

I was in South Africa. The news came to me and four other people in a van, on the way to an airport, via a mobile phone. Our driver's wife called from Johannesburg, where she was watching TV, to say a plane had apparently hit the World Trade Center. She called again to say another plane had hit the other tower, and yet again to report the attack on the Pentagon. We arrived at the Port Elizabeth airport in time to watch, live and in horror, as the towers disintegrated.

The next day our party of journalists, which the Freedom Forum, a journalism foundation, had brought to Africa to give talks and workshops about journalism and the Internet, flew to Lusaka, Zambia. The BBC and CNN's international edition were on the hotel television. The local newspapers ran considerable news about the attacks, but they were more preoccupied with an upcoming election, charges of corruption, and other news that was simply more relevant to them at the moment.

What I could not do in those initial days was read my newspaper, the *San Jose Mercury News*, or the *The New York Times*, *San Francisco Chronicle*, *The Wall Street Journal*, or any of the other papers I normally scanned each morning at home. I could barely get to their web sites because the Net connection to Zambia was slow and trans-Atlantic data traffic was overwhelming as people everywhere went online for more information, or simply to talk with each other.

I could retrieve my email, however, and my inbox overflowed with useful news from Dave Farber, one of the new breed of editors.

Then a telecommunications professor at the University of Pennsylvania, Farber had a mailing list called "Interesting People"[30] that he'd run since the mid-1980s. Most of what he sent out had first been sent to him by correspondents he knew from around the nation and the world. If they saw something they thought he'd find interesting, they sent it along, and Farber relayed a portion of what he received, sometimes with his own commentary. In the wake of the attacks, his correspondents' perspectives on issues ranging from national-security issues to critiques of religion became essential reading for their breadth and depth. Farber told me later he'd gone into overdrive, because this event obliged him to do so.

"I consider myself an editor in a real sense," Farber explained. "This is a funny form of new newspaper, where the Net is sort of my wire service. My job is to decide what goes out and what doesn't...Even though I don't edit in the sense of real editing, I make the choices."

One of the emails Farber sent, dated September 12, still stands out for me. It was an email from an unidentified sender who wrote: "SPOT infrared satellite image of Manhattan, acquired on September 11 at 11:55 AM ET. Image may be freely reproduced with 'CNES/SPOT Image 2001' copyright attribution." A web address, linking to the photo, followed. The picture showed an ugly brown-black cloud of dust and debris hanging over much of lower Manhattan. The image stayed with me.

Here was context.

Back in America, members of the then nascent weblog community had discovered the power of their publishing tool. They offered abundant links to articles from large and small news organizations, domestic and foreign. New York City bloggers posted personal views of what they'd seen, with photographs, providing more information and context to what the major media was providing.

"I'm okay. Everyone I know is okay," Amy Phillips wrote September 11 on her blog, "The 50 Minute Hour."[31] A Brooklyn blogger named Gus wrote: "The wind just changed direction and now I know what a burning city smells like. It has the smell of burning plastic. It comes with acrid brown skies with jet fighters flying above them. The stuff I'm seeing on teevee is like some sort of bad Japanese Godzilla movie, with less convincing special effects. Then I'm outside, seeing it with my naked eyes."[32]

Meg Hourihan was a continent away, in San Francisco. A cofounder of Pyra Labs, creator of Blogger, another of the early blogging tools (now owned by Google), she pointed to other blogs that day and urged people to give blood. The next day she wrote, in part: "24 hours later, I'm heading back into the kitchen to finish up the dishes, to pick up the spatula that still sits in the sink where I dropped it. I'm going to wash my coffee press and brew that cup of coffee I never had yesterday. I'm going to try and find some semblance of normalcy in this very changed world."[33]

Also in California that day, a little known Afghan-American writer named Tamim Ansary sent an impassioned email to some friends. His message was in part cautionary, observing that while America might want to bomb anything that moved in Afghanistan, we couldn't bomb it back to the Stone Age, as some talk show hosts were urging. The Asian nation, he argued, was already there. Ansary's email circulated among a widening circle of friends and acquaintances. By September 14, it had appeared on a popular weblog and on Salon, a web magazine.[34] Within days, Ansary's words of anguish and caution had spread all over America.

Ansary's news had flowed upward and outward. At the outset, no one from a major network had ever heard of him. But what he said had sufficient authority that people who knew him spread his message, first to their own friends and ultimately to web journalists who spread it further. Only then did the mass media discover it and take it to a national audience. This was the best kind of grassroots collaboration with Big Media.

In Tennessee, meanwhile, Glenn Reynolds was typing, typing, typing into his weblog, Instapundit.com, which he'd started only a few weeks earlier. A law professor with a technological bent, he'd originally expected the blog to be some- what lighthearted. The attacks changed all that.

"I was very reactive," he told me. "I had no agenda. I was just writing about stuff, because the alternative was sitting there and watching the plane crash into the tower again and again on CNN."

He was as furious as anyone, and wanted retaliation. But he warned against a backlash targeting Muslims. He said Ameri- cans should not give into the temptation to toss out liberty in the name of safety. He didn't expect to develop a following, but that happened almost immediately. He'd struck a chord. He heard from people who agreed and disagreed vehemently. He kept the discussion going, adding links and perspectives.

Today, InstaPundit.com has a massive following. Reynolds is constantly posting trenchant commentary, with a libertarian and rightward slant, on a variety of topics. He's become a star in a firmament that could not have existed only a short time ago—a firmament that got its biggest boost from the cruelest day in recent American history. The day is frozen in time, but the explosions of airplanes into those buildings turned new heat on a media glacier, and the ice is still melting.

## Chapter 2

# The Read-Write Web

*Technology that Makes We the Media Possible*

I still remember the moment I saw a big piece of the future. It was mid-1999, and Dave Winer, founder of UserLand Software, had called to say there was something I had to see.

He showed me a web page. I don't remember what the page contained except for one button. It said, "Edit This Page"—and, for me, nothing was ever the same again.

I clicked the button. Up popped a text box containing plain text and a small amount of Hypertext Markup Language (HTML), the code that tells a browser how to display a given page. Inside the box I saw the words that had been on the page. I made a small change, clicked another button that said, "Save this page" and voila, the page was saved with the changes. The software, still in prerelease mode, turned out to be one of the earliest weblog, or blog, applications.

Winer's company was a leader in a move that brought back to life the promise, too long unmet, that Tim Berners-Lee, inventor of the Web, had wanted from the start. Berners-Lee envisioned a read/write Web. But what had emerged in the 1990s was an essentially read-only Web on which you needed an account with an ISP (Internet service provider) to host your web site, special tools, and/or HTML expertise to create a decent site.

Writing on the Net wasn't entirely new, of course. People had done it for years in different contexts, such as email lists, forums, and newsgroups. Wikis—sites on which anyone could edit any page—also predated weblogs, but they hadn't gained much traction outside a small user community, in part because of the techie orientation to the software.

What Winer and the early blog pioneers had created was a breakthrough. They said the Web needed to be writeable, not just readable, and they were determined to make doing so dead simple.

Thus, the read/write Web was truly born again. We could all write, not just read, in ways never before possible. For the first time in history, at least in the developed world, anyone with a computer and Internet connection could own a press. Just about anyone could make the news.

About a year and a half later, on November 8, 2000, I was sitting at my desk at the University of Hong Kong where I teach part-time each fall. It was Wednesday morning in Hong Kong, Tuesday evening in the United States, and I was immersed in the U.S. elections muddle that left Americans unsure for weeks who their next president would be.

The U.S. television networks' news programming was unavailable in the university's Journalism and Media Studies Centre, and local media weren't spending as much time on the story as I, an American abroad, might have liked. So I made do with the tools I had—and I realized something that seems obvious only in retrospect.

I found a National Public Radio streaming-audio feed and listened to it. Meanwhile, I was visiting various web sites such as CNN and key newspapers such as the *The New York Times* for national perspective and my own *San Jose Mercury News* for California and hometown coverage. I watched as the map of blue states and red states changed, and drilled in on articles about individual state races.

I realized I was getting a better overall report than anyone watching television, listening to the radio, or reading a newspaper in the United States. It was more complete, more varied. In effect, I'd rolled my own news.

It was a convergence of old and new media, but the newest component was my own tinkering to create my own news "product"—a compilation of the best material I could find. It was a pale imitation of what we'll be able to do as the tools become more sophisticated, but it worked.

My main focus in this book is on what happens when people at the edges participate in the news-gathering and dissemination processes. Of course, I have to remind myself that most people will remain—and I dislike this word—*consumers* of news.

Yet even if that's all they do, they can do it better than at any time in history because technology gives them more choices. (This is one reason why significant numbers of Americans, believing they weren't getting a fair perspective from the U.S. media, sought out international views during the 2004 Iraq War and run-up to it.)[35]

The news is what we make of it, in more ways than one.

To understand the evolution of tomorrow's news, we need to understand the technologies that are making it possible. The tools of tomorrow's participatory journalism are evolving quickly—so quickly that by the time this book is in print, new ones will have arrived. This book's accompanying web site (*http://wethemedia.oreilly.com*) will catalogue new tools as they become available. In this chapter, we'll look more generically at the fundamental technologies.

For people who simply want to be better informed, the Internet itself is the key. We have access to a broader variety of current information than ever before, and we can use it with increasing sophistication.

For those who want to join the process, the Web is where we merely start.

The tools of grassroots journalism run the gamut from the simplest email list, in which everyone on the list receives copies of all messages; to weblogs, journals written in reverse chronological order; to sophisticated content-management systems used for publishing content to the Web; and to syndication tools that allow anyone to subscribe to anyone else's content. The tools also include handheld devices such as camera-equipped mobile phones and personal digital assistants (PDAs). What they have in common is a reliance on the contributions of individuals to a larger whole, rising from the bottom up.

It boils down to this. In the past 150 years we've essentially had two distinct means of communication: one-to-many (books, newspapers, radio, and TV) and one-to-one (letters, telegraph, and telephone).

The Internet, for the first time, gives us many-to-many and few-to-few communications. This has vast implications for the former audience and for the producers of news because the differences between the two are becoming harder to distinguish.

That this could happen in media is no surprise, given the relatively open nature of the tools, which could be used in ways the designers didn't anticipate. It's always been this way in media; every new medium has surprised its inventors in one way or another.

At their heart, the technologies of tomorrow's news are fueling something emergent—a conversation in which the grassroots are absolutely essential. Steven Johnson, author of *Emergence*[36]—a book about how rich, complex systems such as ant colonies come to exist—explained it this way in a 2002 O'Reilly Network interview:[37]

> Emergence is what happens when the whole is smarter than the sum of its parts...And yet somehow out of all this interaction some higher-level structure or intelligence appears, usually without any master planner calling the shots. These kinds of systems tend to evolve from the ground up.

In no sphere is the whole more intelligent than the sum of its parts than in digital networks, where the basic units are zeros and ones—and where, as David Isenberg explained in his pathbreaking 1997 paper, "Rise of the Stupid Network,"[38] the value soars when you move the intelligence to the edges and away from the center. The Internet, in particular, is becoming the environment in which the new tools function, an ecosystem that is gaining strength from diversity. The Web, as it grew up in the 1990s, was a powerful publishing system that journalists of all kinds used to great effect, and still do. But the larger toolkit is part of an expanding, thriving ecosystem.

Let's look inside that toolkit.


## MAIL LISTS AND FORUMS

Before weblogs we had mail lists, and they have not become less important. As noted in Chapter 1, Dave Farber's "Interesting People" mail list is a news source of enormous value to his readers. It is far from alone.

Because I spend time in Asia every year, including a month teaching in Hong Kong each fall, I was extremely interested in the rise of SARS. I wrote several columns about it in early 2003. Soon after one of the columns appeared, I received an email from a Harvard University bioengineering instructor, Henry Niman, who had created several mail lists. One called SARS Science, he said, "targets medical and scientific information on the epidemic. Members include molecular biologists and scientists from around the world who are studying coronaviruses as well as astroviruses and paramyxoviruses." Many of the reporters covering the outbreak also subscribed to this list. A second mailing list was for sending news articles about the disease. I joined both.

This sequence of writing about something and then hearing from an expert in the field has been a common one for Net-savvy journalists lately. But in a sense, journalists were late finding out what nonjournalists had been doing for years.

At last count, there were thousands of mail lists, covering just about every topic one can imagine. Mail lists differ from blogs and standard web sites in at least three respects. First, they serve a specific community, the subscribers, and the community can make the list private. Second, they tend to be narrowly targeted, such as the SARS list. Third, they are "pushed" to subscribers' email inboxes. Some are moderated; most are not. The key thing about lists is that they tend to be populated by a combination of experts in a given field or topic, and by avidly interested lay people. This can be a potent combination.

In 2000, Yahoo! bought eGroups, a primary vendor of mail lists, renamed it Yahoo! Groups,[39] and now hosts thousands of lists. It's trivially simple to create a mail list.

Most mail lists have a small readership, such as the "Blogrollers" group Winer created in 2003 where webloggers tip each other about new postings they think might be especially noteworthy for their peers. Some mail lists have enormous readerships, such as Dave Farber's "Interesting People" list.

Unlike mail lists, online forums, such as Usenet newsgroups, are open to all comers. Individual forums are hosted by companies, user groups, activists, and just about any kind of interest group one can name. Some are moderated, and many are valuable for spotting trends and getting answers to specific questions.

From a journalism perspective, mail lists and forums can amplify the news. They can be an early warning. They can simply be excellent background data. But their value should never be underestimated.

## WEBLOGS

Many to many, few to few. The blog is the medium of both, and all.

Weblogs and their ecosystem are expanding into the space between email and the Web, and could well be a missing link in the communications chain. To date, they're the closest we've come to realizing the original, read/write promise of the Web. They were the first tool that made it easy—or at least easier—to publish on the Web.

So what is a weblog, anyway? Generally speaking, it's an online journal comprised of links and postings in reverse chronological order, meaning the most recent posting appears at the top of the page. As Meg Hourihan, cofounder of Pyra Labs, the blogging software company acquired by Google in February 2003, has noted, weblogs are "post-centric"—the posting is the key unit—rather than "page-centric," as with more traditional web sites. Weblogs typically link to other web sites and blog postings, and many allow readers to comment on the original post, thereby allowing audience discussions.

Blogs run the gamut of topics and styles. One blog may be a running commentary on current events in a specific arena. Another may be a series of personal musings, or political reporting and commentary, such as Joshua Micah Marshall's TalkingPointsMemo.com. A blog may be pointers to other people's work or products, such as Gizmodo, a site devoted to the latest and greatest gadgets,[40] or a constantly updated "what's new" by a domain expert, such as Glenn Fleishman's excellent Wi-Fi Networking News and commentary page.[41] While some blogging software permits readers to post their own comments, this feature has to be turned on by the blogger, and a significant number of prominent bloggers have not enabled the comment feature. At the other extreme, the Slashdot weblog, featuring news about technology and tech policy, is essentially written by its audience.

What the best individual blogs tend to have in common is voice—they are clearly written by human beings with genuine human passion.

Blogs are, as New York University's Jay Rosen puts it, an "extremely democratic form of journalism." On his PressThink blog,[42] a site that has become essential for anyone looking at the evolution of journalism, he offers 10 points to explain why. Here are the first three:

1. The weblog comes out of the gift economy, whereas most (not all) of today's journalism comes out of the market economy.

2. Journalism had become the domain of professionals, and amateurs were sometimes welcomed into it—as with the op-ed page. Whereas the weblog is the domain of amateurs and professionals are the ones being welcomed to it.

3. In journalism since the mid-nineteenth century, barriers to entry have been high. With the weblog, barriers to entry are low: a computer, a Net connection, and a software program like Blogger or Movable Type gets you there. Most of the capital costs required for the weblog to "work" have been sunk into the Internet itself, the largest machine in the world (with the possible exception of the international phone system.)

The nature of journalistic authority is shifting, he told me.

In a "bottom-up, chaotic system like weblog world, certain sites are important without anyone designating that," Rosen said. Moreover, when the people formerly called the audience are now participants, "that's a different kind of relationship."

Businesses have joined the conversation because blogs fill a gap. A few years into the commercial Internet, companies discovered the value of email for marketing and customer support, not to mention internal communication. Then came the plague of spam, which threatens email as a tool for external contacts. Most corporate web sites, meanwhile, are like most annual reports: static, stiff, and turgid, with the most revealing information hidden in footnotes—sometimes to disguise the truth, not tell it—and led by a "Letter from the Chief Executive" (or vacuous mission statement) that appears to have been written by a committee of lawyers and marketing people.

To the extent that even a business blog can bring information to the audience—internal or external—with more style than we tend to see on business web sites, enterprises will benefit. But what brings people back to personal weblogs is their individualized perspective.

Personal blogs also tend to be part of running conversations. One blogger will point to another's posting, perhaps to agree but often to disagree or note another angle not found in the original piece. Then the first blogger will respond, and other bloggers may join the fray. As tools are developed to help people follow those discussion threads across different sites, the cross-fertilized conversations will spread both in numbers and complexity even more quickly than they do today.

To date, blogs have been a medium mainly for individuals, though group blogs are proving to be a smart medium in some circumstances. The most popular individual bloggers draw tens of thousands of visitors daily. It's safe to say that several million people have at least tried blogging. How many do it regularly is unclear, but the best bet is several hundred thousand.

The addition of audio, video, animation, and other multimedia to weblogs has been an obvious move. But it's taken some time for these mediums to become part of the blogging toolkit. Bandwidth (or lack thereof) is the main reason. But as networks improve, we can take for granted that what technologists call "rich media" formats will infiltrate. (I've added audio and video to my own blog, with limited success.)

Blogging software has evolved a great deal from the first products of Dave Winer, Evan Williams, and other pioneers to the genre. The most popular, as of this writing, are Movable Type from SixApart;[43] Radio UserLand,[44] Live Journal,[45] and Blogger,[46] but a number of competitors such as 20six[47] have emerged.

## WIKI

Can absolute editorial freedom result in anything but chaos? Yes, when it's in a Wiki.

Ward Cunningham, who invented Wikis, defines them in many ways, calling them composition systems, discussion mediums, repositories, mail systems, and chat rooms. "It's a tool for collaboration," he writes. "In fact we don't really know what it is, but it's a fun way of communicating."[48]

"WhatIs.com" (an online information technology dictionary) defines them this way: "A wiki (sometimes spelled "Wiki") is a server program that allows users to collaborate in forming the content of a Web site. With a wiki, any user can edit the site content, including other users' contributions, using a regular Web browser."

The crucial element is that any user can edit any page. The software keeps track of every change. Anyone can follow the changes in detail. As Cunningham so aptly puts it, all Wikis are works in progress.

The Wikipedia, a massive encyclopedia, is the biggest public Wiki, but far from the only one. There are Wikis covering travel, food, and a variety of other topics. You can find a Wiki category page on Cunningham's site.[49] One of the best examples of a Wiki as a collaborative tool to create something useful is the WikiTravel site,[50] which brings together a variety of viewpoints from around the world.

Wikis are going private, too. They're increasingly used behind corporate firewalls as planning and collaboration tools. And entrepreneurs are even starting to form companies around the technology, extending it for wider uses.

Wikis are making inroads on campuses as well. My colecturer at the University of Hong Kong set up a Wiki for our students to use as a planning platform for the 2003 class project. The project looked at a controversial proposal to fill in more of the harbor for development. Students posted their outlines and story proposals on the Wiki and used the site to flesh out the ideas. Instructors could watch over their shoulders without interfering except to offer guidance. The Wiki was perfect for this task.

Their use in journalism, at least the traditional kind, is almost nonexistent. But as Wikis become easier to use, they will become a particularly well-suited tool to compile information from disparate sources, collected by people in different physical locations.

## SMS

If weblogs are becoming the opinion pages and, sometimes, even the newspages of the Net, short message services (SMS) are becoming the headlines. For bulletins, there's nothing better.

Think of SMS as instant messaging without being tethered to a PC.[51] SMS isn't a product *per se*. It's a service offered by network providers that allows customers to send text messages over their cell phones. About the only things that differ from carrier to carrier are price and the kind of device a customer will use.

SMS has been a staple of the information diet just about everywhere where mobile phones have penetrated markets, except in the United States. That is surely changing. Forward-looking newspapers in the U.S., along with other kinds of information providers, including companies that have time-sensitive information (such as airlines), have begun offering an assortment of SMS services. *The San Diego Union-Tribune*'s SignOn-SanDiego.com, for example, offers SMS alerts on local news. And I've signed up with United Airlines and American Airlines, the carriers I use most frequently, to be notified if flights are delayed.

Journalists can use SMS in any number of ways; again, this is much more common outside the U.S. The first inkling among journalists of China's SARS epidemic came in an SMS from sources inside the medical profession there. Was this significantly different than simple phone calls in its fundamental nature? Not really. But in a place where being overheard can lead to big trouble, it's much safer—as long as one's messages aren't being intercepted—to simply send a quick SMS.

Over time, perhaps the most important value of SMS will be of the kind described by Howard Rheingold in his prescient book *Smart Mobs*:[52] a self-organizing information system in which individuals and small groups tell each other important news. Rheingold relates, among other examples, how citizens in the Philippines used SMS to organize and overthrow a corrupt government.[53] On a more prosaic level, young people in countries with advanced wireless communications have used SMS for social organization. We're just at the beginning of this technology's development. As networks and handsets improve, SMS will give way to video messaging, with yet to be understood implications.

Professional news people will need to be plugged into tomorrow's smart mobs, just as they must be plugged into today's informal organizations. This is already a natural state of affairs in much of Europe and Asia, which lead the U.S. in the development of wireless messaging; certainly it was for the Chinese journalist who received news of SARS via SMS. Technology moves so quickly that before long it will also seem natural to the men and women who enter professional journalism in America.

## MOBILE-CONNECTED CAMERAS

Pictures are part of journalism, and most organizations employ professional photographers. As cameras become just one more thing we all carry everyday, everyone's becoming a photographer. We haven't begun to think through the societal implications of this fact, but the implications for journalism are serious.

Digital cameras are a staple of amateur photographers, and well-financed professional journalists use high-end digital cameras for their flexibility and the ability to transmit photos quickly. Video is also going digital at a rapid pace. The size of high-quality digital cameras, still and video, is decreasing along with the cost. Connecting them to personal computers for image and video editing is simpler than ever, too. As broadband Internet access becomes more common, quick publishing becomes simple.

Now combine cameras with true mobility, and the ability to instantly send an image to someone else or to the Web. This is the world camera-equipped mobile phones are creating. The images from early models were low resolution and lacked professional quality, but even a bad picture can be newsworthy, and the quality of phone cameras is getting better at a rapid pace. Once again, it's vital to remember technology's rapid pace of innovation and improvement to understand just how soon it will be when most phones aren't just equipped with still cameras, but video cameras. Tomorrow's mobile phones will be able to send information and images to individuals and groups, and publish to web pages in close to real time.

Keep in mind that public photos and videos are not new. The beating of Rodney King captured on videotape is a precedent for what's coming. Citizens have been capturing videos of tornados and other natural disasters for years as well, and cable television caters to voyeurs with a variety of shows featuring citizen-captured police chases, embarrassing moments, and the like. News organizations have increasingly resorted to using hidden cameras—an ugly trend, in my view, because only in the most extreme circumstances, such as when someone's life is in danger, should reporters even consider such subterfuges.

We are only beginning to understand the consequences of this technological development. There will be gross invasions of privacy. The barring of mobile phones with cameras from health-club locker rooms is a testament to the improper ways people have already used these devices.[54] But faster networks and nearly ubiquitous cameras in the hands of average people means that big events—the ones that have some element that can be captured on camera—will be seen, and captured, by several or many people. Keeping secrets, moreover, will be more difficult for businesses and governments. We'll look at these possibilities in the next chapter.


## INTERNET "BROADCASTING"

At one time, Internet Broadcasting was seen as the next big thing, with individuals and groups spawning Internet radio and news stations with the same ease they create weblogs and Wikis. But the entertainment industry has all but killed the possibilities of Internet radio, at least the kind with music, by persuading copyright regulators in the U.S. to impose unaffordable royalties on Net radio.

News radio via the Net is another matter entirely, and there's a big opportunity for people to create their own shows featuring interviews, audio documentaries, and other formats in which royalty-free content is the goal. Christopher Lydon, a longtime professional journalist who has taken to blogging in a big way, posted a series of superb interviews on his "The Blogging of the President 2004"[55] site.[56] *IT Conversations*, a Net-only program, has been posting interviews in various audio formats along with transcripts.[57]

Web-based talk radio is another possibility, and it doesn't need to be expensive. Two staff members on Howard Dean's 2004 presidential campaign created an Internet talk-radio program by patching together some low-cost equipment. They showed that anyone can do this, inexpensively and fairly easily. Look for others to put all the pieces together in a coherent package that anyone can use.

Internet video is a different matter. While the cost of producing video news programming is dropping all the time, delivering it online is extremely expensive, because Internet service providers charge for uploading bandwidth at rates amateurs can't afford. This is where peer-to-peer networking may come into play.


## PEER-TO-PEER


Remember Napster, the music file-sharing web site? It started a revolution with its file-sharing model, also known as peer-to-peer (P2P). If one person had a particular song on his computer, his Napster software would (if he allowed it to) tell a central computer at Napster that the song was available. Then other people who wanted the same song would check the Napster database, find who had the music, and log directly onto the computer of the person who was offering the song.

This system, while having some legitimate (and therefore theoretically legal) uses, was also a haven for copyright infringement. The music industry sued, ultimately killing the company. What the industry could not stop, however, was the idea, and other technologists filled the gap with increasingly sophisticated file-sharing systems, some of which will be difficult to stop because they'll have no central points of control.

There are a number of reasons why P2P is important for tomorrow's journalism. One of the most prosaic is cost, because P2P solves a serious problem: the more successful your web site becomes, the more it costs you to keep it going. Internet service providers charge web site publishers in several ways, but one way is based on how much traffic your site receives and the bandwidth required to serve the text, images, audio, and video to viewers. Even a modestly successful video can create a huge bill for the site owner. This is a unique situation in media history because in the past, the more successful you were, the lower your marginal costs.

P2P solves this by spreading popular material around the network. With technologies such as BitTorrent, a free software product, every downloader's computer is also a content server.[58] So the more popular you are, the less it costs, not the other way around.

P2P is also valuable in a political sense. New P2P systems under development will provide the closest thing to anonymity that we've seen so far. Repressive governments want to keep Internet content under control, but anonymity will make censorship more difficult.

As we'll discuss in Chapter 11, the entertainment media barons of today utterly loathe P2P, at least the kind they can't control, largely because it can be a platform for copyright infringement. I also believe they fear it because of its assistance in democratizing media. Either way, they want to put a stop to it. They must not be permitted to succeed, however, because in the name of preventing copyright infringement, they are taking away other rights—including our right to make what's known as "fair use" for quoting and personal backups—and they could ultimately dampen or even wreck the possibility of grassroots journalism talking hold.

*Put this but in New Media Tech, Chapter.*

## THE RSS REVOLUTION

For people who want to "roll their own" news reports, nothing may be more important for them to understand than a little known technology that is beginning to transform the delivery of Internet content. And they can thank the bloggers, in large part, for its growing success.

Early in the development of blogging software, programmers baked in a content-syndication format called RSS, which stands for (among other things) Really Simple Syndication. This syndication capability allows readers of blogs and other kinds of sites to have their computers and other devices automatically retrieve the content they care about. It's spawning a content revolution that is only now beginning to be understood and appreciated. It could well become the next mainstream method of distributing, collecting, and receiving various kinds of information. If the Web is a content warehouse, the blogging world is a conversation—and RSS may be the best way to follow the conversation.

Imagine your own "Presidential Briefing"—with only the topics you want, updated whenever you want, and with the added ability to drill down for details. No need to go to your browser and reload a bunch of sites. RSS does the heavy lifting.

So don't think of RSS as just another technology abbreviation. "Think of it as a Rosetta Stone to tomorrow's information—or at least some of it," said Chris Pirillo, founder of LockerGnome, a provider of tech-oriented email newsletters.[59] "RSS suddenly makes the Internet work the way it should. Instead of you searching for everything, the Internet comes to you on your terms."

RSS, or a technology like it, is baked into almost every weblog software product. Create a blog, and you're creating RSS. There is a critical mass of content just from bloggers. But traditional news organizations and businesses are realizing its value, too, and they're creating RSS "feeds," as the files are called, of their own material.

If you want to see the RSS feed of my (or any other) weblog or other RSS-enabled web site, you have to subscribe yourself. I can't force it on you. This is one reason why RSS is so important: the user is in control.

The web site accompanying this book has links to a variety of RSS-related software and how to use it. But let me offer an example to demonstrate how simple it is to get it running. In my own case, on a Macintosh computer, I downloaded and installed NetNewsWire,[60] a type of program known as a newsreader or aggregator. NetNewsWire came with a large collection of RSS feeds to which I could subscribe with a couple of mouse clicks. For several that weren't included with the software, subscribing was trickier. I had to find each site's RSS feed web address, copy it, and paste it into NetNewsWire's subscription chooser.

Like other newsreaders, NetNewsWire has three "panes," much like most email programs. In the lefthand pane is a list of sites I follow. I click on one of those site names, and the pane at the top right of the screen shows the headlines from that site. I click on a headline, and in the bottom-right pane I see a summary of the article or the entire piece, depending on what the owner of the site has decided to provide. If I want to see the original page or article, I need only double-click on the site name or headline.

Because newsreaders pull together various feeds into one screenful of information, they are incredible time savers. I can pull the headlines and brief descriptions of postings from dozens of blogs and other sites into a single application on my Mac. I don't need to go surfing all over the Web to keep an eye on what all the people I'm interested in are writing. It comes to me.

The formatting and structure of an RSS feed tends to be bare bones, making RSS a great way to make material available on non-PC platforms such as smart phones and handheld organizers, as well as providing a way for web sites to syndicate content from one another. For example, I have an RSS reader on my Treo 600, a combination phone and personal organizer. It scoops up a bare minimum of material from the RSS feeds—just the headlines and summaries—and provides a great service.

The extensibility of RSS creates some drawbacks. Many weblogs expose only headlines and summaries to newsreaders, requiring the user to click through to the source (the original web site) to read the full text. The irony here is that the newsreader actually undoes the idiosyncratic feel of many weblogs by stripping them of visual elements such as layout or logos, as well as eliminating the context produced by blogrolls (blog authors' links to other weblogs) or the author's biographical information (and any advertising). The same drawback, or benefit, exists with text versions of email newsletters.

Newsreaders also assign equal weight to everything they display. So the headlines and text from Joe's Weblog receive roughly the same display treatment as material from, say, *The*

*New York Times*. For some users, this will be entirely appropriate. But others will demand—and vendors will surely provide—more nuanced newsreading tools, with the ability to highlight by topic, by writer, by metrics such as how many other people subscribe to a particular blog (its popularity), or by other parameters. The world is waiting for such creative approaches, and RSS and related tools will make them possible. Nick Bradbury, who wrote the popular HomeSite HTML editor and site-design tool, has taken the first steps in that direction with Feed-Demon,[61] a Windows RSS reader that creates a newspaper-like view of RSS content; for better or worse, it controls display details and takes layout flexibility away from the human reader.

As exciting as RSS has become in the personal weblog context, its possibilities are much wider. Information from all kinds of sources can and should be syndicated this way. *The New York Times* makes some of its content available via RSS. Microsoft, while slow to embrace weblogs, latched onto RSS recently in a way that was useful and honored the spirit of the community. The company is making available feeds of its Microsoft Developers Network (MSDN) articles, so a programmer can subscribe to MSDN rather than hunting through the Microsoft site. Similarly, Cisco Systems has begun making some material available via RSS. Several sites provide lists and descriptions of what's available, including NewsIsFree[62] and Syndic8.[63]

MAKING SENSE OF IT ALL

If tomorrow's journalism is an infinitely complex conversation, keeping track of it will require an assortment of new tools going well beyond RSS that will allow us to search for and organize what we discover. A few have already arrived in what can only be called "Version 0.5"—what techies call beta form: promising and useful to a degree, but not quite ready for the average user.

One that shows the way is Feedster,[64] a web-based application that indexes RSS files. I've found it useful for keeping track of what some bloggers are saying about my own work. Feedster has been experimenting with aggregating and sorting through discrete collections of RSS feeds to create what it calls "Feedpapers," which the site calls up-to-the-minute digests of RSS-based news and blog commentary.

Another is Technorati,[65] which mines information about the weblog world. It was designed by San Francisco technologist Dave Sifry to fill a personal need. "I had been running my own blog for about a year, and referrer logs [information about site visitors and the pages they viewed on the site] weren't enough," he said. "I wanted to know what people were talking about, and what they were saying about me, and about the people I cared about." So he wrote some code to crawl the blogs and find out.

The Feedsters and Technoratis, and projects like them, have become a vital part of a larger ecosystem. But like mail lists, blogs, Wikis, SMS, and the other tools of our journalistic future, they are only tools. They must not be confused with journalism itself. Certain values must remain: fairness, accuracy, and thoroughness.

At the same time, services such as Feedster and Technorati are helping us envision what amounts to a new architecture for tomorrow's news and information. They may enable "consumers" of journalism to sort through the opinionated conversations and assemble something resembling reality, or maybe even truth, if they are willing to seek out sources from a variety of viewpoints. We'll look at this architectural potential in more detail in Chapter 8.

More intriguingly, we have to ponder a world where many kinds of devices connect relatively seamlessly, and where social and business networks can be formed in an ad hoc way. The spreading of an item of news, or of something much larger, will occur—much more so than today—without any help from mass media as we know it. The people who'll understand this best are probably just being born.

In the meantime, even the beginnings of this shift are forcing all of us to adjust our assumptions and behavior. The people who make news, as we'll see next, are at the forefront of this adjustment.

Chapter 3

# The Gates Come Down

A peculiar silence reigned in most major newspapers and TV networks the first few days after Trent Lott, celebrating fellow Republican Senator Strom Thurmond's 100th birthday in late 2002, seemed to wax nostalgic for a racist past. Lott, then majority leader of the U.S. Senate, recalled Thurmond's presidential campaign in 1948, a race in which he called for the preservation of segregation. The nation would be better off if Thurmond had won, Lott said.

It was an outrageous assertion, but barely noticed at the outset. ABC News mentioned it. *The Washington Post* had a story but buried it. And that was about all we heard from the major media. But the silence didn't last, because Lott got a taste of tomorrow's media: the swarm of webloggers, emailers, and other online journalists who are changing some long-established rules.

The flow of outrage and information was complex.[66] But the bottom line was that webloggers and other online commentators, far more than mainstream journalists, kept the story of Lott's remarks alive despite the major media's early disinterest. Liberal bloggers, such as Joshua Marshall on Talking Points Memo,[67] were early to sound off, but several conservatives also chimed in. In some cases, bloggers were almost as outraged by Big Media's inattention as by the senator's statements and initially weasely expression of regret for his remarks.

A few days later, the story that didn't go away was running, full-bore, in the national media. Even President Bush was obliged to denounce Lott, a key congressional ally. In the end, no one was surprised when Lott, under enormous pressure, resigned as majority leader.

While bloggers could not have brought down Lott on their own had Big Media not taken up the story, the Lott debacle was, by all accounts, a watershed. Weblogs claimed "their first scalp," said card-carrying establishment conservative John Podhoretz in his *New York Post* column.

Call them newsmakers. Call them sources. Call them the subjects—and sometimes, in their view, the unwilling victims—of journalism. But however we describe them, we all must recognize that the rules for newsmakers, not just journalists, have changed, thanks to everyone's ability to make the news.

Most of today's politicians and business people, and virtually all powerful institutions, accumulated their status and authority in a different era. They see the news media's traditional hierarchies reflecting their own centralized, top-down model, with distinct control points. In this model, public relations and marketing departments deal with the press and the public. Executives deal with reporters when necessary. News is controlled from within the organization and managed when outside forces intervene.

It's an industrial age model: manufacturing news. It still works, to some degree, but it's less and less effective. If markets are conversations, as the *Cluetrain Manifesto* authors have noted, then journalism—the information people need to manage their lives—will increasingly be part of those conversations.

Newsmakers need to understand that the swirling eddies of news are not tiny pools on the shoreline. Information is an ocean, and newsmakers can no longer control the tide as easily as they once did.

So they must face at least three new rules of public life.

First, outsiders of all kinds can probe more deeply into newsmakers' businesses and affairs. They can disseminate what they learn more widely and more quickly. And it's never been easier to organize like-minded people to support, or denounce, a person or cause. The communications-enabled grassroots is a formidable truth squad.

Second, insiders are part of the conversation. Information no longer leaks. It gushes, through firewalls and other barriers, via instant messages, emails, and phone calls.

Third, what gushes forth can take on a life of its own, even if it's not true.

## SPREADING THE WORD

As noted earlier, modern communications have become history's greatest soapbox, gossip factory, and, in a very real sense, spreader of genuine news. At one time, an individual with an issue had few options. He could stand on the corner and rant, or post a sign, or write a newsletter, or pen a letter to the editor. Today, if his argument is sufficiently moving and/or backed up with facts, the tools at his disposal can make it a global phenomenon. The autonomous linking machine—consisting of people who care enough to spread the word, plus new tools such as RSS, which widely disseminate what they write—launches into action. And how the word does spread.

Even before the Web rose to prominence, the online world was making companies pay attention. In 1994, Usenet, the system of Internet discussion groups, helped teach a lesson to Intel, which makes most of the processors that are the central brains of personal computers. News of the "Pentium bug," a math-calculation flaw in a version of the Pentium processor, first spread via Usenet before it was picked up in the popular press. At great expense financially and to its reputation, Intel had to replace many of the flawed chips. "Our immediate lesson was from that moment onwards, you cannot ignore that medium [the Internet] and that that medium was going to get more and more important at setting opinions," an Intel executive told the CNET news service in 1999.[68]

A decade after the Intel debacle came another relatively trivial, but still revealing, example. In early 2004, with great fanfare, including a Super Bowl commercial, Pepsi announced a "free songs" promotion. Buyers of Pepsi could look at the underside of the bottle cap and, about one out of three times, win a free song download from the Apple iTunes music web site. But someone noticed a flaw in the bottle design. He or she figured out how to tilt the unopened bottle just so and discover whether the bottle contained the code for the song. Once upon a time that information would have remained within a small community of people, but in the Internet age, that information was almost instantly available to anyone with an Internet connection in the form of a document titled "How to never lose Pepsi's iTunes giveaway."[69] And there was nothing Pepsi could do about it. If someone knows something in one place, everyone who cares about that something will know it soon enough.

Consider a far more profound example, a case with true life-or-death implications: the SARS epidemic that began in the Chinese province of Guangdong in November 2002. The repressive government, accustomed to controlling the news, at first didn't allow the medical community to tell anyone what was happening. But in early February 2003, the news began to leak out anyway, not through newspapers or television or official announcements, but through SMS, or short messaging through mobile phones, a modern form of word-of-mouth. And the word was grim: people were sick and in some cases dying from a particularly virulent form of pneumonia. That led to some news coverage, probably much earlier than might have happened had the people not literally taken news delivery into their own hands.[70]

Once SARS became a household word and panic began to set in, SMS became a medium of choice for the government, too.

Hong Kong authorities used it to attempt, not very successfully, to dampen unfounded rumors that were spreading on the Internet.[71]

Now add "moblogging" and its kin to the equation—the use of camera-equipped mobile devices by just about everyone, in a world where we must assume that people are constantly taking pictures in public places.

Newsmakers, especially Hollywood stars and other celebrities, already loathe the "paparazzi" photographers who follow them around and snap pictures in unguarded moments. What will happen when 10 average citizens aim their phones at the stars and zap the images they take to their friends or to web sites? Still images are only the beginning; video cameras will become part of our phones soon enough. The paparazzi have better cameras and are better picture-takers, but the swarms of amateur paparazzi will satisfy most of the public's insatiable hunger for news about their favorite celebrities. And for the people who live in the public eye, that eye will never blink when they're outside of their homes.

That, of course, is a relatively trivial example of what's coming. Camera phones and other carry-everywhere photographic and video devices may give people powerful tools to prevent crime; as CNN reported in 2003, a 15-year-old boy snapped a camera-phone picture of a would-be abductor, helping the police find the man.[72] These devices will also greatly accelerate the way we document history.

As of early May 2004, it was still unclear who took the digital photographs of Americans abusing Iraqi prisoners in Abu Ghraib prison, but their escape into the public sphere was already seen as a negative pivot point not just in the conflict but in the world's view of America. Even if the military and the Bush administration had wanted to keep the near-torture covered up, once the photos had been taken and started to make their way around, their wider distribution was almost inevitable.

We are a society of voyeurs and exhibitionists. We can argue whether this is benign or repugnant, but when secrets become far more difficult to keep, something fundamental will have changed. Imagine Rodney King and Abu Ghraib times a million. Police everywhere must already wonder if they are being taped. Soon they will have to assume they're being caught on digital video. This has obvious benefits, such as curbing police misconduct. But everyone who works, or moves around, in a public place should consider whether they like the idea of all their movements being recorded by nosy neighbors. We may not be able to choose between the benefits of ubiquitous cameras and their drawbacks.

It's worth reflecting how events of the past would have looked had tomorrow's technology been available at the time. Let's apply that to the horrific events of September 11, 2001. Our memories of that awful day stem largely from television: videos of airplanes slamming into the World Trade Center, the fireballs that erupted, people falling and jumping from the towers, the crumbling to earth of the structures. Individuals with video cameras captured parts of this story, and their work ended up on network TV as well. The big networks stopped showing most graphic videos fairly quickly. But those pictures are still on the Net for anyone who wants to see them.

We also learned, second-hand, that people in the airplanes and Trade Center towers phoned loved ones and colleagues that awful day. What would we remember if the people on the airplanes and in those buildings all had camera-phones? What if they'd been sending images and audio from the epicenter of the terrorists' airborne arsenal, and from inside the towers that became coffins for so many? I don't mean to be ghoulish, but I do suggest that our memories would be considerably different had images and sounds of that kind ricocheted around the globe.

## TRUTH SQUAD

In September 2002, Microsoft posted a semi-bogus web page advertisement featuring a winsome young woman, identified as a freelance writer, who'd supposedly switched from a Mac to a PC. The page was entitled "Mac to PC: Mission Accomplished, Convert Thrilled," and was a response to Apple's "Switch" (from PCs to Macs) campaign. A commenter on the Slashdot site[73] discovered and reported that the picture of this supposed freelancer was from a Getty Images archive.[74] The Associated Press's Ted Bridis then scoped out the rest of the story, which was, of course, not the one Microsoft had been floating. A Microsoft PR man, weaving around some direct questions from me, said: "It was a mistake that it was posted, and Microsoft took it down as soon as it came to the attention of the Windows XP marketing team. Microsoft regrets any confusion it may have caused."

I suggested at the time that people might be making too much of the half-fake nature of the ad. After all, the people who pitch products in TV and print advertisements are usually actors. But when Apple's PC-to-Mac converts were apparently all real, including their pictures, Microsoft's phoniness was all the more obnoxious.

What made the incident stand out was the way the untruth unraveled. Slashdot's readers, members of a powerful online community, got on the case. They were the first to show that something wasn't kosher with the Microsoft page. And they deserved much of the credit for the story coming out in the first place.

The accumulation of data is a powerful research tool for anyone who wants to drill deeper into an issue. The earnest pamphleteer can now do more than challenge something. He can build an online encyclopedia of detailed information on any topic and keep expanding it—a vibrant archive and organizing tool that others use and augment. Combined, this becomes an impossible-to-ignore force.

And it's been happening for some time. In the mid-1990s, McDonald's Corp. faced some angry online citizens and never quite figured out what to do about them. The fast-food behemoth took two activists to court in London, arguing that the company had been libeled by their pamphlets. The activists counter-sued, and then created the path-breaking "McSpot-light" web site[75] to support their side in what became the longest-running such court case in British history—a trial that became a referendum on the McDonald's empire and its some-times unseemly actions around the world.

One of the most useful aspects of McSpotlight was its bril-liant deconstruction of McDonald's marketing materials. Using web frames, an online display technique, the site showed McDonald's public-relations message on one side of the screen. The McSpotlight rebuttals appeared on the other side.

McDonald's officially won the trial, or at least a portion, in part because British libel laws are tilted toward plaintiffs. The company was trying to extract money from a stone, however, so after its enormous legal bills, it had lost a serious financial battle. And, crucially, the company took a beating in the court of public opinion. The McSpotlight court case and web site revealed a multinational giant that, at the very least, had an occasional deficit in ethics. More people knew about that record after the trial than before.

McSpotlight didn't fold with the end of the trial. It expanded its mission even as the trial was proceeding to include a wider look not just at McDonald's, but multinational corpo-rate behavior.

The tobacco companies, another widely criticized multina-tional industry, also felt the weight of web-based documentation in the mid-1990s when the University of California, San Fran-cisco created the Tobacco Control Archives, an assortment of documents that antismoking forces have found valuable in their war against the industry.[76] Stanton Glantz, a UC San Francisco professor who's been studying the tobacco industry and its con-tributions to political candidates, said the university's librarians solved several problems by posting the material on the Web, thus getting the material to people who wanted it while saving time for university personnel. Only later did the power of the new medium become clear, he said, when antismoking forces else-where started using the material in their own campaigns.

The Web is "a very important development," he told me in 1996, not long after he'd created the archive. "It allows people like me—kind of detail nerds—to make the resources available, fairly inexpensively and in however much depth we want."

And it's allowed more and more activists to shine a light on material that powerful institutions would prefer to hide. Government officials are as secretive as companies, perhaps more so. Which is why we should thank people such as Russ Kirk for his Memory Hole site,[77] a growing archive of important material. The site's home page declares its mission is "rescuing knowledge, freeing information." It achieves its goal brilliantly. In a journalistic coup, Kirk put Big Media to shame in April 2004 by using the Freedom of Information Act to get the military's photos of America's Iraq war dead—the moving and dignified pictures of flag-draped caskets that other media hadn't thought to request.

The repositories continue to expand, and they're moving an information imbalance closer to equilibrium for everyday citizens, not just for activists and scholars. In his 1914 book *Drift and Mastery*,[78] Walter Lippmann warned that civilization was becoming so complex that "the purchaser can't pit himself against the producer, for he lacks knowledge and power to make the bargain a fair one." The knowledge equation has unquestionably shifted back towards the purchaser, and the power is following. Users of appliances and devices, whose inner workings were once trade secrets and inaccessible to consumers, have been tapping that power.

A couple of years ago, I wanted to upgrade the hard disk on a video recorder I use at home. It was a DishPlayer, attached to my Dish Network satellite system. The original drive held 17 gigabytes, storing roughly 12 hours of video, and a new 40 gigabytes drive was on sale at the local electronics store for about $120. Unsurprisingly, Dish Networks wasn't especially interested in telling me how to do it. And there were no traditional sources either, such as printed hobbyist magazines devoted to upgrading DishPlayer recorders, or newsletters that explained how to fire up the various diagnostic modes using the remote. The Web—and discussion groups in particular—was my go-to source. I found solid instructions online,[79] gave them a try, and, voila, I had a 30-hour storage system. (I also found instructions on other bulletin boards where users had posted warnings to avoid instructions that hadn't worked for some users—advice I took; the instructions I ultimately followed came with a warning that the upgrade might fail if I wasn't careful, but others posting to the board agreed the fix would work if done properly.)

What I did was minor-league tinkering compared with what others are doing every day. The hacking phenomenon—and I use the word "hacking" in its most benevolent sense—has expanded into the world of gadgets and everyday tools. People who want to improve what they've bought are studying how things work, whether the products are traditional electronics or things with a software component, and these customers are making adjustments—hacks, as they're known—that either make the products better or change their nature entirely. And they're doing it by informing each other, in an open source manner that brings the community's best minds to bear on common problems.

In early May 2003, Apple Computer released a new series of iPod handheld music players. It took no time for the iPod mavens to run tests and discover functions that Apple hadn't mentioned in its product literature. "Well," a report began on the iPoding site,[80] "we couldn't wait so we went to the local Best Buy and picked up a new Gen 2 15 GB. It's going to be taken apart soon, but we first ran Diagnostic Mode on it. It has a recording feature! There is also a test for LINEIN that does recording too."

As a journalist who frequently uses a digital recorder for interviews, this was interesting news for me. But the point was that it was news, period, and it was broken by the people who used the device most ardently, not by the company that made it. Apple may have thought it was keeping future plans to itself (though that's debatable), but it couldn't keep smart people from figuring things out for themselves or from broadcasting what they discovered.

The process has something in common with the car-defect reports that eventually make their way back to manufacturers. In the old days, we'd learn of those defects if we encountered one, if the manufacturer told us, if the defect was sufficiently major to warrant news coverage, or if the government ordered a recall. Now we learn about them from user groups and from the Internet.

One of the more notable examples of learning about unauthorized things over the Internet has been the tinkering of automobile electronic systems, a trend automakers universally dislike. Earlier auto enthusiasts tinkered with carburetors and manifolds; now they tinker with software code. "Much to the chagrin of the automobile manufacturers and in spite of tight security, computer hackers have been able to reverse-engineer the code for most engine controllers within just a few months of the code's appearance," wrote Warren Webb, technical editor of EDN Access, a trade magazine.[81] "By adjusting the control-system parameters, hackers can defeat the California-emissions controls and increase automobile performance." And people doing the hacking tell others what they've done. A quick web search will turn up dozens of sites where people share their knowledge of various tweaks, such as how to boost horsepower.[82]

Now the automakers have a legitimate concern, especially if the hackers disable smog-control systems or introduce some behavior that might make the car unsafe. For the most part, however, the people doing the hacking are learning ways to make car engines and other systems more efficient and reliable. Banning such information sharing—sometimes through the use of obnoxious copyright lawsuits—is tantamount to giving manufacturers unprecedented control over customers. Which, of course, is something they want to have—but they are risking more than just customer unhappiness if they push the control too far. They are risking their businesses.

Eric Von Hippel, business professor at the Massachusetts Institute of Technology, thinks businesses should encourage some level of hacker behavior, not shun it.[83] He told me companies should be doing everything they can to support and encourage the "lead users"—people like me with my Dish-Player—to find flaws in products and improve them. Just as journalists should not be threatened by a more knowledgeable audience, companies should not be threatened by smart customers who care enough to make products better. When your customers offer their expert assistance, the smart move is to say Thanks.


## LOOKING DEEPER


If customers exchanging information wasn't a big enough change, consider the new category of self-organized customer information erupting around us.

In his research labs, University of Tokyo Professor Ken Sakamura has been experimenting with tiny chips that contain short-range radios, embedding them in various products and other items. In his Ubiquitous Networking Laboratory,[84] he scans them and links the product identification to a database with much more information, including the product's history. Someday, he told me, everything will have these ID tags, and we'll be able to get vast amounts of information about what we touch and buy. For example, a head of lettuce could tell us where it was grown and whether the farmer used pesticides. Or a bottle of pills could tell us whether the drug would pose risks if taken with another drug we've been prescribed.

Marc Smith, a Microsoft researcher,[85] has offered another glimpse of the future with his "Aura" system. Using what is essentially off-the-shelf technology, he's equipped a handheld computer with a wireless Internet connection and a bar-code scanner that he uses to scan products in stores. His computer then connects to a server that collects data from Google and other sources, and shows him the results on the handheld screen.

Suddenly, far more than the price is available. Data about the product, and its maker, is available in a far wider information ecosystem. Was a shirt made by slave labor? Did the can of processed food come from a company with a record of poisoning streams in its factories' backyards? Did the company have a reputation for being good to employees and the environment? Smith likes to show a supermarket scan he once did of a cereal box. The top item in Google reveals that the maker had at one point recalled the product because a significant ingredient wasn't on the label. That might be interesting information to someone hyper-allergic to that ingredient. If every object can tell a story, Smith said, "One of the more profound stories is 'If you eat me I will kill you.'"

Now add location to this notion. During the SARS crisis of 2003, a Hong Kong mobile phone company created a system to alert people if there had been any cases of SARS in the building they were about to enter. They used publicly available data and combined it with location-based software in the phones.[86]

It all suggests a higher level of transparency, not granted willingly by the "newsmaker"—a government or corporation—but captured by the user. It's possible because all kinds of data and metadata (information about information) is now escaping into the wild. The downsides are plain, including the consequences of erroneous information and potential invasions of privacy. But the positive uses are also evident.

## BUBBLE, BUBBLE, TOUT AND TROUBLE

The name Jonathan Lebed doesn't mean much to people anymore, but it should hang on the wall of every corporate public-relations executive's office. Lebed was a stock market player, one of many in the bubble days of the late 1990s whose recommendations of shares online helped fuel price rises before the crash. He was hardly alone in manipulating the market. Famous analysts on Wall Street issued absurd recommendations to buy stocks—including some they considered dogs privately—that then plummeted. Lebed didn't travel in such elevated circles. He was a New Jersey teenager who, under false names in Internet chat rooms, made hundreds of thousands of dollars by touting various shares. He ended up settling with securities regulators, who allowed him to keep much of his loot. As Michael Lewis noted in *The New York Times Magazine*, it was never really clear whether he was doing something flat-out illegal or just ethically questionable.[87]

Companies should remember is that this kind of activity—and much worse ways of playing the system—hasn't gone away. It's still rampant.

But it's part of a wider phenomenon: the ability of anyone to join in a global dissection of corporate behavior and finances. The problem for the average person entering this cyberworld, as I discuss at greater length in Chapter 9, is distinguishing between truth and falsehood. The problem for the subject of the discussion—the newsmaker—is bigger.

For honorable public companies, some of the worst dilemmas arise in forums where people discuss stock prices and corporate financial performance. The urge to boost the value of one's own portfolio, or to spread information that helps depress the price and make short-selling more lucrative, is too obvious to ignore. But even in these forums you can find nuggets of useful information. Journalists who cover companies and fail to monitor such places are guaranteed to miss relevant data.

Companies should monitor these discussions carefully, of course, even when there's no obvious participation by corporate officials. Most do, and for the same reasons the journalists watch the discussions—to learn something—but also to see if people are spreading misinformation or worse.

Almost everyone on these systems uses a pseudonym. Sometimes it's insiders who are doing the posting. At least insiders posted more frequently before companies started going to court to get the names and addresses of—depending on one's view—whistle blowers or revealers of trade secrets and other confidential information. Sometimes postings become a target of corporate lawyers, as we'll discuss in Chapter 10. But courts are beginning to tell companies they can't require the identification of anonymous chat-room posters unless there's some actual evidence of libel.

Companies should ponder a more interesting question than whether they should chase down and respond to every rumor they see online. What if, instead, trade secrets are simply a vestige of a dying era? With few exceptions, I'd suggest that the more transparent a company is, the more likely it will succeed in a networked world. I wouldn't take this so far as to say companies should bare all; that's obviously absurd. But Doc Searls's shot at the Segway, inventor Dean Kamen's two-wheel scooter that won so much publicity when it emerged from a massive rumor mill, was well-deserved. Searls, not coincidentally a *Cluetrain Manifesto* coauthor, wrote on his blog[88] in December 2001:

> I believe that Dean Kamen's creation is so original, and his vision so personal, that there is no way anybody else could have cloned it or stolen its thunder before it came out. So it annoys me that he and his crew were so deeply secretive about the thing, even though I know secrecy is pro forma in the invention business.
>
> But did it do any good?
>
> Yes, there was some nice buzz about "Ginger" (aka "IT") when it was in development, [but] there wasn't much to talk about. And now that it's out, there still isn't. We don't know enough. We haven't been talking about it.
>
> If Kamen and crew kept no secrets about Ginger when she was in development, I'd betcha there would now be far more demand, and far more creative thinking about what could be done with it.

And I'll guarantee you this: the most original uses for this original machine will be ones Kamen didn't imagine when he created it.

This is heresy for many, but it's going to be more and more obvious as time passes. Maybe the discussion boards, far from being a threat, are a boon. Of course, they'd be even better if companies participated officially. In fact, the best examples are support forums hosted by the sellers of products in which designated staff members participate and postings are not censored, except in cases of obvious libel or deeply offensive language. One company that has grasped this fairly well is EchoStar, which makes the home satellite TV system I use. A spokesman told me the company's technical people participate indirectly in the online news chatter, letting webmasters know when there's misinformation on their sites. In effect, Dish Networks winks at the users' activity but tries to prevent people from causing real damage.

In an article explaining the surprising showing by Howard Dean in the early stages of the 2004 presidential campaign, Ed Cone, a journalist in North Carolina, made some telling observations that apply far more widely:

> Television, radio, print and mail can create awareness and desire for a product. Senders control the presentation and, if intelligently worded and presented, the messages cause an individual or company to vote with its dollars, by buying the product. But the lesson of Dean's campaign is that the Web is not for micromanagers. With the Internet, an effective campaign creates a community that will on its own begin to market your product for you. Properly done, you won't be able—or want—to control it.[89]

## SWARMING INVESTIGATORS AND SPIES

In breaking down barriers and secrecy, our weapons have several edges. In his important book, *The Transparent Society*,[90]

David Brin suggested that privacy is becoming a relic of a pre-technological time. Preserving old-fashioned privacy was impossible, he said, because modern technology would overwhelm us with its snooping power and the collection of vast amounts of data. Our only recourse, he suggested, was to turn the same tools back on the watchers, to create what would amount to a détente in which we all reserved some dignity. I don't believe it will happen this way because governments and large organizations will never permit citizens to have the same access to their inner sanctums and methods that they insist on having to our personal and professional lives.

Even so, regular people are beginning to discover ways to redress the balance. Witness the case of former U.S. National Security Advisor John Poindexter, who helped dream up the grotesquely invasive "Total Information Awareness" program. Thanks to new technologies, he got a taste for himself.

Total Information Awareness, you may recall, was the Bush administration's data-mining program, designed to ferret out suspicious activities by potential terrorists. It would gather vast amounts of data on individuals by collecting and linking records from financial, driving, criminal, court, medical, and other databases. Poindexter, the former rear admiral and Iran-Contra scandal figure from the 1990s, was in charge of putting this program together.

Civil libertarians picked up and amplified a column by Matt Smith from the December 3, 2002 *San Francisco Weekly*, an alternative newspaper.[91] The column, wrote Net activist John Gilmore, "points out that there may be some information that John M. and Linda Poindexter of 10 Barrington Fare, Rockville, MD, 20850, may be missing in their pursuit of total information awareness. He suggests that people with information to offer should phone +1 301 424 6613 to speak with that corrupt official and his wife. Neighbors Thomas E. Maxwell, 67, at 8 Barringon Fare (+1 301 251 1326), James F. Galvin, 56, at 12 (+1 301 424 0089), and Sherrill V. Stant (nee Knight) at 6, may also lack some information that would be valuable to them in making decisions—decisions that could affect the basic civil rights of every American."

Gilmore took it a step further. He downloaded publicly available satellite photos of Poindexter's neighborhood and posted them on the widely followed Cryptome web site.[92] He also urged people with access to databases containing information on Poindexter and other privacy invaders to expose it as an example of what would go wrong with Total Information Awareness.

A few days later, privacy activist Richard Smith chimed in on the Cryptome site. "It looks like members of the Total Information Awareness (TIA) development team at DARPA don't like the lime-light. All of their bio's [sic] were removed from the Information Awareness Office[93] Web site sometime during the past couple of weeks. However the Google cache still had all of the bio's cached, so I have put copies on my Web site." He listed the web address.

Was this Total Information Access, judo-style? Not entirely. The program was officially put out to pasture, but the snoops are still trying to make it happen via other means, and they'll always have much more data than their opponents. But in the future, they will understand that looking over shoulders is no longer the sole province of the spics. In this case, the swarm of activists and commentators, who individually could make scarcely a dent, was collectively making itself heard.

## WATCHING JOURNALISTS

What industry is traditionally among the least transparent? Journalism. We have been a black box, and have become only slightly more transparent in recent years. But the public is demanding more transparency in our own field, and is doing some reporting of its own when we fail to respond in satisfying ways.

Jim Romenesko's Poynter Institute media blog,[94] the first and still the best of its genre, has become a water cooler not just for journalists but for people who observe journalism. Generally, the blogging community is not shy to go after newspapers, magazines, and broadcasters for real and imagined offenses against fairness and accuracy. For journalists, who are among the most thin-skinned people around, this trend has been something of a shock. We are not accustomed to being scrutinized the way we scrutinize others, however healthy it is that we are.

Even *The New York Times* was forced to pull down its veil in 2003, when the infamous Jayson Blair's journalistic cons become one of the newspaper's worst scandals. The *Times'* appropriately scathing internal analysis of the mess, the "Siegel Report,"[95] revealed a horror show of missed communications and lax management on top of plainly corrupt behavior by Blair himself. But the Siegel Report appeared briefly online and then disappeared, prompting Jay Rosen at New York University to ask what had happened to it. Eventually, and in large part because of Rosen's prodding, the document reappeared online.

In early 2004, amid political reporting that many in the blogosphere found wanting, a suggestion emerged to improve journalism in general. The idea was to follow individual reporters' political coverage on web sites, relentlessly tracking errors and omissions and exposing them to the world. I commented in my own blog, and on Rosen's PressThink site, where the notion first got some traction:

> I like the idea that people are watching what I say and correcting me if I get things wrong—or challenging my conclusions, based on the same facts (or facts I hadn't known about when I wrote the piece.) This is a piece of tomorrow's journalism, and we in the business should welcome the feedback and assistance that, if we do it right, becomes part of a larger conversation.
>
> But if the idea is to create some kind of organized collection of Truth Squads, I'm less comfortable. Here are just three of the many, many questions/issues that come immediately to

mind (and as you'll see, I'm not alone in wondering these things):

1) Who's doing the watching? A self-appointed "watcher" is an antagonist in most cases, convinced before he/she starts posting criticisms that the journalist in question is getting things wrong, whether due to incompetence or animosity. Journalists confronted with this kind of attitude don't respond well, and probably won't respond at all.

Paul Krugman has a cadre of online critics who make my own look benign. Occasionally they make a sound point. Much of what they say is incorrect. And some of it is debaters' tricks: using straw men to shoot down things he didn't say, or saying something that may be true but is off point, etc.

2) Will journalists who do participate in the online discussion of their work—and many will be forbidden to do so by their organizations, probably for legal reasons—hit the law of diminishing returns?

I recall the quasi-religious debates over the OS/2 operating system back in the early and middle 1990s. I was a fan of OS/2 but not sufficiently infused with the religion. Once in a while I'd post a note in a Usenet discussion where something I'd written was either being misinterpreted or had been seriously twisted. I'd then get hammered by one of the more fervent OS/2 acolytes who'd deconstruct every sentence and ask further questions, few of which were actually relevant (in my view) to the issue. I quickly learned that I had time for correcting outright mistruths and not much else. (I also had defenders in the newsgroup, which helped.)

3) Why should anyone trust what critics say any more than what the journalist says? An assertion that a journalist has a fact wrong is not, in itself, true. It's just an assertion.

Do we need Truth Squads watching the Truth Squads? There are, amazingly, sites that deconstruct the anti-Krugman stuff. But you'll forgive a casual reader for ignoring almost all of it.

None of these issues means that Web watchers are a bad idea. But if the idea is to really make journalism better, I'm just not convinced this will work.

This prompted Donald Luskin, an investment officer and a prominent Krugman debunker who writes an entertaining and frequently instructive economics and policy blog[96] to write: "Wouldn't it be nice for journalists like Dan Gillmor if everyone who disagreed with their pronouncements just sent friendly little emails and let them decide how and whether to respond? How unseemly that, instead, some of us have become 'organized Truth Squads.' Apparently only Big Media has the right to be organized."

I responded on mine:

First, I welcome comments on this blog, and have had some lively debates with some fairly angry critics here from time to time; Luskin could have posted a copy of his remark right on this page, but that would have contradicted the implication that the only good feedback is happy-face e-mail. (Note that Luskin doesn't allow people to post comments directly, and seems to prefer more of an echo chamber than actual debate in the letters he does post.) Second, I've been arguing for some time that the little guy needs to get active and organized to have a chance against Big Everything (including Big Media). Luskin either doesn't know that or doesn't care, and somehow I'm not surprised.

I'm having some second thoughts about the comments feature, for many reasons that I'll discuss in Chapter 9. But this much is clear: the trend toward media transparency is inevitable, and it will engender debates that help users of journalism understand a process that has been hidden from view. Will we ever be entirely transparent? Not likely. But we can't avoid—and shouldn't try to avoid—more openness.

## TURNING THE TABLES

We've seen how modern communications give anyone who cares the tools to learn more—far more—about people and organizations that in the past tried to ration the news. What's more, once someone finds out something, she can spread the word globally. But newsmakers need to embrace this new reality, not fight it.

They should also realize that they are far from helpless in the new era. They can use the same tools, in fact, to bring their message to the outside world, and to improve the way they communicate internally, as we'll see in the next chapter.

These changes are, at the least, disconcerting on all sides. However, I strongly believe that they are a positive trend because they encourage openness instead of paranoid secrecy. And in the end, like it or not, they're inevitable.

*Chapter 4*

# Newsmakers Turn the Tables

On January 9, 2002, reporters Bob Woodward and Dan Balz of *The Washington Post* sat down with U.S. Secretary of Defense Donald Rumsfeld. The journalists were working on a series of articles about the hours and days immediately following the September 11, 2001, terrorist attacks on New York and Washington—"the best serious history we can do of these 10 days," they told the secretary.

Rumsfeld said he understood from Secretary of State Colin Powell that he, Rumsfeld, was at the end of the interview trail: "He said you've talked to everybody in the world on this."

The two reporters were indeed prepared for their session. They asked a series of questions, probing deeply into what Rumsfeld had thought, said, and done in those days. Their homework was, in a word, exceptional.

How do we know? Because immediately after *The Washington Post* series appeared later that month, the Department of Defense posted a transcript of the interview on its DefenseLink web site.[97] Anyone who cared to know about the journalists' interviewing style could see it firsthand. Moreover, anyone who wanted to see which small pieces of the interview had made it into the newspaper could also do that. It turns out that the Defense Department posts every major interview with Rumsfeld and his chief deputy, Paul Wolfowitz.

Why this practice? It's to make sure that the full context is available, according to a Rumsfeld aide. What she didn't say—

but didn't have to—was that posting these interviews serves a multitude of purposes for the department. First, assuming the transcriptions are accurate (and sometimes they are not),[98] they provide valuable history for anyone who cares and not just context for the interview itself. Second, if an interviewer writes or broadcasts a story that doesn't reflect the substance of the interview, or outright misleads the audience, the department can point to the transcript in its own defense. Third, the process helps keep reporters on their toes.

It will also make journalists uncomfortable. Our little priesthood, where we essentially have had the final word, is unraveling. But as software people say, that's a feature, not a bug.


Newsmakers have always possessed a certain leverage in the give and take with the press. After all, they are the ones we write and talk about; we're only the observers. Moreover, in a world where too many reporters serve as little more than stenographers, newsmakers can create and hold onto the agenda.

Now it's true that newsmakers can use the tools of new journalism in old ways, such as the old-fashioned trial balloon, to trick the press and mislead the public. Many will do just that because they continue to live in a world where all interactions with the media that can't be controlled are by their definition hostile. The ones who behave this way will be missing a profound point, but they've been missing it for years.

The point has *Cluetrain*-ish echoes—that markets are conversations. It has realpolitik echoes, too, because the stakes are so high in such interactions. But the bottom line is a change, for companies, for politicians, and for other newsmakers brave enough to get it. This evolution from a broadcasting view of the world to a conversational view will not be neat and clean. But its inherent messiness will open communications in ways that will benefit everyone, assuming it's done correctly.

As I noted in Chapter 3, the old rules of newsmaking are no longer the only ones in force. What made them work in the first place—news flowing through a select group of heavily controlled mass-media conduits, mainly television—is still very much alive and largely in control of how most citizens perceive the news.

But the press release culture is beginning to die, and nothing could be better news than that. News and commentary from the edge of networks, from average people who want to be part of the conversation, from bloggers to activists, are facts of life for the newsmakers. Professional journalists remain very much a part of the action, and I expect we will continue to do so, but a wider constituency is emerging.

Newsmakers of all kinds—corporate, political, and, I'd argue, journalistic—need to listen harder, and in new ways, to constituents of all kinds, whether voters, customers, or the general public. Then they need to learn from what they hear. Marketing and customer service no longer work as simple lectures. Businesses need to engage in the conversations that are already occurring about their products and practices. Using weblogs and other information tools such as discussion forums, companies can engage customers, suppliers, and employees in a dialogue in which everyone learns from each other. Mass media remains a vital tool of modern communications, but understanding the evolving world I've been describing will become just as necessary. For example, a well-targeted approach to a weblogger who's become an expert in a given area may be more effective than a magazine ad.

And companies need to realize that being open and truthful is not just the right thing to do; it's the smart thing. In the emerging world of Internet-enabled communications, obfuscation and lies will work even less well than before. Activists and informed customers will catch the cheaters and hold them accountable. McDonald's may have won the McSpotlight libel trial, but I hope and trust that the company will, in the end, be a better—not just craftier—corporate citizen as a result of this and other citizen action. Politicians such as Trent Lott will remember that nostalgia for a segregationist era is unacceptable to the vast majority of Americans.

Making this shift in thinking will feel, at times, like three-dimensional chess. Consider the multiple audiences business serves: traditional media, new media, other businesses, customers, regulators, politicians, and political constituents. Now add the varying communication tools—email, weblogs, short messages, syndication via Net-based tools such as RSS—and you get a sense of the new landscape and its complexity.

In this chapter, I'll offer some specific advice and examples to the newsmakers of tomorrow, ideas on how to conduct genuine conversations with their constituents, who include everyone from journalists to employees to the general public. I hope business people and politicians, in particular, will use them for the right purposes, and not to mislead and deceive.

## LEARNING BY LISTENING

While it's possible to learn something from a focus group, or a scientific survey, those techniques don't add up to listening. Consider the case of Phil Gomes, a public-relations professional in the San Francisco Bay Area.[99] About two years into his career, his agency put him onto an account dealing with enterprise software. He was told to handle media relations and industry analysis for a suite of programs that ran on IBM's AS/400 midrange computers, which had a huge market presence and were known as sturdy and reliable machines. The software firm was looking into rewriting its software to run on computers running the Unix and Windows operating systems. Some of the AS/400 customers, then representing 90 percent of the customer base, were worried that they might be left behind.

Gomes found a "listserv" (an online mailing list) for users of the software in question where they were creating their own news report, in effect, by conducting well-informed discussions about the product, gaining knowledge that once might only have come from a journal or a user group. Gomes and his client needed to understand what they were saying.

"By monitoring this list, I gained an incredibly rich perspective on what the customers' needs, concerns, and decision-making processes were," Gomes said. "Thus, I was able to then bring that intelligence back to the client and tune communications accordingly. Were it not for the perspective the list offered, the company might have pursued the communication of the open systems strategy so vigorously that the AS/400 customers (who were never in any danger of losing support) might have felt like stepchildren."

Did Gomes' employer fully appreciate his effort? Not exactly. Some of his supervisors "did not see much value in me subscribing to these lists and monitoring the discussions. 'Oh, jeez,' they'd say. 'Gomes is in his chatrooms again.'"

More recently, Gomes has become one of the better-informed PR-industry observers of blogging and other new media. He's written useful papers and weblog postings on the topic, but said he's been greeted by "some degree of disdain. There's a knee-jerk tendency in the corporate communications field to treat every new online media development as the next CB radio instead of fully exploring it."

But some companies are catching on and learning to use new communication tools. Technologies such as RSS have given companies new ways to monitor what's happening. Buzz Bruggeman, the lawyer I mentioned in the *Introduction*, also sells a software product called "ActiveWords," an application that automates a variety of tasks in the Windows operating system.[100] He uses the Feedster service (discussed in Chapter 2), which searches for mentions of ActiveWords. It creates an RSS feed that goes into his newsreader, NewsGator. Every half hour, NewsGator checks with Feedster for anything new. If there is:

> I immediately scan it, read it and figure out what to do, i.e. respond, comment, thank, forward to our team, etc.

When I respond to a blogger, he/she is thrilled, and typically writes more about us, and tells his/her readers that we are great people, responding to users and customers and the net leverages all the time. If there are user problems, we solve them quickly; on balance it is brilliant stuff.

My total involvement in this process once the query is done is almost zero. Probably weekly I check out Google news, Google newsgroups, but the Feedster stuff is vastly more important.

If you assume that bloggers really are "intelligent human agents", then this model is sensational as you don't have to go look for anyone or anything; it comes to you.

At one time, this kind of service cost a bundle. Now anyone can get it at almost no cost.

## BLOG IT

The average corporate web site has much in common with the average annual report. It's loaded with information, too much of which is hidden or disguised in an effort to minimize problems and maximize what's going right. To that end, particularly in the case of companies with problems, it seems designed to thwart the casual visitor who wants to look deeply into the enterprise and its doings. The least interesting feature of a corporate site, with few exceptions, is the typical "Letter from the Chief Executive," a content-free missive that does nothing to reveal the character either of the company or its leader. Creating an impression of openness isn't the same as actually being open.

"Blogging is an opportunity for Public Relations, not a threat," wrote public-relations pro Tom Murphy on his PR Opinions blog.[101] "Blogging provides a unique means of providing your audience with the human face of your organization. Your customers can read the actual thoughts and opinions of your staff. On the flip side, consumers increasingly want to see the human side of your organization, beyond the corporate speak."

When Groove Networks Ray Ozzie explains something on his blog,[102] the reader is gaining insight into the CEO's way of thinking, not just the company's products. The indirect trajectory of Ozzie's blog is what makes it so worthwhile. He's not pitching Groove so much as explaining what he's thinking about on matters relating to the company and its ecosystem.

On July 17, 2003, Ozzie posted an item about the poor security in wireless computing, linking first to an article he'd seen in the trade journal *Infoworld* as support. That article, he said, was one reason why "people are discovering why compartmentalized security such as that implemented by Groove is so important moving forward," he wrote. "The alternative is more than a bit frightening: Recognizing their valid concerns, would you allow your employer to 'lock down' and remotely manage your home computer?"

I don't cite this posting because it's earthshaking information, but because it illustrates how one executive used this channel to talk about an important issue in today's computing world—security—while simultaneously making a subtle pitch for his own product. Only because Ozzie already had some credibility was this effective, since there's an element of hyperbole in his message. He addressed an issue and reflected a viewpoint—in his own words, not a PR person's. The pitch fit the context of the posting. It was relevant. It didn't have to lead directly to more sales to be useful.

The blog gave Ozzie "a communications channel under my control," he told me, where he could say what he wanted (within limits, such as keeping trade secrets secret). He can post quickly and without limits on length. "I feel as though there's a conversation—many conversations—going on out there. It lets me feel like I'm part of that conversation, and when I get calls and emails, there's confirmation that I'm part of the conversation."

Not long after we discussed all this, Ozzie put his blog on a hiatus due to a heavy work schedule but then revived it many weeks later. "It's been a very busy past few months," he emailed me in early 2004. "The biggest difference between where my head is at these days versus about a year ago is that I used to feel guilty for not posting. At this point, knowing how effectively RSS works, I know that when I start posting again—even if it's only once in a blue moon—I won't have to regenerate the audience from scratch. When I first started posting, I really felt as though I would 'disappear' from the community if I needed (for whatever reason) to take a break, but RSS aggregators really only impose a small burden for continuing to monitor people who can only post rarely."

A more recent executive recruit to the blogosphere is Mark Cuban, owner of the Dallas Mavericks franchise in the National Basketball Association. An Internet billionaire (cofounder of broadcast.com, a Net company acquired by Yahoo!), Cuban became famous as the demonstrative sports team owner, though he's also kept investing in the technology and television arenas. His "Blog Maverick"[103] attracted instant attention when he launched it in March 2004, and no wonder: he took on sportswriters and offered pungent commentary on sports and investing, and generally took to blogging like no other CEO I've seen. (He also needed a copy editor, but most bloggers do.)

I was intrigued and, on the spur of the moment, shot a quick email to him with five questions. He responded almost immediately.

Q: What prompted the blog in the first place?

A: I was tired of reading incomplete information or misinformation about what I was doing in the sports media. This was one way to get the facts out.

Q: From your observations, are business people and folks in the public eye generally aware of their own ability to frame the discussion, or at least respond to what's being said?

A: Yes and No. I think everyone with any awareness of the Internet from a business perspective is aware of blogs. The issue is, "If you write it, will they come?" It's one thing to write a blog to set the record straight, but if no one reads it, it's not worth the effort. That creates a Catch 22 that I'm sure most don't think is worth the risk.

Q: Should all CEOs do their own blogs? If so, why? If not, why not?

A: Probably not. Being in sports is different than just being in business. The local newspapers write about the Mavs every day. They might write about a company once a quarter at most.

Q: What kind of thing wouldn't you say on a blog? What are the limits, if any?

A: I don't know yet.

Q: What else should I have asked you about the new world of communications?

A: It's not a new world. We all have been able to create our own websites for years. This is just a content management system, verticalized for diary entries. That diary-like format has caught the attention of the voyeur in all of us. Whether or not it's a long-term impact, I have no idea.

CEO blogs are useful. Even better, in many cases, are blogs and other materials from people down the ranks. For journalists, some of the most valuable communications from inside companies come from the rank and file, or from managers well below the senior level. Why not let them communicate with the public, too?

A growing number of smart companies understand why this is a good idea. Perhaps the best at this early on was Macromedia, maker of popular web-design tools such as Dream-Weaver and Flash. Macromedia programmers and product managers contribute to a variety of blogs. For example, John Dowdell offers a "news service for people using Macromedia MX",[104] one of Macromedia's key products. Macromedia also aggregates its blogs onto one page for convenience and allows anyone to read them.[105]

Microsoft has set a new standard in several ways. In May 2004, Bill Gates touted the advantages of blogs and RSS in a speech to corporate chief executives. Noting the convenience factor, he said, "The ultimate idea is that you should get the information you want when you want it..." Walking the talk, the company allows hundreds of staffers to blog on personal sites. I'm especially impressed with Channel 9,[106] run by several of the company's software developers. They're putting a distinctly human face on what they do, and use videos, audio, and text conversations to augment basic text blogs. (The name "Channel 9" comes from some airlines' policies of letting passengers listen in to cockpit-tower conversations on the planes' audio systems.)

The public sector can use these techniques, too. Phil Windley served as the state of Utah's Chief Information Officer for about 21 months ending in December 2002.[107] He'd encountered weblogs at a conference in California and was intrigued by what they might represent. He started his own personal blog and then realized the format could have value in an enterprise setting. So he bought 100 licenses for Radio Userland, one of the major weblog software packages, and offered one to any state information technology (IT) people who wanted to start a blog. Almost three dozen took him up on the offer, and about a third of those remain active, he says. His own blog gave him better visibility among the IT workers who read it from around the state. And he, in turn, learned from their blogs about the challenges they were facing.

Of course, it's not as simple as just telling an executive (or having the executive volunteer) to write a blog, or offering blogs to others in the organization. Enter the lawyers.

Even in an era of openness, governments, companies, and other big organizations still have trade secrets. They don't want to air dirty laundry. That's why companies and governments have strict email policies, nondisclosure agreements, and other measures to prevent valuable inside information from migrating into the wrong hands. (Groove has rules on which topics bloggers can write about and which they can't.)

Sometimes what you can't post outside the firewall—where the public can see it—is fine to post inside. An internal blog or Wiki can help an organization's workers keep up to date on projects and each other's individual discoveries. Utah's IT blogs were for the IT workers only, and they served their purpose.

Weblogs, internal or external, are not for everyone or every enterprise, Windley says. "You have to decide how comfortable you are with people being candid," he says. "Weblogs are about people being candid. Some organizations don't like that."

Robert Scoble, one of the most prolific Microsoft bloggers, has become well-known in the technology field because of his Scobleizer blog.[108] In a comment he posted on my blog, he said:

> "Others will either figure it out, or will lose the benefits of participating in the marketplace. But, it really requires you to hire smart people and give them access to the most sensitive of internal information. Not every company will figure this out, but Microsoft is uniquely positioned to really take advantage of the new conversational marketing. Why? We all have access to executive-level views of the company. That's quite unlike other places I've worked."

I've had my battles with Microsoft over the years. But as one of the company's louder critics, I can say with certainty that its willingness to let employees have this conversation with the public is a smart move for marketing and PR purposes. It tells me, among other things, that the empire is trying to be a little less evil.

After companies decide blogging is a good idea, they have to come up with a corporate policy that includes what employees can say and how they can say it. They should also decide on a writing style and come up with policies of how to respond to offensive statements and threats. Finally, and most importantly, the leader of the organization has to be committed to the process. He doesn't have to write a blog, but he must make it clear that blogs and other kinds of lateral communications are important.

In 2003, Scoble posted a manifesto for corporate bloggers on his own blog.[109] Some of his suggestions may not be practical for most companies (and it's evident to me, at least, that Scoble's own company frequently ignores his suggestions), but the list has some valuable ideas. Here are several of the better ones:

— Tell the truth. The whole truth. Nothing but the truth. If your competitor has a product that's better than yours, link to it. You might as well. We'll find it anyway.

— Post fast on good news or bad. Someone say something bad about your product? Link to it—before the second or third site does—and answer its claims as best you can. Same if something good comes out about you. It's all about building long-term trust. The trick to building trust is to show up! If people are saying things about your product and you don't answer them, that distrust builds. Plus, if people are saying good things about your product, why not help Google find those pages as well?

— Have a thick skin. Even if you have Bill Gates' favorite product people will say bad things about it. That's part of the process. Don't try to write a corporate weblog unless you can answer all questions—good and bad— professionally, quickly, and nicely.

— Talk to the grassroots first. Why? Because the mainstream press is cruising weblogs looking for stories and looking for people to use in quotes. If a mainstream reporter can't find anyone who knows anything about a story, he/she will write a story that looks like a press release instead of something trustworthy. People trust stories that have quotes from many sources. They don't trust press releases.

Skilled professions may be the most ideal for this kind of communication. For example, over the past several years, the number of high-quality legal blogs has exploded. Most started out simply because the author enjoyed writing about the law. But legal blogs turn out to be superb marketing tools as well. Ernest Svenson, a New Orleans lawyer, didn't have marketing in mind when he started his blog,[110] but it's been modestly helpful there, too, he told me, generating referrals and requests for bids on services.

"In general, I do it because it puts me in touch with attorneys who are interested in how technology is changing the practice of law," he said, noting that there aren't very many lawyers in New Orleans who are eager to talk about such things.

## THE CELEBRITY BLOG

Wil Wheaton is not, repeat not, Wesley Crusher.

Now in his early 30s, Wheaton isn't a bit sorry he played the role of the brainy but somewhat annoying teenager on *Star Trek: The Next Generation* back in the 1980s and early 1990s. He's proud of it. But some fans of the show utterly loathed the Crusher character. A once notorious Internet discussion group was called "alt.ensign.wesley.die.die.die"—and the tone of the postings fit the newsgroup's title.

In 2001, the Pasadena resident launched a weblog,[111] in part to "undo a lot of the misconceptions directed toward me because of the character I played on Star Trek," he said. His online journal mixes intensely personal observations with commentary on modern life, politics, technology, and entertainment. It tells you a lot about who he really is: a thoughtful and intelligent family man, with a bent toward geekiness and political activism.

The blog has become Wheaton's portal into a new career as a writer. And Wheaton has established a new kind of connection with his audience. Call it the Celebrity Blog. And think of it as the evolution from the celebrity as a manufactured product to the celebrity as something more genuine in a human sense.

Wheaton's is highly personal. It's helped people get to know him, as opposed to the *Star Trek* character. (A personal observation: *The Next Generation* remains by far the best of the many series in the long-running franchise.)

Wheaton was no fan of the Hollywood system that creates stars and spits them out after using them. The blog has reflected that sentiment. "I'd struggled so much as an actor, and felt like I was running out of time to be a successful actor," he said. "I'd done lousy movies to support my family. I started writing about that, the ups and downs, mostly downs—what it's like to be someone whose first half of life is being famous, and the second half, being famous for being famous."

Nor is he a fan of the Hollywood trade press, to put it mildly. "I'm cynical about entertainment press," he said.

"I don't think the press on the whole is truly objective with researched, hard-hitting journalism. It's basically an extension of the studio publicity machine." When new films are released, there's lots of coverage, but hardly anything negative, because writers who express skepticism tend to lose their access in the future.

And while the trade press won't beat up on popular actors, Wheaton said, "they'll beat up on me all the time because I'm a minor celebrity. What am I going to do, threaten? I don't have a publicist."

He recalled an *Entertainment Weekly* story about blogs. "The writer was snotty and dismissive and condescending," he said, taking some quotes "totally out of context, and portrayed me in a really negative light. In the grand scheme I could care less. It's just lazy journalism. But everyone in the entertainment industry read it. So perception is important."

"In a situation like mine, having a blog is useful," Wheaton said, "because it allows me to get my story out."

He lost his passion for acting and found a new one in writing. The blog has spawned one book, *Dancing Barefoot*,[112] and another was on the way in early 2004. He was making a living from his writing, an enormously satisfying turn of events. (Disclosure: Wheaton's new publisher is also the publisher of this book. He was self-publishing when I first wrote about his blog in my newspaper column.)

Wheaton has been using computers much of his life. He's conversant with the Web's current programming languages of choice, he's an advocate of open source software, and he uses the Linux operating system at home. He's also taken up some causes dear to the hearts of many in the tech community, such as reform of the copyright system that has been tilted so drastically toward copyright holders and against customers and users. He's a strong supporter of the Electronic Frontier Foundation (EFF), which fights for liberties in a digital era; he stirred up the crowd at a 2002 EFF fundraising event with a rousing call to arms against industry abuses and an endorsement of EFF's mission.

Writing a weblog like his carries a responsibility. Authenticity matters. Lots of his readers "feel they know me, which is weird," he said, citing an email that had just arrived when we spoke in mid-2003. The correspondent mentioned an incident in his book, which Wheaton calls "a love letter to my wife." As Wheaton recounts the story, the couple was on a Santa Barbara street as it began to rain. He opened an umbrella. "She grabbed the umbrella, closed it, and said, 'Let's walk in the rain,'" he recalled. "I wrote about it. It was definitely sappy. I'm head over heels for my wife and have been for eight years."

Wheaton's online correspondent wanted him to understand something: "He said, 'We read this for your honesty, and if we find out this is being written by some clever writer, we'll all feel betrayed.'"

"They always say to write what you know," said Wheaton. "That's really good advice."

## TALKING TO THE AUDIENCE

What business needs to use from-the-edges technology most of all? Public relations. Yet in the past few years, the PR industry has graduated from mere cluelessness to only a semi-conscious understanding of the Internet's possibilities. To the extent that PR professionals view their jobs as only pretending to give out genuine information, what follows will not be useful. I have a more charitable view of the industry, and suspect there are plenty of PR pros who see the possibilities in entering this new era in a smart way.

It's astonishing to see how bad most corporate web sites are after all these years. In my "Dear PR People" letter on my weblog, I offer the following simple guidelines:

Make sure your clients have a ton of information on their Web sites. This should include not just press releases but also links to articles written about the client by other publications; bios and high-definition photographs of leaders and detailed information, including pictures (and videos) of products; and anything else you think might be useful.

Don't bury the PR contact information so far inside the website that no one without an advanced degree in Library Science can find it. I look for the "About the Company" page, then look for the "Press" page and then for the "Contact Information" page. Maybe there's a more logical place for such information, but wherever you put it, don't hide it.

I used to request email contacts instead of phone calls, faxes, and snail mail. Now, unless someone has some news or a pitch aimed specifically at me—and I mean me alone—I no longer want even email due to the spam plague. I want RSS. Even if a company doesn't want to create a weblog, it absolutely should create RSS feeds of its major news. This is not optional anymore; it's essential.

On April 2, 2002, networking giant Cisco Systems' "News@Cisco" PR operation created RSS feeds of its press releases.[113] The intended audience, said Dan Teeter, the engineer who set them up, was just about everyone from reporters to analysts to investors to partners to customers. Microsoft has RSS feeds aimed at developers. Slowly but surely, companies are learning.

If public-relations people start creating RSS feeds of releases, journalists and the public at large could see the material they want, and the PR industry would be able to stop blasting huge amounts of email to people whose inboxes are already over-cluttered. There will continue to be a use for email in PR, but the volume could be cut substantially—*if* PR people can be persuaded to do so. In 2002, Jon Udell, an *Infoworld* columnist, described (in his blog, of course) a communication he'd like to receive: "Hi, I'm [NAME], [CTO, Architect, Product Manager] for [COMPANY] which does [PRODUCT

OR SERVICE]. I have started a weblog that describes what we do, how we do it, and why it matters. If this information is useful and relevant, our RSS feed can be found here. Thanks!"[114]

The spam scourge has also made life next to impossible for email newsletters. By some estimates, somewhere between 15 and 30 percent of legitimate email is now blocked by spam filters. If a newsletter is treated as spam, it's no good to anyone. Thank goodness for RSS, said Chris Pirillo, publisher of the LockerGnome newsletters. "RSS is evolving as a replacement for email publishing and marketing," he told me.

There's a right way to do RSS, and a distinctly wrong way. Some companies do both. Apple Computer, for example, has an RSS feed of its press releases. But when you look at them in my RSS newsreading software, all you see is the headlines, without text, so if you want to read the things, you have to go visit Apple's site. Stupid. Conversely, Apple's iTunes people have created an RSS feed of the top-selling new songs. In the pane of the newsreader that contains the body of the message, you see the album cover and some details about the song. Not stupid.

## FINE-GRAIN PITCHING

In April, 2001, Apple Computer's public-relations agency got a request from a blogger, Joe Clark, who wanted to interview someone inside the company about the Macintosh operating system. Clark had written for tech magazines, and his now dormant NUblog[115] was an increasingly popular site, but the PR agency didn't know this. Frustrated by the negative response, Clark posted the email exchange on his site, which in turn prompted a cease-and-desist letter from the agency's regional vice president. The entire episode showed how fundamentally clueless Apple and its PR people were about a medium that was growing in importance.

To be fair, this was 2001, before weblogs were well-known. Clark, a tech writer and published author, was a relatively early player in what Azeem Azhar, a principal in 20six, a European weblog tool company, calls the "eBay-ization of media—everyone can be a buyer and a seller." Others call it "nanopublishing"—small sites, run by one or very few people, focusing on a relatively narrow niche topic. A niche blogger may lack the influence of a major publication. According to Azhar, a niche blogger in this context is "a teenage boy who drives the mobile-phone purchase decisions of his group of teenage friends; or the London yoga practitioner who has 60 or 80 fellow yogi readers on his blog, and who influences their yoga-related purchasing."

But they do make a difference.

For example, people in the Wi-Fi wireless networking arena have learned that at least two weblogs—Glenn Fleishman's Wi-Fi Networking News, which I discussed earlier, and Alan Reiter's Wireless Data Web Log[116]—are as important to their readers as any print publication. These sites provide the latest Wi-Fi news, along with highly informed commentary by their authors. In fact, they're better than any print publication I've seen.

The influence of effective bloggers transcends technology. In the world of baby strollers, a southern California woman named Janet McLaughlin moves markets.[117] "While she doesn't earn a dime for her efforts," The Wall Street Journal reported on September 2003, "Ms. McLaughlin—better known to her followers as Strollerqueen—has attained celebrity status in the underground world of stroller watchers and gained outsize influence on new buyers. Shoppers around the globe seek her counsel with Internet postings titled 'Wise strollerqueen give us your expertise!!,' 'ALL HAIL THE STROLLERQUEEN!,' and 'Stroller queen: thanks for making me look normal.' She has referred so many customers to two West Coast stroller stores that they both periodically offer 'Strollerqueen discounts.'"[118]

Another influential niche publication is Gizmodo, a weblog about the latest and greatest electronic gadgets. It's part of the small but growing collection of sites run by Nick Denton, a financial journalist turned entrepreneur. Gizmodo's influence far exceeds its relative size, and its first writer, Peter Rojas, was an experienced tech journalist who worked at publications such as *Red Herring* magazine. Rojas, who has since moved to another niche blog, Engadget,[119] said companies did pick up on what he was doing, though "it took a few months to really get noticed (except for Microsoft, they picked up on Gizmodo within days of our launch)." He told me in mid-2003:

> I'll have to say that the pitches aren't exactly pitches *per se*, more like PR people emailing me to let me know about a new product or to invite me to have lunch with someone who is going to be in town, that sort of thing. I do get a lot of press releases that aren't relevant to Gizmodo, that's mainly because I made the fool mistake of registering for CeBIT America [a giant trade show], so now I get all sorts of "enterprise application" bullshit. Still, I very rarely blog something because a PR person "pitched" it to me. Most of the fodder for Gizmodo comes from trawling my trusty newsreader a million times a day, with the rest coming from tips from readers (who I supposed could be PR people in disguise. You never know).
>
> I'd have to say, though, the PR people who do contact me seem smarter and more respectful than those who barraged me back when I was at Red Herring. Whether that's because they're clued in to the world of blogs, and thus have a better understanding of how they work, or whether the tech bust left only the best flaks in business, I can't say for certain. But overall, my experience with PR people has been pretty positive, and those I've dealt with seem to be taking Gizmodo very seriously as a technology news outlet. I even once had the VP for Global Marketing at Kyocera write me an angry email after I dissed one their new phones.

Denton thinks blog pitches are ideal for "marketers who are inclined toward a PR-centric word-of-mouth strategy." He offers an example: a maker of high-end bicycles can't effectively advertise in newspapers or television, which go to a mass audience; the coverage from bicycle magazines doesn't meet the manufacturer's needs either. Without the resources to hire an expensive PR agency, the bicycle maker might look online for "the 15 people most influential in writing about bicycles and extreme sports—to identify who writes about this stuff, who's listened to [by the Web community] and who spreads memes," and approach those bloggers for coverage.

Or businesses can find the influential bloggers themselves. As noted, the blogging world has spawned services designed to help bloggers—and others—keep track of things. Technorati and Feedster are probably the most useful among the early entrants.

## SOME RULES FOR NEW-WORLD PR AND MARKETING

I'm always glad not to be doing PR or marketing. Unless I was pitching something I genuinely believed to be important, I'd have trouble making the pitch. And never mind the chore of dealing with journalists.

But if I were doing this, given the tools now available, I'd offer to my boss or client the following rules for using tomorrow's media:

1. Listen hard, because people outside your organization may know things you don't. Keep an eye on chat rooms, discussion boards, email, blogs, and everything else from the edge, both outside and inside the operation.

2. Talk openly about what you're doing, and why. Start a weblog, or 10 weblogs, from inside the company. Explain, in plain English (or whatever your local language), what's going on inside the place. Get the CEO to post, too. Create internal blogs and Wikis behind the firewall.

3. Ask questions, because there will be people who are willing to answer. After you've listened and talked, take the next step and turn on the comments feature in your weblogs so customers can post back. Ask for help from your various constituencies. Set up discussion groups, but don't censor them except to remove libelous, obscene, and totally off-point postings.

4. Syndicate your information to the widest audience in the most efficient way. Create RSS feeds for everything useful to journalists and the rest of us, including press releases, speeches, blog postings, and other material.

5. Help out by offering more, not less. Make sure your web site has everything a journalist might need. This includes pictures, audio, video, charts, and plain old text—and make sure it's easy to find. If journalists can find it, customers can, too. That's a good situation, not a negative one.

6. Post or link to what your people say publicly, and to what is said about you. When your CEO or other top official gives an interview, transcribe it and post it on the web site. If it's an interview being broadcast, put the audio or video online as well. If an article about you is unfriendly, link to it anyway (because other people will find it even if you pretend it doesn't exist) but also post a reply.

7. Aim carefully at people who really care. Find out which micro-publishers are talking about your product or service. (Use Google, Technorati, Blogdex, and Feedster, not just Nexis and clipping services.) Also ask around about whom you should be contacting. Then make sure you keep these people well-informed. Treat them like professional journalists who are trying to get things right, and they'll be more likely to treat you with similar respect.

8. Correct your mistakes promptly and honestly. When a major news outlet or serious blogger posts something inaccurate, respond immediately. Point to source material that backs you up. Send an email to bloggers who have pointed to the errant item, and tell them about your response. If it's a matter of opinion, not fact, be judicious in your replies.

9. Thank the people who teach you new things. Congratulate them publicly when they offer a great suggestion, and do it again when you put it into effect. And when someone finds your mistake, don't be defensive. Tell the world—and the person who told you—how much you appreciate the assistance.

10. Experiment constantly, because risk is a part of growth. This is a new medium we're all learning. As Esther Dyson says, "Always make new mistakes."

## Chapter 5

# The Consent of the Governed

On Feb. 17, 2004, Ben Chandler won a special election to the U.S. Congress. A Democrat in a race targeted by both major parties as a must-win seat in the House of Representatives, Chandler racked up a smashing 11 percentage point margin.

Markos Moulitsas Zúniga, author of the Daily Kos weblog,[120] was ecstatic. "This wasn't just a victory. It was a mauling," he wrote late that evening as the results became clear. "And we ALL made it happen. From the cash, to the volunteers on the ground, to the good vibes."

Moulitsas had reason to celebrate. The California activist/blogger, an ardent Democrat whose blog had become one of the must-read sites for political junkies, was applauding not just a chipping away at the Republican House majority. He was celebrating the role his and other blogs had played in Chandler's win. Blogs did more than lead cheers. They were vehicles for the "mother's milk of politics," namely money.

The previous month, Chandler's campaign had made what turned out to be an astonishingly smart bet. It took out advertisements on the Daily Kos and 10 other popular political blogs, most of which had a left-leaning stance. A $2,000 investment, using the then nascent Blogads online ad agency,[121] had turned into some $80,000 in contributions, mostly in small (around $20) amounts, from around the nation. Chandler was "in disbelief" that so many people outside the district cared, his campaign manager told *Wired News* the next day.[122]

The voices from the edges of the political system—average people with real-life concerns, not just the big-money crowd—had been heard.

Historians will look back on the 2002–2004 election cycle as the time when the making-the-news technologies truly came into their own. Big Media and the forces of centralization retained a dominant role during this period, to be sure. And blogs and other such communications tools didn't, by themselves, elect anybody; the implosion of the Howard Dean presidential campaign demonstrated their limitations. It takes the right combination of circumstances and candidate, as Chandler showed, to win elections.

But even as the pundit class was dismissing the Dean phenomenon and, by implication, the value of the Net, it was increasingly obvious that the political sands were shifting.

Just as the tools of emergent journalism are giving businesses new ways to organize and market, they are helping to transform political life into a virtuous feedback loop among leaders and the governed. Even though the Dean campaign imploded, it broke new ground and became a template for others. And even though governments are not doing enough to take advantage of technology to serve their constituents, they will inevitably see the value in doing so—for financial reasons, if nothing else.

This evolution is also about reinforcing citizenship. The emerging form of bottom-up politics is bringing civic activity back into a culture that has long since given up on politics as anything but a hard-edged game for the wealthy and powerful. The technologies of newsmaking are available to citizen and politician alike, and may well be the vehicle for saving something we could otherwise lose: a system in which the consent of the governed means more than the simple casting of votes.

## BUSINESS AS USUAL

For all the obvious value of Net-based politics, it isn't going to overturn the status quo overnight. The consent of the governed had become a sick joke in the latter part of the 20th century, when "one person, one vote" morphed malignantly into "one dollar, one vote"—in which the dollars were spent on TV to appeal to the masses with increasingly truth-free attack ads. And by all evidence, the 2004 campaign season showed that big money and media were still largely holding sway.

Exhibit A was the spate of attack advertising that helped sink Howard Dean in the first contest for delegates, the Iowa caucuses. And even Dean, who used the Net brilliantly to raise money in mostly small, sub-$100 donations, turned around and used much of that money to buy television advertising. In a media world where TV still wields great power, and in a campaign season in which the Democrats had front-loaded to make the winner of Iowa and/or New Hampshire virtually unstoppable, he was only doing the rational thing.

Exhibit B was Arnold Schwarzenegger's winning campaign for governor in California, when incumbent Gray Davis was ousted from office in the October 2003 recall election. The actor's victory had almost nothing to do with grassroots activism and almost everything to do with a Hollywood-style, Big Media sales job by a candidate who happened to have a box office hit in the theaters. Schwarzenegger did have popular appeal, and the recall campaign got its start online, but in the end, the pitch was to an electorate that—sadly, but typically in modern America—didn't care about the candidate's paucity of experience and qualifications, or his refusal to offer any specifics on what he'd do if elected. He hid from serious journalists, substituting appearances with Jay Leno and Oprah Winfrey, and almost laughed in the faces of newspaper reporters who tried to address the details of actual issues.

Exhibit C, George W. Bush's 2004 reelection campaign, has been an even more pronounced version of the top-down, big-money affair from four years earlier, though his advisors did use the Net to some degree. Bush raised several hundred million dollars, most coming from the wealthy elite that had put him into power in the first place.

The message from these examples was clear: Americans as a whole weren't buying edge politics, at least not yet. It seemed that late 20th century politics, a time when choosing our political leaders was little more than a television show where voters were nothing more than consumers, still had some serious legs.

## WHAT'S NEW IS OLD

The use of online technologies to organize politically is hardly new. As far back as the early 1980s, the radical right was using bulletin boards to keep people in touch and to spread its message.

Ross Perot's 1992 run for president as an independent had one little noticed but important feature. He proposed "electronic town halls," a concept that apparently stemmed from his founding and running of Electronic Data Systems. The idea didn't go very far, in part because of Perot's mainframe-era understanding of technology: he understood central control, not true grassroots activity. "Had Perot been using today's pervasive technology and literate base (of supporters) would he succeed?" wondered Peter Harter, a former Netscape executive who wrote a law-school thesis on the subject in 1993. "Probably not, as he yanked power and authority away from his volunteers." Yet Perot had still shown the way for subsequent campaigns.

People at the network's edges—using mobile phones, not PCs—helped bring down a corrupt Philippines government in 2001, Smart Mobs[123] author Howard Rheingold wrote. "Tens of thousands of Filipinos converged on Epifanio de los Santas Avenue, known as 'Edsa,' within an hour of the first text message volleys: 'Go 2EDSA, Wear blck.' Over four days, more than a million citizens showed up, mostly dressed in black. Estrada fell. The legend of 'Generation Txt' was born."

In 2000, America saw the first serious demonstration of the Internet as a fund-raising tool. Republican challenger John McCain raised the then unprecedented amount of $6.4 million online in his campaign against George Bush. McCain lost, but the lessons of his effort weren't lost on the next clutch of contenders. Internet fund-raising had become just one more arrow in the political quiver.

The 2002 elections were the first to see serious use of weblogs. In that year, Tara Sue Grubb, a resident of North Carolina's Sixth Congressional District, decided to challenge the long-term Republican incumbent, Howard Coble, who hadn't had a serious opponent in years. One of her top issues was Coble's obsequious kowtowing to the wishes of Hollywood's movie studios on the issue of copyright protection. She had no money or visibility, but she had the passion of Netizens who were fighting for fairer copyright laws.

She didn't find those Netizens. They found her, via weblogs and email. And they went into action. Ed Cone, a magazine tech writer and part-time columnist for the *News & Record*, a leading North Carolina newspaper, introduced Grubb to software developer Dave Winer, who helped her set up a weblog. Grubb's site drew attention from other weblogs and media, including my column. News of her campaign hit Slashdot, bringing thousands of visits to her weblog, plus some money for her campaign fund. By the end of the campaign, the newspaper was quoting her, and Coble had to explain his fealty to the movie industry.

It would have been poetic justice if blogs and Grubb's engaging energy had carried the day. The reality was far different. Coble won overwhelmingly, though for the first time in years he'd had to sweat just a little. What mattered most about Grubb's candidacy was the way it formed, a small but pathbreaking Net coalescence.

## ELECTING A PRESIDENT

There is wide consensus that smart use of the Net was a principal reason for the election of Roh Moo Hyun as president of South Korea in 2002. Running as a reformer, he attracted support from young people who deftly used tools such as short text messages (SMS) on mobile phones, online forums, and just about every other available communications technology in the nation widely considered to have the planet's best communications infrastructure.

Roh also attracted the interest of an online publication that hadn't even existed when his predecessor was elected. OhmyNews.com, an online newspaper written mostly by its readers, had achieved a strong following for its tough, skeptical reporting in a nation where the three major newspapers—all conservative and accounting for some 80 percent of all daily circulation—had ties to the government and rarely rocked the boat. Korean political observers agree that OhmyNews' journalism helped elect Roh. It was absolutely no coincidence that Roh granted his first post-election interview to the publication, snubbing the three conservative newspapers. (We'll look more closely at OhmyNews in Chapter 6.)

In 2004, the Legislature impeached Roh. But the Korean cyber-citizens had their say once again. In an April legislative election, voters decisively voted into power a party allied with Roh, and by all accounts the Internet activists again played an enormous role.

By 2004, American politics was approaching a tipping point. Enough people were online, and for the first time they had the tools to seriously shake things up themselves. And it was the Dean campaign that did the shaking. It's worth spending some time understanding how this happened, why it happened, and what lessons we can learn.

## DEAN MEETS MEETUP, BLOGS, AND MONEY

"Broadcast politics tells people they don't count," said Joe Trippi. As Howard Dean's campaign manager during the candidate's rise and fall, he wanted to change that.

Trippi's qualifications were unique. He was a self-professed techno-junkie who attended San Jose State University in the heart of Silicon Valley and had developed close ties to the tech industry. He'd also been a long-time heavyweight political operative, having worked many local, state, and national political campaigns. (I first encountered him in Iowa in 1988 when I was covering U.S. Rep. Richard Gephardt's first presidential contest. He was Gephardt's deputy campaign manager.)

In the latter half of the 1990s, Trippi worked both as a political and marketing consultant, the latter role mostly with technology companies. Trippi, McMahon & Squier, a consulting firm, had handled Dean's Vermont gubernatorial races, and as much by coincidence as anything else it fell to Trippi to manage what just about everyone understood as the longest of long shot runs for the presidency.

Trippi had been online for years, and lately he'd become a fan—and frequent denizen—of chat rooms, forums, and other online conversations. He'd also started reading political weblogs and was intrigued by their authors' knowledge and fervor.

Dean's rise to such a prominent national role was unlikely, and it stemmed initially from his politics, not the Net. He struck a powerful chord with several activist groups, including those who opposed the Bush administration's Iraq war policy and others who'd concluded that the Democratic establishment was little more than a watered-down version of the Republican Party. Dean more than compensated for his somewhat awkward campaigning style by offering a choice for, as he put it in a phrase borrowed from the late Minnesota Democratic senator Paul Wellstone, the "Democratic wing of the Democratic Party."

The candidate's initially lonely stance against the war brought him condemnation from the right and disdain from many in his own party. But it galvanized activists who despaired that they were being ignored by the government and even their own party's leaders. And for the first time, they had easy-to-use ways of finding each other and reaching out to others.

One way was Meetup,[124] a web site that helped people organize physical-world meetings. Scott Heiferman, Meetup's founder, had never expected politics to be one of the service's markets. He'd envisioned it as a way for people to gather to discuss things like knitting, medical issues, or other topics through which connecting in the real world would improve on the online experience. But like so many other things in our new world, people out at the edges of the network had their own ideas and acted on them. The Dean Meetups started small but grew quickly, in part with the help of pro-Dean bloggers who'd let people know about local meetings.

Trippi and his boss had been watching it all with some fascination, but they weren't sure where the action would lead. Sure, it would be great if more bloggers would lend their support and more Meetups would help generate excitement. But they didn't fully grasp how quickly the grassroots were shooting skyward. A turning point came on March 15, 2003, when Dean supporters in New York City used Meetup to absolutely flood what the campaign had expected to be a routine, relatively small rally. By several accounts, Dean truly got the power of the Net that day.[125]

The Dean rise could not have happened without three independent factors, which became mutually reinforcing and fueled the grassroots fervor.

The first was a candidate who energized people. Second, the Net had become mature enough, with sufficient presence in people's homes and workplaces, for it to be a tool people readily used. Maybe most important, Trippi said, was "understanding how not to kill it," meaning the effectiveness of grassroots activists, and knowing not to impose—at least not at first—the traditional command and control system on which campaigns have operated for so long.

There was still a traditional campaign hierarchy at the center of Dean's national headquarters in Burlington. But the profound insight in the campaign's Net-working—which raised huge risks along with the opportunity—was trusting people out at the edges to almost literally become the campaign, too. "What's going on in Austin?" Trippi asked rhetorically in midsummer. "We don't have a clue. We're just assisting."

Trippi assembled a smart, dedicated staff for the online operations. It included webmaster Nicco Mele, who'd been working on technology for several progressive groups in Washington. Karl Frisch moved from California after rejuvenating the state Democratic Party's once lifeless web site. Zephyr Teachout, a lawyer and activist with deep Vermont roots, started as a field director and had to learn basic hypertext markup language when she moved to the Internet outreach job, and quickly grew comfortable talking with computer programmers about system requirements.

Early in 2003, Mathew Gross, an environmental studies graduate and author in Utah, was contributing to a popular pro-Democratic (and largely pro-Dean) blog called MyDD.com, when he decided he wanted to blog for the campaign itself. He made his way to Vermont and talked his way into Trippi's office where he stammered about his goals. Gross was on the verge of being dismissed when he told Trippi he'd been writing for MyDD. "You're hired," Trippi shot back. "Go get your stuff and get back here."

Gross' campaign blog became a template for others to follow.[126] It was nervy and chock-full of useful information about the campaign as well as pleas for support. It linked to other pro-Dean blogs. One especially smart move was encouraging Dean supporters to post their own comments at the end of blog postings. Comments on blogs often attract trolls, people whose purpose is to disrupt an online forum, not make it better. Yet comments to the Dean blog, which were numbering more than 2,000 a day by early October, tended to stay civil and high-minded. A genuine community had formed, and people were watching out for each other. Was it, as critics later charged, an echo chamber? To an extent, yes, and that may have limited its reach. But the self-reinforcing forum helped create the campaign in the first place.

A more legitimate criticism of the Dean Internet effort was that it didn't seem to draw much in the way of policy assistance from the grassroots. Perhaps this was inevitable; after all, candidates are supposed to take stands, and voters then can make decisions about whom to support. But a true conversation between a candidate and his public would involve the candidate genuinely learning from the people. That process wasn't prominent in the Dean enterprise.

The Dean campaign blog also drew criticism for not reflecting Dean's own thoughts, except for the rare (and largely unrevealing) times when the candidate posted something. In fact, Dean would have been wise to do more blogging himself in order to make his thought process more transparent. But running for president is time-consuming, to put it mildly, and the blog reflected the campaign, which was far more open than most, by revealing the personalities of the people who became vital communicators with the activists and readers who wanted to understand the Dean phenomenon and take part in it.

Trusting the outside campaigners included risks. As *The Washington Post* reported, the self-proclaimed "Dean Defense Forces"[127] urged supporters to send email to journalists whose coverage was deemed inaccurate or otherwise unworthy. (Reporters who have covered companies with cult followings—people who post incessantly in online discussion forums—know the routine. Someone will post a comment "suggesting" that everyone send an email to the reporter who's insufficiently worshipful of the company in question.) It's one thing to be told of a mistake, but another to be harangued by followers of a cause, however well-meaning, who end up harming their own movement. A Texas supporter, meanwhile, sent what was widely regarded as an email spam. He was soundly attacked even by his own fellow Dean-folk and promptly issued an abject apology.[128]


## CASH COW, AND CATCHING UP


The blog and web site in general had another, essential purpose: raising money. Mostly through small donations, Dean's campaign raised millions via the Net. In one classic frenzy, responding to a $2,000-per-plate fundraiser headlined by Vice President Dick Cheney, the Dean campaign blog urged supporters to counter the Republicans' one-evening, multimillion-dollar haul with a slew of small contributions. They did, and Dean got a new burst of positive publicity in addition to the funds.

By the fall of 2003, Dean soared to a huge lead in raising money and support among the Democratic rank and file. But after he made some big mistakes and his campaign imploded, common wisdom held that the "Internet thing" had been just another bubble-like event. Dean, the cynics said, was another Webvan. The absurdity of this should have been obvious. Were it not for the Net, an unknown former governor of Vermont would never have reached such heights in the first place.

I cannot emphasize the money angle strongly enough. The Democratic Party's front-loading of the presidential primary season—party leaders' determination to get someone nominated early and to keep insurgents out of the running—meant that there was only one way for an outsider like Dean to have a shot. Trippi, who took a great deal of abuse for the failure of the Dean candidacy after being forced to leave the campaign in February 2004, pointed out that Dean's sole shot was to capture the nomination at the start. The tactics almost worked.

Moulitsas, of Daily Kos fame, makes a strong case that the McCain-Feingold campaign-finance reform law of 2002, which looked like a bad deal for Democrats, actually spurred his party's increasingly effective Net fund-raising. The Democrats' main fund-raising method prior to the law had been big "soft money" donations from wealthy benefactors, money that went into national party coffers, allegedly for basic party-building functions but actually to elect candidates.

McCain-Feingold banned soft money, making small donations from average citizens far more important than before—donations that the Republicans were especially adept at getting from a better-organized grassroots network. As Dean's coffers filled, mostly with small donations, it suddenly occurred to the Democratic national party that "we had this great machine, able to turn out small-dollar donations," Moulitsas said.

Some people on the political left are convinced, meanwhile, that the Net is a progressive antidote to talk radio, which is now dominated by the right wing. Is this wishful thinking? After all, it was George McGovern's 1972 presidential campaign that made early and creative use of direct mail, a tactic that not only didn't elect McGovern but was also quickly adopted—and ultimately co-opted—by the Republicans, who to this day have made far better use of the medium.

Yet there may well be reasons to think that the Net is better suited to progressives. First, the Republican rank and file tend to stay "on message"—maintaining a coherent party line despite disagreements on peripheral issues. Republicans are also a party of centralization—thoroughly in bed with Big Business and all too happy to use government power to regulate the most private kinds of behavior.

The Democratic Party's lack of unity may have provided one of the openings for Net politics. There's more genuine debate, I sense, in the left-wing blogs than on right-wing blogs—more willingness to allow comments, for one thing. "Republicans have a more cohesive caucus," conceded Moulitsas, "but we hash out the issues."

## OPEN SOURCE POLITICS

I have no doubt that the 2004 campaign will be seen, in retrospect, to have shown the first glimmerings of open source politics. What does that mean? Open source politics is about participation—financial as well as on the issues of policy and governance—from people on the edges. People all over the world work on small parts of big open source software projects that create some of the most important and reliable components of the Internet; people everywhere can work on similarly stable components for a participatory political life in much more efficient ways than in the past.

The Dean campaign is hardly the only example of people using the Internet to take action in innovative ways. Perhaps the most intriguing idea, from an open source perspective, was an experiment by MoveOn.org.[129] This left-of-center nonprofit was formed during the Clinton impeachment drama—"Censure the president and move on," was the mantra that launched one of the Net's most powerful political organizations.

The experiment was a contest staged in the spring of 2004, called "Bush in 30 Seconds,"[130] in which MoveOn invited regular people to create their own anti-Bush commercials. The 15 finalists were an incredible display, not just of activist sentiments but of the power of today's inexpensive equipment and software for making videos. It was a demonstration of how personal technology had begun to undermine, as Marshall McLuhan had long since predicted, the broadcast culture of the late 20th century. Tools that were once the preserve of Big Media were now in the hands of the many.

Wes Boyd, MoveOn's cofounder, told me that he and his colleagues were deeply impressed by the passion and creativity that went into the "Bush in 30 Seconds" spots, as well as by their technical execution. Whether one agreed with the ads or found them appalling, they compared well, at least in terms of impact, with spots by the pros. "I'm excited about turning the broadcast medium back on itself," Boyd said.

Open source politics was integral to the Dean campaign, which relied on open source programmers who flocked to the cause and wrote software that ran the campaign's online machinery. After the Dean campaign shut down, some of the programmers moved to other campaigns, and some decided to work on new platforms for the future.

Members of an unaffiliated group called Hack4Dean, later renamed DeanSpace,[131] contributed tools including social-networking software designed to connect volunteers. Their work, itself based on an open source project called Drupal, is continuing. Zack Rosen, one of the programmers, later received venture-capital funding from a California firm that looks for public-interest investments. He and his team would build a "groupware tool set" that included content-management, mail lists and forum posting, blogging, and much more. Initially, the goal was to create an analogue to Yahoo! Groups, the online service that lets nontechies set up mailing lists, but to aim its functions strictly at political campaigns. In the long run, the goals were much more ambitious:

> To establish a permanent foundation that can spearhead social software development projects for non-profit organizations. Unless an organization is committed to hiring full time engineers to do Web development, the only and most frequent solution is to pay tons of money hiring firms to provide proprietary 'black box' Web application products. These firms have a conflict of interest—they live off the monthly checks so they have a huge interest in owning the organization's data and locking them into their services.
>
> We want to create a much cheaper, open, and powerful option for these kinds of services. The goal is to have a full-time development shop that spearheads projects inside open-source communities working on the applications these organizations need, and a consulting firm that can support the toolsets. This is a much more efficient and productive way to do this kind of development.

A safe prediction: Net-savvy campaigning will be the rule by 2008, and it will be lower-level candidates who do the next wave of innovating. The Chandler campaign in Kentucky was just the start.

If 2004 was a breeding ground for what's coming, it's clear that the Internet will be integral to every campaign, not just an add-on. For example, every candidate, or at least campaign, will have a weblog or something like it. Keeping supporters up to date and involved in the campaign's activities, will be as much a part of the routine as keeping the media informed. In most cases, there will be little difference. Campaign web sites will be far more interactive than they are today, and will host a genuine discussion instead of the pseudofolksy lectures we are used to. All insurgent campaigns, and some incumbents, will raise most of their money online.

If they're especially smart, campaign managers will take a page from MoveOn's textbook. If I were running a political campaign of any size, I would be asking my candidate's supporters to send in their best ideas and home-brew advertisements.

Campaigns will also improve the mechanics of getting out the vote. For example, SMS messaging will be in the toolkit for local political operatives who want to make sure a candidate's supporters make it to the polls, remind voters with SMS to make sure they remember to vote, and send a car if a voter needs a ride. These are standard tactics, just updated.

## A CHANGING ROLE FOR JOURNALISTS

Professional journalists, by and large, seemed baffled early on by the edge-to-middle politics Dean was using to his advantage. The top-down hierarchy of modern journalism probably played a role because editors probably couldn't relate any better to the notion of a dispersed campaign than to the idea of readers directly assisting in the creation of journalism.

But once the media grasped what was happening, the coverage emerged. Big Media, and the candidates, also started to realize that some of the best political journalism was coming from outside their ranks. Josh Marshall's Talking Points Memo and Moulitsas' Daily Kos, among many others, offered better context than just about anything the wire services were delivering. It was no coincidence that Wesley Clark gave an in-depth interview to Marshall not long before jumping into the race. And the Command Post,[132] originally created to cover the Iraq war, was a superb collector of all things political.

What the third-party sites such as independent blogs showed was the value of niche journalism in politics. The issues of our times are too complex, too nuanced, for the major media to cover properly, given the economic realities of modern corporate journalism. Typically, even good newspapers devote at most two or three stories to candidates' views on specific issues. Television news operations, especially at local stations, tend to ignore the issues and politics outright.[133] Moreover, there are simply too many political races, from the local to national levels, to cover even if TV news stations cared. This is a golden opportunity for citizen activists to get involved, to help inform others who do care about specific topics. Maybe the masses don't care about all the issues, but individuals care about some of them. "The monolithic media and its increasingly simplistic representation of the world cannot provide the competition of ideas necessary to reach consensus," wrote Joi Ito, an entrepreneur and blogger, in an essay entitled "Emergent Democracy."[134]

What would make a difference? It depends on what you want. "If your goal is debate and discussion, a network of blogs is a more powerful medium than a single blog with lots of readers," Cameron Barrett, who was Wesley Clark's presidential campaign blogger, and who then moved to the Kerry campaign, commented in my blog.[135] "When your goal is message or top-down communication, then a few blogs with a lot of readers is more powerful."

We need both. I'd be thrilled to see a million blogs sprout to cover, and be part of, campaigns of all sorts. If you care deeply about health care, for example, start a weblog covering the candidates' views on the subject. Link to their position papers on a page that lets your readers examine those positions. Then link to news articles that a) contain candidates' statements, b) offer context to the topic, and c) can help your reader understand the overall issue better. Open your comments section both to readers and campaign staffers, and welcome the discussion that brings better information to everyone involved. You will have done a service.

Clone that model and apply it to every issue in every race. If enough people join the process, we'll have a flood of valuable information. No doubt, some of it will be biased, or outright wrong. That's where Big Media organizations can help. We in the media can collect the best alternative coverage of the issues and publish it on our sites. We can list blogs by category and, when warranted, by bias of the author. When we learn that a certain blog or site is trying to mislead people, we can indicate the bias, or just drop it from the listing. We should, of course, ask our audience for assistance in all of this. Naturally, we won't be the only ones trying to offer this kind of collected resource, but we may have sufficient credibility to make our aggregation among the most useful.

One of the best examples of this very thing is the British Broadcasting Corp.'s ambitious new iCan project, which aims to fuse citizen activism and journalism. To assist average people in being activists, the BBC has created a web-based platform that combines data on issues with tools citizens can use to push their own agendas in the public sphere. The journalists then observe what average people are doing and focus some of their coverage on what the activists are reporting. I'll talk more about this pathbreaking project in Chapter 6.

## THE TOOLS OF BETTER GOVERNANCE

Politics doesn't stop when the elections are decided. Governing is political, by definition. The tools of many-to-many communications will transform government if politicians and bureaucrats cooperate and lead. How this will occur is still a bit foggy, because a true deployment of e-government is many years away. But the potential may be even more obvious than in campaigns.

To date, e-government has largely consisted of static web pages offering information to taxpayers, businesses, and other constituents of governmental services. The interactivity in such sites tends to be limited to filling out the occasional form or making an appointment. It's the standard top-down approach moved to the Net.

But it doesn't have to offer a substandard result, not when it's done right. For evidence, visit the remarkable "Earth 911,"[136] a site created by an environmental activist that has become indispensable to citizens and governments alike. Phil Windley, the former state of Utah chief information officer, calls it a "public-private partnership that happened unilaterally"— that is, at the instigation of a single motivated citizen.

That citizen is Chris Warner, who's been working at this project for about 15 years from his home base of suburban Phoenix. Operating initially on a shoestring and now with contributions from companies and some government support, he and his team have collected under one virtual roof the most comprehensive array of environmental information you can find anywhere. If you visit the home page and type in your Zip Code, you'll find local data for that community from a variety of federal, state, local and corporate sources. Earth 911 is a clearinghouse that serves governments and people in their communities. Thousands of government employees, from a variety of agencies, send their information to Earth 911. Its staff massages the data and then arranges it so citizens can use it. In other words, what they've created is a highly centralized core with a thoroughly decentralized data-collection system that feels utterly local to the citizen looking for information.

Warner and his team have replicated the system in a pets-oriented site called (what else?) Pets 911,[137] again collecting massive amounts of data and massaging it so it's locally relevant. News organizations have started using Pets 911 on their web sites, a trend Warner is thrilled to support. They've also just finished an "Amber Alert" support project to make the new national missing-child system work more efficiently. The possibilities are almost endless.

"There are hundreds of uses for this medium we've built," Warner said of the open source software platform his team has created. "We want it to be plagiarized. That's the best thing that could happen."

Going from the bottom up, from average citizens to the power centers, is a considerably more difficult, but potentially more rewarding, endeavor. There are several reasons for this, only one of which is obvious: the potential cost savings in letting citizens take on more of the chores. This doesn't have to resemble the use of institutional voice-mail systems, where costs are literally shifted to the caller (assuming the caller's time has some value, as is always the case). The time saved by doing things online can easily outweigh the hassle of doing things in person, especially in a bureaucratic way.

When I renew my car registration every year, I do it through the California Department of Motor Vehicles web site. I can't print the little sticker that goes over the old one on the license plate—a shame, actually, but an understandable decision given the potential for counterfeiting stickers—but I can handle every part of the process except the actual sending of the sticker and new registration to me. What do I save? The cost of the stamp and envelope, for one thing. But the more important value is that I'm not mailing my check to the DMV; I know my payment will have arrived on time.

What's missing from the DMV site, and from just about every other government site I can name, is any sense that a bureaucrat has the slightest concern for what the citizen thinks or knows. And this is where the tools of bottom-up journalism could have a genuine value. The simplest example is a suggestion box—a real one, where people in government listen to the citizens. Just as journalists need to hear what the audience is saying, governments can and should learn from voters and taxpayers.

For the briefest time after September 11, there was a glimmer of precisely this.

On the DefenseLink web site,[138] the public face of the U.S. military, a link appeared. It asked the public for "Your Ideas to Counter Terrorism." The solicitation didn't last long, but it was a smart move, with great potential. Here's why.

The military and law enforcement are, almost by definition, centralized entities. But they're facing a decentralized opponent in a kind of combat known as "asymmetrical warfare"—in which one side is big and powerful by traditional measures while the other side is small, decentralized, and able to leverage technology in horrific ways.[139]

There's growing recognition of the value of decentralizing people and data at a time when big, centralized operations may be targets. But we need to find ways to bring the nation's collective energy and brainpower to bear on the threat. As Sun Microsystems' Bill Joy has said so memorably, most of the brightest people don't work for any one organization. Tapping the power of everyone is the best approach.

The Homeland Security Information Network, under construction as I write this, is built in part on peer-to-peer technology. It's designed to let various levels of governments share information quickly and securely, and on an ad hoc basis when necessary. The furthest the system goes is to local public-safety personnel. What it does not do, at least not yet, is solicit information from average citizens. To me, this suggests insufficient recognition at high levels that in a world of asymmetric threats, the people who are not in official chains of command will be more and more important.

John Robb, who served in a U.S. Air Force special operations unit and later ran an Internet research firm, helped me understand asymmetry and its consequences in the wake of the attacks. I asked him how we could use the power at the edges of networks and society to counteract the bad guys.[140]

Among his suggestions: "Build a feedback loop that greatly expands on the Pentagon's suggestion box but also narrows down the individual questions. Marshall McLuhan first proposed this (and I believe it): For any problem there is a person or persons in a large population of educated people that don't see it as a problem. We need a feedback loop that can filter up knowledge and insight. For example: If you have seen a loophole in airport security and have a solution as to how to correct it, there should be a mechanism for getting that information to the people that can make the change."

Note the direction of the information, from the bottom to the top—or, more accurately, from the edge to the middle.

An extension of the feedback loop, Robb said, is to create much more targeted "knowledge networks" tapping into specific pools of information. "Our foreign service and military units don't have enough Pushtu speakers," he wrote just prior to the U.S. invasion of Afghanistan, referring to one of that Asian nation's dominant languages. "However, I am sure we have tens of thousands [of Pushtu speakers] living in the U.S. right now. Why not tap them for expertise in real-time?" How? By giving soldiers satellite phones to call Pushtu speakers who could serve as translators.

The public-health world could take advantage of these kinds of techniques. Bioterrorism, in fact, may absolutely require them. Ronald E. LaPorte, a public-health expert at the University of Pittsburgh, has proposed an "Internet civil defense" using the power of networks to help neighbors watch out for each other. As USA Today's Kevin Maney described it in October 2001:[141]

In an attack, the millions of Net users could act as sensors, feeding information about illnesses, suspicious activity and so on to the captain, who would feed it to the system. Authorities would instantly know what was happening. Experts everywhere — whether a molecular biologist at a university or a grandmother in Dubuque, Iowa, who lived through smallpox—would instantly be tapped, so they could see the information and try to help. Sure, it could be used fraudulently, but the risks would be outweighed by the rewards.

In reverse, officials could send the captains instructions on what to tell people to do and real-time information about events. By disseminating reliable, trusted information, the system might prevent panic. Individual Internet users would have to take the responsibility of passing information to non-Net users.

When the stakes are this high, and the threat this different, we should be looking for the best ideas wherever they originate. I'm betting that the center won't hold if we waste power at the edges.

## Chapter 6

# Professional Journalists Join the Conversation

In October 1999, the *Jane's Intelligence Review*, a journal widely followed in national security circles, wondered whether it was on the right track with an article about computer security and cyber-terrorism. The editors went straight to some experts—the denizens of Slashdot—and published a draft. In hundreds of postings on the site's message system, the technically adept members of that community promptly tore apart the draft and gave, often in colorful language, a variety of perspectives and suggestions. *Jane's* went back to the drawing board and rewrote the entire article from scratch. The community had created something, and *Jane's* gratefully noted the contribution in the article it ultimately published.[142]

I started my weblog the same month. It was an experiment, one of the first blogs by a mainstream journalist. But it proved to be the linchpin in my understanding that my colleagues and I—and my profession as a whole—were entering a new stage of development. My readers, I realized, had become my collaborators.

Four months later, Oh Yeon Ho and a small team launched OhmyNews.com, a Korean online newspaper. From the beginning, they assumed that their readers weren't just passive vessels for other people's work. "Every citizen's a reporter," Oh wrote on February 22, 2000, as he announced the new site. "Journalists aren't some exotic species, they're everyone who seeks to take new developments, put them into writing, and share them with others."[143]

What was happening? In an emerging era of multidirectional, digital communications, the audience can be an integral part of the process—and it's becoming clear that they *must* be.

It boils down to something simple: readers (or viewers or listeners) collectively know more than media professionals do. This is true by definition: they are many, and we are often just one. We need to recognize and, in the best sense of the word, use their knowledge. If we don't, our former audience will bolt when they realize they don't have to settle for half-baked coverage; they can come into the kitchen themselves.

In this chapter, we'll look at how the news industry can adapt to an evolution that is turning some old notions on their heads. It may be painful for some of us, but I will argue that the rewards are worth it. We really have no choice, anyway.

"More and more, journalism is going to be owned by the audience," said Jeff Jarvis, a prolific blogger who heads Advance Publications' Advance.net online operation. "That doesn't mean there isn't a place for pro-journalists, who will always be there— who need to be there—to gather the facts, ask questions with some measure of discipline and pull together a larger audience. What I've learned is that the audience, given half a chance, has a lot to say. The Internet is the first medium owned by the audience, the first medium to give the audience a voice."

As I noted in the *Introduction*, we shouldn't see this as a threat. It is, rather, the best opportunity in decades to do even better journalism.

The business questions are much more difficult to answer because many of the same developments affecting newsrooms are also, as noted earlier, having a massive and ultimately negative impact on the bottom line of Big Media news organizations. I hope we can survive what's coming because I believe in the mission of journalism and fear that serious investigative reporting will diminish, and perhaps nearly disappear, if big newspapers and other serious outlets wither; what blogger will take on the next Watergate scandal the way *The Washington Post* did?

## TRADITIONAL MEDIA'S OPPORTUNITY

When most Big Media companies consider having a conversation with their audience, they tend not to push many boundaries. For example, it astonishes me that some organizations still don't put reporters' (much less editors') email addresses at the end of stories. There is no plausible excuse for leaving out contact information when the articles are posted on the Web. A news operation that fails even this test is not remotely serious about engaging its audience.

Bulletin boards don't fully cut it, either. *The New York Times'* forums[144] frequently contain valuable insights, but it's doubtful that many (if any) of those ideas ever reach the actual journalists inside the *Times* newsroom. If the staff isn't part of the discussion, it's just readers talking with each other—and they can do that without the *Times*. Contrast the paper's forums with *Times* columnist Nicholas Kristof's "Kristof Responds" discussions,[145] a truly valuable addition to the paper's repertoire.

Slate, the online magazine owned by Microsoft, has come up with one of the most useful ways of handling readers' input. The "Fraywatch" page[146]—"What's happening in our readers' forum"—is a compilation of what Slate editors consider the most interesting comments posted by readers. Snippets from comments are reassembled, with context from the editor plus links to the original postings, in a coherent and entertaining way. This is useful journalism in its own right, even as it demonstrates the value of readers' contributions.

Web chats featuring journalists are a step in the right direction, but are once again only a step. *The Washington Post*'s frequent online Q&A sessions,[147] in which reporters answer questions from readers, are a useful addition to the online operation, but they aren't the only kind of interactivity we must adopt.

My own experience may be instructive. Covering technology in Silicon Valley is a humbling but rewarding job. In most gatherings, I'm taking up the far-left data point on the intelligence bell curve. Of course, being the least knowledgeable person in the room has its advantages; I always learn something.

That's one reason why my blog has been so helpful. It's sparked deeper conversations with my sources and my readers, who are always telling me things I don't know. This is interactive journalism.

As a columnist, writing a weblog has been easier for me than it might have been for a beat reporter. I was already putting my opinions in the newspaper, so it wasn't much of a stretch to put them online in what amounted to a bunch of mini-columns. But there's no requirement that blogs be opinionated. A reporter can easily post items relating to her beat, the kinds of tidbits that once made it into a "reporter's notebook," as well as news that won't make it into the paper for space reasons.

Occasionally, I ask readers for their ideas on columns I haven't written yet; I explain the topic and say what I think I understand about it. No, I don't tip off the competition when I have a genuine scoop but, as a columnist, I'm usually talking about things that are already known in a general sense. My online readers, who include a surprising number of traditional sources, are never shy about noting the angles I might have missed or telling me I'm dead wrong. I consider it all, and the resulting column is better for the process. Recall our earlier discussion of "open source" software, a process in which the code itself is developed by a community and is then freely available. Think of this as a form of open source journalism.

One of the most significant differences between print and the Web is that web-based conversations transcend geographical boundaries. Steve Outing, a longtime observer of online news, as well as a blogger and columnist, wrote in late 2003 in his "Editor and Publisher" magazine column that my blog has helped give me a global reach instead of a local one. That's gratifying if true, but the major value has been in the way my readers have made me better at my job.

When readers first began commenting on my blog in mid-2003, I didn't know what to expect. Here's how it tends to work in the best case. I post an item. Someone responds to me. Someone responds to the first or second comment, and before long, the people commenting are talking with each other, not just with me. I think of it as a mini-Slashdot, a small set of mostly literate and thoughtful comments. The blog does attract its share of trolls (people whose aim in life seems to be to ruin public discussions), but by and large the process works well.[148]

Blogs have been slow to take off in the mainstream media. I attribute this more to the innate conservatism of the Big Media business than anything else. But there is another reason, too: mistrust among traditional editors of a genre that threatens to undermine what they consider core values—namely editorial control and ensuring that readers trust, or at least not assume there is an absence of, the journalists' objectivity and fairness. This hasn't been an entirely wrong-headed worry, but it is overblown.

Despite the resistance, dozens of mainstream journalism organizations have adopted blogs, a trend that seems likely to accelerate. Not a week goes by without me getting a call from someone in the business who's thinking about doing a blog and who wants to hear about the advantages and potential pitfalls. CyberJournalist.net keeps a comprehensive list of blogs by and about journalists.[149] They run the gamut of topics, from politics to arts to technology to pure commentary.

The most successful blogs by professional journalists have shared some of the characteristics that make any blog worth reading: voice, focus, real reporting, and good writing. Dan Weintraub's California Insider political blog[150] at the *Sacramento Bee* became a must read during the 2003 California recall election that installed Arnold Schwarzenegger as the state's governor. (Weintraub had an unfortunate run-in with *Bee* editors, who now insist on editing his blog postings before they go out on the Web.) James Taranto's Best of the Web Today blog[151] for *The Wall Street Journal*'s editorial page is another classic; I don't agree with much of the conservative doctrine he highlights, but he does it with great style. Sheila Lennon's Subterranean Homepage News,[152] affiliated with *The Providence*

*Journal,* offers perspectives on a variety of topics, many of which are media-related. The quintessential journalism blog needs no introduction to journalists. It's a safe bet that most working American journalists with web access visit Jim Romenesko's Poynter Institute blog at least once a day; it has become the water cooler for the profession. There's something liberating about the blog form for journalists. The format encourages informality and experimentation, not to mention the valuable interaction with the audience that makes coverage better.

Group blogs, where more than one person can submit postings, lack the voice of the single individual, but they can work. A smart approach here has been the "event blog"—a one-off effort pegged to some major news event. Probably the first such blog by a newspaper was the *Charlotte Observer*'s "Dispatches from along the coast," which provided coverage of Hurricane Isabel in August 1998.[153] On December 31, 1999, and January 1, 2000, SiliconValley.com (where my blog appears) pulled together everything it could find on the Web to cover a New Year's Eve and Day that had enormous emotional impact and, many people feared (wrongly, as it turned out), might bring a variety of computer-related disasters due to the "Y2K bug."

Breaking news is one of the great opportunities for using these techniques. My colleague at the *San Jose Mercury News,* Tom Mangan, had a blog (now retired) for copy editors, delightfully named "Prints the Chaff,"[154] on which he urged newsrooms to create what might be called insta-blogs for big local stories. It's partly a competitive issue, he wrote:

> If we have a blog up and running within minutes of a big story breaking, we cut Google and the [other] bloggers out of the equation. If we make it interactive, we make our site the go-to location for breaking news. We will open ourselves up to the problem of people entering comments that later prove untrue, but readers will learn to distinguish between the feedback—half of which is nonsense—and the work of the pros, which, hopefully, will have a much smaller nonsense factor.

Many journalists, unable to get official permission to do blogs on their organizations' sites, have launched their own. There are risks in doing so, as CNN's Kevin Sites discovered in Iraq when CNN forced him to quit writing his blog. A spokesman sniffily told *Online Journalism Review*: "CNN.com prefers to take a more structured approach to presenting the news. We do not blog. CNN.com will continue to provide photo galleries, video clips, breaking stories and interactive modules as ways to involve readers in learning about the war."[155] This attitude, a classic top-down approach to the news, ended up hurting the network more than the correspondent, who later went to work for MSNBC (which welcomed the blog). By killing Sites's blog, CNN was showing how a network that once was at the cutting edge of journalism had become another widget in the Time Warner assembly line.

The case of Steve Olafson was more about what he was writing than the fact that he was blogging in the first place. Olafson was a political reporter for the *Houston Chronicle*. Using a pseudonym, he also published a blog that contained political commentary—sometimes going after people he covered as part of his regular job. The *Chronicle* was right to call this unacceptable and, in mid-2002, requested that the blog be taken down on the grounds that it might compromise his credibility. But then the newspaper fired Olafson.[156] This was an overreaction. The paper could have shifted him to another position or disciplined him in some other way. The message was unambiguous: blog at your own risk.

Dennis Horgan, an editor at the *Hartford Courant*, wasn't fired, but he was ordered to stop posting commentary on his blog.[157] The *Courant*'s top editor, Brian Toolan, attempted to justify this move in a 2003 essay in the *Nieman Reports* magazine, saying, in part:

> This is not an issue of freedom of speech. It is about professional expectations and, when they are ignored, as in this case, the newspaper's standards and public responsibilities are compromised. Like most newspapers, the Courant has an

ethics code. It has language that directs that "an individual's interests outside the paper should not come into conflict with, or create the appearance of conflict with, the staff member's professional duties at the Courant." Horgan, and others, argued that since he now edits the Travel section, his public views on public matters don't interfere with the newspaper's coverage of those same issues.

I don't accept that logic. I know some readers, who depend on the paper, would not accept it either, and I recognize how readers' perceptions can hurt.[158]

We can applaud Toolan's wish to keep high ethical standards, but where was the conflict of interest? I can't see one in this situation. If a few readers' perceptions were misguided, that's their problem, not the newspaper's. Toolan was clearly correct that there was no free-speech issue, however. He had the right, as Horgan's employer, to make this mistake. (The paper later attempted what looked like a clumsy compromise, giving Horgan a web-only column that resembled a blog.)

Newspapers are moving ahead nonetheless.[159] The family-owned *Spokesman-Review*[160] in Spokane, Washington, has some excellent staff blogs but also makes a practice of pointing to blogs written by people in the community. One of the most forward-looking is the *Journal-World*[161] in Lawrence, Kansas. Rob Curley, general manager of *World Online*, runs both the newspaper's web site and Lawrence.com (an affiliated site), and deserves kudos for the innovations he and his smart staff have brought to a hidebound industry. In every way possible, they've engaged the community. Forums have brought forth new voices. So has blogging.

Lawrence.com—which is deliberately distinct from its newspaper parent—runs several blogs by members of the community in addition to a blog written by one of the paper's political reporters. Curley told me:

When we started the blogs on Lawrence.com, we intended them to be fairly similar to what most think of when they think of blogs ... frequently updated posts with an immediate interaction between the writer and the readers. But that isn't what they've become.

The blogs on Lawrence.com have pretty much become columns on steroids. They're almost always fairly long. And though the writers will respond to the readers several times a day, they rarely post more than one new thing a week.

They're kind of interactive columns.

Why I like them is because they feel so real to me—from the language to the topics to the responses.

There is a real sense of community in our blogs, and it's a community that more than likely doesn't read the daily newspaper, and it probably doesn't visit our newspaper site.

More important than anything else, our blogs make Lawrence.com feel and taste like Lawrence—maybe not the Lawrence that a 50-year-old resident knows, but definitely the Lawrence that a 20-year-old knows. And that's exactly what we were after.

Curley and his team have won just about every award there is for online journalism. No wonder. They get the Web.

## AUTHORITY FROM LINKING, LISTENING

The most web-like activity is linking: pointing to other people's content. Newspapers and other journalism organizations have been learning to do a better job of this on their sites, offering pointers to articles and data that reside outside their sites. We need to do more than that.

On my blog, I frequently point at other news organizations' stories, including a local competitor, the *San Francisco Chronicle*. If I have the choice of pointing to an equally good story on my newspaper's own site, I'll naturally do so. But when the competition has done a better job than we have on a topic I care about, I'd be shortchanging my readers if I didn't take them to the best coverage. No one from my company has ever suggested I do otherwise.

I also point to sites of nontraditional journalists and, whenever possible, I post or point to the deepest source materials, such as transcripts and other data that provide more context. We in pro-journalism tend to do this on big projects when we post things such as affidavits, interactive maps, and the like. But the authority of a story increases with the links to the best original material from which it was derived. We can learn more from the bloggers about this.

Increasingly, I'm glad to say, news organizations are catching on. While online versions of news stories that have run in the newspaper rarely link to competitors' work, newspaper bloggers have been more wide-ranging in pointing outside. Dan Froomkin's "White House Briefing"[162] on *The Washington Post*'s site, which started in early 2004, was especially active in this regard, though he tended to ignore blogs in favor of establishment media. Similarly, *The New York Times*' "Times on the Trail,"[163] a column that looks like a blog but isn't officially called one, has sometimes been generous in outside pointers.

We can also increase our credibility by listening to our online critics, and we're beginning to do just that. Long gone are the days when criticism was handled, except in extreme cases, by just two publications of note, the *Columbia Journalism Review*[164] and the *American Journalism Review*.[165]

A right-leaning blogger who calls himself "Patterico"[166] has made it one of his missions to critique *The Los Angeles Times* for what he sees as an assortment of left-leaning sins. In early 2004, he took the *Times*, which he calls the "Dog Trainer," to task for its coverage of Supreme Court Justice Antonin Scalia's conflicts of interest, including the judge's hunting vacation with Vice President Dick Cheney, an old friend, when the court was hearing a pivotal case involving Cheney's Energy Task Force. Patterico observed that Justice Ruth Bader Ginsburg also had a conflict of note, a connection to the National Organization for Women (NOW). His correspondence with the *Times* got results. On March 11, 2004, he wrote, proudly: "On the one hand, I have to hand it to *The Los Angeles Times*. They have run a front-page story about Justice Ginsburg's speech to the NOW Legal Defense Fund. On the other hand, why did I have to be the one to tell them about it?"[167]

For me, this follow-on complaint doesn't hold up. Journalists find out much of what we print and broadcast from people who tell us things—people like Patterico, who helped make the news.

## ASKING THE FORMER AUDIENCE FOR HELP

Inviting the audience to contribute isn't a new phenomenon. After all, we've asked readers to write letters to the editor for a long time, and we generally answer the phones when readers call with tips or complaints. In other words, some conversation has always taken place; we just need to have more.

Some of the most important photos and videos in recent news history were the product of amateurs; we can scarcely imagine the second half of the 20th century without the gruesome Zapruder film of John F. Kennedy's assassination. More recently, as video cameras have become popular, we have seen what happens when average people captured important events such as police beatings of suspects and approaching tornados. And it was amateurs who caught the most horrific images of the United Airlines 767 fireball as it crashed into the second World Trade Center tower on September 11, 2001.

In each of those cases, the public was communicating through the mass media; the amateur videos rapidly made it, as in earlier events, onto CNN and the other major TV networks. For the foreseeable future, this will continue to be the case because TV is our gathering place in national crises, because of the high bandwidth costs for offering video over the Web, and for the simple fact that mass media still reaches the biggest audience. But as more and more members of the former audience make and capture the news, their contributions will be understood as essential to the news-gathering process at all levels.[168]

We can still learn a thing or two from nonjournalism organizations. In February 2003, after the space shuttle broke up on reentry to the Earth's atmosphere, NASA put out a call to anyone who had photographs that might help in the investigation of the accident, and thousands responded.[169]

Then, in the weeks before the launch of the 2003 Iraq war, the BBC asked its audience for pictures having anything to do with the conflict.[170] It received hundreds, some of which it posted in a photo essay that was both journalistically smart and emotionally moving for viewers.

Those were obvious things to do, though not many traditional journalism organizations bothered even to try. It will soon be a no-brainer, I believe, for every news web site to prominently post an email address to which people can send their pictures, whether from phones or personal computers. The newspaper (or broadcast outlet or whatever kind of news service) should periodically post the best pictures online and in the regular news product. In this way, they can get the public accustomed to using the medium in this manner. Then, when some big event occurs, the organization will have trained at least some people to use the posting service almost by reflex.

Readers of the *San Diego Tribune*'s "Sign On San Diego" online operation were an essential part of that city's biggest local story of 2003: the wildfires that raged through southern California. The readers, urged on by the site, posted photos of and messages about what they were seeing. Some used the forums to create discussions aimed at the residents of a single block in a suburb; neighbors were filling each other in on what was happening. This was local news at its finest, and the people were doing it for themselves, assisted in the best possible way by their local newspaper.[171]

In addition to photos, news organizations can make it easy for readers to send them tips through SMS (short text messages

thorough attempt yet to bring tomorrow's journalism to life with a project called iCan.[174] At its heart is a fairly daring notion: equip the audience with some of the tools of political activism. Then watch what they do and report on it.

iCan was an outgrowth of both journalistic and political considerations, project leaders told me when I visited London in October 2003. First, the BBC and other media organizations were missing big stories. For example, huge fuel-price protests in 2000, which led to turmoil on the British roads, came as a surprise, even though the issue had been boiling up on the Internet. The 2001 national elections in the United Kingdom were another major catalyst. Turnout was low, by British standards, at about 60 percent. One of the BBC's core missions is to help the electorate make informed decisions, and the service's leadership wanted to know what it could do better.

"We found some interesting things," said Martin Vogel, the iCan project codirector. For instance, the 40 percent of the electorate that didn't vote was "by no means apathetic" about the issues of the day, but rather unhappy with the candidates and policies being offered. With younger audiences moving away from traditional media to new media, the BBC looked for a way to use new media to foster political involvement.

So iCan aimed to create a platform to help citizen activists influence the system from the local level on up. Local was especially important, because it's where people feel the most impact. BBC journalists spent months pulling together a host of information aimed at citizen activists, including pointers to various resources on and off the Web. Journalists wrote guidelines and instructions on everything from how to start a campaign to dealing with troublesome neighbors. "We let people know they can do things for themselves," said Samanthi Dissanayake, a broadcast journalist who signed on for the iCan experiment.

But iCan's users, not the staff, are expected to write the bulk of the guides as time goes on. The editorial staff will monitor what emerges and will exercise some editorial control, such as removing libelous or flagrantly inaccurate information. "The job of the journalist, more than ever, is to be a filter," said Tim Levell, iCan's editorial project leader.

iCan launched in early November with a national web site and five pilot areas where the BBC was focusing additional resources. One was in the county of Cambridgeshire, an hour's train ride north of London that spans the demographic gamut. It includes a university city, a somewhat downtrodden urban center, and farmland. As in three of the other four pilot areas, a journalist was dispatched from regular duties to focus exclusively on iCan. The journalist helped to seed local activism, monitored the citizen campaigns, and then reported the news to reflect local concerns.

One of the first campaigns created by citizens was an initiative to curb schoolhouse bullying. This came as a surprise to Levell. Of everything iCan's researchers imagined in their planning process, "we never modeled bullying as the first thing to bubble up," he said. But the BBC was listening.

iCan may or may not turn out to be a model for other news organizations, but it's a valuable experiment. While news companies make it their mission to inform the public, few have made it a mission to arm them with tools they can use to make a public ruckus. To watch what people can do with such tools, and to report on it, takes the process even further. The BBC isn't just making the news with iCan; it's helping citizens make their own.

## CASE STUDY: THE CITIZEN REPORTERS

Lee Pong Ryul had a day job in engineering at a semiconductor company near Seoul, South Korea. In his spare time, he was helping to shape tomorrow's journalism.

Lee was an active "citizen reporter" for OhmyNews, the online news service. OhmyNews has shaken up the journalism and political establishments while attracting an enormous audience by melding 20th century tradition—the journalism-as-lecture model, in which organizations tell the audience what the news is and the audience either buys it or doesn't—into something bottom-up, interactive, and democratic. This is an important experiment, and when I visited in the spring of 2003, it was clear that the bet was already paying off.

The influence of OhmyNews, just four years old at the time, was substantial and expanding. It had been credited with having helped elect the nation's current president, Roh Moo Hyun, who ran as a reformer. Roh granted his first post-election interview to the publication, snubbing the three major conservative newspapers that have dominated the print journalism scene for years.

If OhmyNews is a glimpse into the future, so is South Korea—and that's no coincidence. It's a wired nation; more than two-thirds of households are connected to the Internet, most with high-speed links. The Internet is an always-on part of everyday life, not an afterthought. That deep digital pool has spawned some 21st century kinds of media, from complex, multiplayer online games to publications such as OhmyNews.

Even taxi drivers who don't have time for newspapers have heard of OhmyNews. The site draws millions of visitors daily. Advertisers support both the web site and a weekly print edition, and the operation had been profitable in recent months, its chief executive and founder, Oh Yeon Ho, told me.

He was a 38-year-old former writer for progressive magazines. With a staff of about 50 and legions of "citizen reporter" contributors—more than 26,000 had signed up when I met him, and more than 15,000 had published stories under their own bylines—Oh and his colleagues were creating real value in an emerging journalistic reality.

"The main concept is that every citizen can be a reporter," he said. "We changed the concept of the reporter."

The old way meant becoming a professional journalist and getting a press card. Journalism was a credentialed and, in Korea, a somewhat elevated position in society—bizarre as that sounds to readers in the U.S., where we journalists enjoy roughly the same public esteem as politicians and used-car salesmen. The new way, Oh said, is that "a reporter is the one who has the news and who is trying to inform others."

The paper's citizen reporters go into issues that the mainstream media haven't covered, said Jeong Woon Hyeon, chief editor. The site posts about 70 percent of the roughly 200 stories submitted each day, after staff editors read the stories. Postings work on a hierarchy corresponding to the place on the page; the lower the headline appears, the less important or interesting the editors consider it. The higher, the more newsworthy—and the more the freelance contributor is paid.

When OhmyNews started, the idea wasn't entirely new. News organizations have long used stringers, people who contribute freelance articles. What was so different with OhmyNews was that anyone could sign up, and it wasn't difficult to get published. On the Web, space for news is essentially unlimited,[175] and OhmyNews welcomed contributions from just about everyone. The real-people nature of the contributors lent further appeal to the site.

The melding of old and new was extensive. The company issued temporary staff press cards so some of the more active contributors could cover specific events. Full-time professional staffers, meanwhile, worked in a time-honored manner. They jockeyed with reporters from big newspapers, magazines, and broadcast outlets for scoops in government and business, then lobbied for the best possible display of their work.

OhmyNews reflected its bosses' passion for going beyond conservative newspapers' constrained view of the world. Its coverage of events such as the death of two schoolgirls, crushed by a U.S. Army vehicle in an accident during the summer of 2002, forced the hand of mainstream media, which was downplaying the story. Protest demonstrations after that incident evolved into nationwide anger against America, and a profoundly nationalist fervor that helped elect Roh.

Oh's rise from underground magazine writer to powerful media figure had any number of ironies. One is that the government he disliked was instrumental in wiring the nation for high-speed data access, creating the conditions that ultimately gave OhmyNews an opening. Then there was the way he came to realize that he should start OhmyNews. He went to the U.S. in 1997–99 to get a master's degree at Regent University in Virginia. The school's president was Pat Robertson, the evangelist and right-wing political figure.

To know America, a journalist friend told Oh, you have to know how the conservative right operates. In Robertson's case, part of his strategy was counteracting what he saw as a liberal-biased press, and so offered media courses through Regent.

"I learned their techniques," he explained. "But my approach is quite different."

In one course, students' homework was to create a new media organization on paper. Oh's imaginary company was the genesis of OhmyNews, and "I got an A+," he said wryly.

The vision was to use the Internet, which was then growing like mad in Korea, and to capture the power of average people who, Oh strongly believed, did not back South Korea's government and overall policies—people who also weren't being represented by the conservative media companies that controlled about 80 percent of daily circulation. A 50-50 liberal-conservative balance would be much better, he said.

Oh and his colleagues were well aware that the interactive nature of the medium extends far beyond OhmyNews' appeals for contributions from citizen reporters, and their approach reflected that understanding. Each story had a link to a comments page. Readers could, and did, post comments ranging from supportive to harsh, and they voted on whether they approved or disapproved of specific comments.

Sometimes the journalists replied directly on the comments page. Lee Pong Ryul, one of OhmyNews' most active citizen reporters, regularly replied to clarify points and to answer questions He also said he got plenty of email responses to his work.

In previous writing jobs, Lee focused on family topics, often mentioning his two daughters, because his political writings on other online sites had gotten little or no response.

OhmyNews, he says, changed the equation. Here, at last, was a publication that reflected some of his views of politics and society—and that was glad to publish what he wrote to a readership hungry for such information. In about three years of contributing to OhmyNews, he averaged about 100 stories a year. Editors at the publication check spelling, he said, but not much else. Fact checking by OhmyNews staff is reserved for "hard" news stories, not personal features such as his.

He certainly didn't do it for the money. Stories that make the OhmyNews equivalent of the front page earned him a little less than U.S. $20, the top rate at the time. He got commensurately less for stories that ran lower on the page, and figures he made between $50 and $100 a month in freelance payments—not a pittance but hardly a fortune.

Lee had no ambitions to be a professional writer. "I don't think I'm qualified," he said. But he believed he won, on balance, a greater response for the kinds of stories he was writing—about regular people's lives—than some of the professional journalism that was running in the newspapers and on the site every day.

OhmyNews' ambitions aren't limited to print. It runs video webcasting services and plans to expand its multimedia presence. Someday, citizen reporters such as Lee will be contributing video reports, not just text, in a dazzling, multidirectional sharing of information.

The easy coexistence of the amateurs and professionals will, soon enough, seem natural. Publications such as OhmyNews will pop up everywhere because they make sense, combining the best of old and new journalistic forms. OhmyNews is an experiment in tomorrow. So far, it's a brilliant one.[176]

## NEWSROOM TOOLS

Even as we invite the former audience into the process, journalists must first embrace the technology that makes collaborative reporting possible. We've been fairly good at this in the past, but technological changes are accelerating.

Writing on the Web would be simple if text was all that mattered. The next generation of multimedia tools will give journalists more options—and vex editors in the process. The advent of camera phones and small, high-quality digital cameras has given professional journalists great new tools that transcend the desktop. News organizations should issue a camera phone and digital camera to every member of the staff and urge people to shoot anything that even resembles news. In addition to the camera in my phone, which takes generally lousy pictures, I also carry a small digital camera that not only takes high-quality photographs but also 30-frames-per-second video with sound.

We should be encouraging reporters to get audio and video snapshots. I'm not suggesting that we turn reporters into videographers (not yet, anyway), because anything that distracts from the reporting mission in a big way will harm journalism. But it only makes sense to get a quick video of a scene, such as the office of someone we're interviewing; maybe it'll go on the web site with a little editing, but even if it's unsuitable for general consumption, it can remind the reporter of some physical details for the actual story. Similarly, audio clips can amplify a subject, giving a better sense of the person being interviewed; since reporters increasingly make audio recordings of interviews, there's no reason not to turn them into transcripts or extended excerpts to be posted online (and they should be whenever possible).

Will this threaten the professional photographers who capture images so well for news organizations today? I hope not. Their skills are far beyond mine and most other amateurs. But we have to be ready to capture images when the pros aren't around; even a poorly composed photo of a pivotal event is better than no picture at all.

The next generation of mobile phones will give reporters more than the ability to capture pictures and short videos. They will be publishing tools as well. The BBC, leading the way as it so often does, issued "3G" mobile phones to some of its journalists in late 2003.[177] The phones worked on the latest high-speed mobile data networks, enabling the reporters to file video interviews from the field in real time.


## TEACHING NEW TRICKS

Meanwhile, there is a gap in journalism education, an often hidebound institution in its own right. It's not that the better journalism schools lack technology or don't know how to use it, but rather they tend to serve such a conservative and slow-moving industry.

I confess to some skepticism about undergraduate journalism degrees in the first place. Some of the best journalists I know never took a course in the subject; then again, others have. Whatever your view of this endlessly debatable topic, the fact is that journalism schools are the main source of new staff. But we can't allow them to crank out a new generation of reporters, editors, photographers, and broadcasters who don't understand and appreciate how the profession has changed. The problem is actually more serious among faculties than students. It doesn't surprise me that the students I've met, in guest lectures at U.S. universities and through my own experience teaching a new media course at the University of Hong Kong for five weeks each fall, are more open to this new style than most faculties and deans.[178]

Interactive, online reporting and editing is becoming a staple of the curriculum. Teaching the use of tools is relatively trivial, however. Teaching students how to be relentlessly inquisitive with a sense of fairness and a genuine wish to inform the public is harder. There's a lot to be said for the traditional liberal-arts education in that regard, and better undergraduate journalism programs offer precisely that kind of education.

Jay Rosen at New York University makes a persuasive case for a new kind of journalism education, not just an updated understanding and practice of the trade itself. He envisions a journalism school that takes its inspiration from, of all places, the Yale School of Drama, not from the quasi-science the information profession pushes in most universities.

"The Yale Drama School has two halves," he told me. "One says, here's how to study drama and become an actor or director. The other side says, here's the Yale Repertory Theater and cabaret, and does productions." He wants NYU to replicate some of this.

With a foundation grant, NYU is trying to create what Rosen calls a "portfolio model of journalism education." One idea is to attract students, some of whom are already professional journalists, who believe they know what kind of journalists they want to be—for example, a human rights reporter or a music journalist. Then they create an online portfolio showing what they can do.[179] NYU provides some basic training, but the focus is on creating a body of work that will be displayed on the Web, complete with the student's contact information. This method, which needs to be more interactive, runs somewhat counter to the traditional model of journalism education, in which the student tends to learn how to be a generalist. But in this age of specialty blogs and publications—and at a time when more people from other fields are joining news organizations as specialist reporters—this approach is at least worth exploring.

Moreover, journalism schools need to reflect the evolution from a lecture mode to a conversational mode. At a minimum, journalism schools should insist that students understand genuine interactivity, which is the basis for a conversation with the audience. They can start by making the conversation richer among faculty and students on campus; the lecture mode of education still has value in some circumstances, but only some.

At Northwestern University's Medill School of Journalism, widely recognized as one of the best in the world, Rich Gordon, formerly a reporter and editor with several major U.S. newspapers, including the *Miami Herald*, is an evangelist for the conversation and is practicing what he preaches. He told me in April 2004:

> I teach new media in a variety of contexts—I teach classes focused on new media's impact on journalism, I make guest appearances in other classes to talk about how the Internet is changing journalism, and I make presentations to media company executives on new media strategy. In all of those kinds of classes, I talk about the unique capabilities of new media. And clearly one of the most powerful is the way in which it changes the relationship between the journalist and what we've historically called the audience. I point them to interesting examples of this kind of journalism, including Weblogs, discussion forums, ohmynews, photo blogs, etc. And I raise the question of why more traditional journalists and media companies are not seizing the opportunity to change their relationships with the audience.
>
> All that said, I think this quarter is the first one where I've led a class that is focusing entirely on this subject. I have a group of six new media master's students who are working with Advance.net (and Jeff Jarvis) to explore the proposition that "hyperlocal citizens' media" can help meet the information needs for a town or neighborhood. As you know, communities this size (say, under 100,000 residents) tend to be undercovered by the mainstream media. The major metropolitan dailies can't afford to staff newsrooms in dozens or hundreds of communities this size, can't zone the local section enough ways to provide coverage at this level, and charge too much for ads to get the kind of local merchant advertising that would pay for journalists in these communities—and the kind of advertising that people in these communities value as useful information. If a community this size is lucky, they have a good weekly or small daily that understands its

mission is to provide this kind of hyperlocal journalism. But even in places that have good community newspapers, there is information that doesn't make its way into print.

Gordon's students picked Skokie, Illinois, a city of about 54,000 people near Northwestern's home in Evanston, to launch their experiment. After soliciting help from local residents and organizations, they launched "goskokie.com" (a blog with forums and other features) with a motto of "news for the people by the people." Gordon said the students contacted local organizations and individuals there for assistance. This will be fascinating to follow, and it may be a model for journalism education.

## A QUESTION OF TRUST

Using the tools of multidirectional journalism doesn't mean we have to cross ethical lines. We have plenty to deal with already on that score, as the infamous Jayson Blair proved with his fabrications and plagiarism while reporting for *The New York Times*. When cyber-gossip Matt Drudge reported rumors of investigations that Senator John Kerry, the Democratic presidential candidate, had been romantically involved with a former intern, few responsible news organizations picked up the story. Drudge, we recognized, didn't have a sterling record for accuracy. The old-fashioned publications and broadcasts that disdained the story were, it turned out, making the right call both online and offline. (I'll talk more about this in Chapter 9.)

No matter which tools and technologies we embrace, we must maintain core principles, including fairness, accuracy, and thoroughness. These are not afterthoughts. They are essential if professional journalism expects to survive.

Even as we listen better to our former audience and converse more freely, we are still obliged to gather as many facts as possible. We are obliged to be fair. We are obliged to correct our mistakes. Fortunately, it turns out that we'll be even better equipped to maintain those principles if we listen and participate in the conversation.

And we still need editors. Bloggers who disdain editors entirely, or who say they're largely irrelevant to the process, are mistaken.[180] The community's eyes and ears on weblogs are fine for what they provide. As noted, my readers make me a better journalist because they find my mistakes, tell me what I'm missing, and help me understand nuances.

Good editors add their own experience in a different way. They are trained, mostly through long experience, to look for what's missing in a story. They ask tough questions, demand better evidence for assertions, and, ultimately, understand how this thing we call journalism comes together. Sometimes they can help us see that less is more: I can't count the number of times an editor of my column has suggested that a sentence is unnecessary or inflammatory without purpose, leading me to agree that its removal would strengthen the piece, not weaken it. They make my work better in different ways, and I would not want to see them disappear.

We can help the new journalists understand and value ethics, the importance of serving the public trust, and professionalism. We can't, and shouldn't, keep them out.

*Chapter 7*

# The Former Audience Joins
# the Party

On December 10, 2003, thousands of Iraqis marched on the streets of Baghdad to protest bombings by insurgents, violence that had caused far more civilian than military casualties. For all practical purposes, *The New York Times* and other major media outlets missed the march and its significance.

But some local bloggers did not. They'd been trumpeting the prodemocracy demonstrations for days prior to the event. Blogs, it turned out, became the best way to get the news about an important event.

Some of the most prominent coverage came from a blogger named Zeyad, whose Healing Iraq site[181] had become a key channel for anyone who wanted to understand how occupied Iraq (or at least that part of Baghdad) was faring. His reports were thorough and revealing, and his readership grew quickly once word got around.

"I was surprised that people would rely on my blog as a source of information together with news," he told me in an email. "Many of my readers have confessed to me that they check out my blog even before checking out news sites such as CNN, BBC, etc. What I find people more interested in is first-hand accounts of daily life in Iraq, and coming from an Iraqi they give it more credence than if it were coming from western journalists."

Zeyad's reporting was just one more example of how the grassroots have emerged, in ways the professional media largely still fail to comprehend, as a genuine force in journalism.

Indeed, the grassroots are transcending the pallid consumerism that has characterized news coverage and consumption in the past half-century or more. For the first time in modern history, the user is truly in charge, as a consumer and as a producer.

This chapter focuses on two broad groups. First are the people who have been active, in their own way, even before grassroots journalism was so available to all. They are the traditional writers of letters to the editor: engaged and active, usually on a local level. Now they can write weblogs, organize Meetups, and generally agitate for the issues, political or otherwise, that matter to them. Once they know the degree to which they can transcend the standard sources of news and actually influence the journalism process, they'll have an increasing impact by being, more than ever before, part of a larger conversation.

I'm most excited about the second, and I hope larger, group from the former audience, the ones who take it to the next level. We're seeing the rise of the heavy-duty blogger, web site creator, mailing list owner, or SMS gadfly—the medium is less important than the intent and talent—who is becoming a key source of news for others, including professional journalists. In some cases, these people are becoming professional journalists themselves and are finding ways to make a business of their avocation.

## CITIZEN JOURNALIST: BLOGGERS (AND MORE) EVERYWHERE

On February 19, 2004, Rex Hammock was ushered into the Old Executive Office Building in Washington. He and four other small-business people sat down with President George W. Bush for a short discussion on economic issues. It was another in a series of Bush meetings with supporters of the administration's policies. This one, unlike previous sessions, was closed to the press.

But what White House officials apparently didn't know—or didn't care if they did know—was that Hammock, owner of a small publishing company in Tennessee, was a citizen journalist in his own right. On his way back to the airport that day, he wrote on his laptop computer a long and somewhat rambling essay that he soon posted on his weblog.[182] There was no breaking news, but rather a folksy kind of reporting. He wanted to report his impressions rather than discuss policy.

"He is definitely not a wonk, but he knows clearly what he believes needs to happen for the country and its economy to prosper," Hammock wrote of Bush. "I don't think the circular arguments regarding 'what ifs' and 'what abouts' interest him. Nor me, for that matter."

The blog posting, and the media coverage of what this citizen reporter had done in the absence of standard media coverage, became a mini-story in its own right. One lesson was obvious: excluding The Media from coverage no longer necessarily means much.

Walt Mossberg and Kara Swisher, columnists at *The Wall Street Journal*, had learned this nine months earlier at the *Journal*'s D (All Things Digital) conference in southern California. To the annoyance of "official" members of the press who attended the event, including me, the main sessions were off the record. Of course, that didn't stop any number of regular attendees from reporting in their weblogs what various speakers, including Microsoft's Bill Gates and Apple's Steve Jobs, said. (In my blog, I later pointed to the unofficial coverage.[183]) The restrictions were lifted for the 2004 conference.

These cases show the increasing futility of the expression "off the record" in large groups or when dealing with nonprofessional journalists who aren't steeped in the nomenclature of what can be disclosed and what can't. Recall the incident I noted in the *Introduction*, when bloggers helped turn an audience against a telephone company CEO. At another conference the next autumn,[184] Howard Rheingold was asked if the real-time feedback and commentary typified by the Nacchio blogging might lead conference speakers to be less candid in such circumstances. In other words, the questioner wondered, would this kind of thing create a "chilling effect" on public discourse?

On the contrary, Rheingold said to laughter and applause, "I would think it would have a chilling effect on bullshit."

The coverage of important events by nonprofessional journalists is only part of the story. What also matters is the fact that people are having their say. This is one of the healthiest media developments in a long time. We are hearing new voices—not necessarily the voices of people who want to make a living by speaking out, but who want to say what they think and be heard, even if only by relatively few people.

One of the main criticisms of blogs is that so many are self-absorbed tripe. No doubt, most are interesting only to the writer, plus some family and friends. But that's no reason to dismiss the genre, or to minimize the value of people talking with each other. What excites me in this context, however, is that the growing number of blogs written by people who want to talk intelligently about an area of expertise is a sign of something vital. Blogs can be acts of civic engagement.

They can also be better, or certainly offer more depth, than the professionals who face the standard limitations of reporting time and available space (or airtime) for what they learn. A case in point is the work of Pamela Jones, a paralegal who runs a blog called Groklaw,[185] which has become probably the best overall source of information about the legal battle between the SCO Group, a software company, and the free software community. In this suit, the SCO Group is claiming ownership of software that was the precursor of the Linux operating system. It has sued several companies, including IBM, and has threatened users of the Linux operating system. The fight could determine the future of open source software itself. No professional journalism organization has covered this enormously complex case as well as Jones and a team of volunteers. Their prodigious research is nothing short of amazing. In an interview on Linux Online,[186] Jones explained her motives:

> All right, I said to myself, what can I do well? The answer was, I can research and I can write. Those are the two things attorneys and companies hire me to do for them. I decided, I will just do what I do best, and I'll throw it out there, like a message in a bottle. I didn't think too many people would ever read it, except I thought maybe IBM might find my research and it'd help them. Or someone out there would read it and realize he or she had meaningful evidence and would contact IBM or FSF [Free Software Foundation]. I know material I have put up can help them, if they didn't already know about it. Because of my training, I recognize what matters as far as this case is concerned. Companies like IBM typically hire folks to comb the Internet for them and find anything that mentions the company, so I assumed they'd notice me. That's all I was expecting. By saying all, I don't mean to diminish it as a contribution. I just wasn't expecting thousands of readers everyday.

What she did hope for, and got, was "the many-eyeballs power in this new context." This was a crucial insight. "Many-eyeballs power"—open source journalism—worked because the work, while centered on one person's passion for the subject, had been spread among the community. This is another example of a passionate nonexpert using technology to make a profound contribution, and a real difference.


## EVOLUTIONARY AND REVOLUTIONARY

Americans, protected by the First Amendment, can generally write blogs with few consequences. However, in country after country where free speech is not a given, the blogosphere matters in far more serious ways. This is the stuff of actual revolutions.

If Iran's famously repressive political system ever sees true reform without suffering another violent revolution, the contributions of people such as Hossein Derakhshan will have played no small role. Derakhshan goes by the name Hoder. A 20-something expatriate who'd moved to Toronto after leaving Iran, he may have been the first Persian-language weblogger when he launched his site in December 2000.[187] By tweaking some settings in the Blogger software configuration, "I could post and publish in Persian"—something that hadn't been possible before, given the difficulties of using the Persian character set.

Emboldened, Hoder decided to help other Iranians set up their own blogs. "I published the simple step-to-step guide on Nov. 5, 2001, and wished 100 people could start blogging by one year," he told me. "Then just after one month, we already had more than 100 Persian weblogs. It was unbelievable."

Not as amazing as it would get, though. PersianBlog.com, a service created in 2002, grew to have more than 100,000 user accounts in less than two years. Hoder estimated that more than 200,000 Iranian blogs had been created by early 2004, though not all are written in Iran and many aren't being maintained. Again, what matters most is what the Net made possible: Iranians, who live in a repressive country with strict controls on media, were able to speak out and access a variety of news and opinions.

The blogs are a cross-section of Iranian society. Many focus on topics people are not allowed to freely discuss in the nation's media: relationships, sex, culture, and politics. They are a communications network for a repressed people and speak volumes about a regime that is struggling to control how modern technology is used by its citizens.


Repressive regimes certainly can, and do, silence individual voices. China's information minders discovered the power of personal publishing some time ago and have been trying to keep the most widely listened-to voices—at least those critical of the regime or who discuss forbidden topics—out of general circulation. A young Chinese woman writing under the pen name "Muzimei"—a blog featuring frank descriptions of her sexual exploits—lost her job as a columnist at a newspaper in Guangdong Province.

Stopping truth is difficult, though. Sina Motallebi, an Iranian blogger, discovered this when he was jailed for his blog in 2003. Bloggers and some journalists around the world protested his jailing; he was released after 23 days and moved to Europe.[188] But what he was talking about didn't disappear from the consciousness of Iranians who wanted more than their local party line because Persian bloggers are still challenging the status quo.

Those of us with First Amendment protections in the U.S. shouldn't get too smug. Americans' passion for liberty, including truly free speech, swings on a pendulum that at the moment is moving in an alarming direction. Secrecy has become the norm in the halls of power, and big companies, notably in the entertainment industry, have been asserting "intellectual property" rights that take big whacks out of free speech. We'll look more at this in Chapter 9.

Yes, technology has made it possible for millions to speak freely and be heard, many for the first time. But the struggle to keep that freedom, which brings new risks even in free societies, is only beginning.

## NONPROFIT COMMUNITY PUBLISHING

The Melrose Mirror is not a weblog.[189] The web publication, updated the first Friday of each month, resembles a community newsletter more than anything else, but it's a fine example of tomorrow's journalism. "The World Wide Web is not for couch potatoes," the Mirror says on its Welcome page. "It's for people who care and share and are aware."

The Mirror was founded in 1996 to serve the community of Melrose, Massachusetts. It is edited by the Melrose Silver Stringers, a collection of senior citizens who've devoted their time and energy to community affairs. The site isn't much to look at, especially when compared to glitzy commercial news sites. It's not interactive. But this is true grassroots stuff, filled with articles and pictures that give its readers a distinct sense of place along with plenty of useful information for their lives and community.

The Mirror was the original testing ground for a project started by the Massachusetts Institute of Technology's "News-in-the-Future" Consortium at the famous Media Laboratory. MIT created the web-based software, also called Silver-Stringer,[190] to make community publishing easier.

It worked in a big way. "SilverStringer software has been used pretty much around the world by seniors, teens, and children," said Jack Driscoll, visiting scholar and Editor in Residence at the Media Lab and advisor to many of the groups using the software. Besides the United States, countries where the platform has become the basis of grassroots journalism include Finland, Italy, Brazil, Thailand, Ireland, India, Mexico, and Costa Rica. By far the biggest installation is operated by the *La Repubblica* newspaper in Italy; its "Kataweb" online affiliate[191] uses SilverStringer to help publish some 4,200 online school newspapers.

Probably the best-known site using the software is Junior Journal,[192] which is run by children from around the world with no adult involvement apart from Driscoll, a former top editor at *The Boston Globe*, serving as advisor. More than 300 children from 90 nations have worked on Junior Journal in the last five years.

The Junior Journalists rigorously edit their work, Driscoll told me. Each story has three editors, sometimes as many as five. The process fuels a sense of both responsibility and ethics.

"One kid wrote about a multinational corporation," he said. "The original piece said there was a history of bribery. They checked this out. They [the company] were accused once of bribing an official, but never charged. The kids did the homework"—and ended up toning down the piece.

In another case, the staffers vetoed a story that had lyrics from the rap singer Eminem. One young reporter wrote a review with a stanza that contained some offensive content. With some nine-year-olds in the audience, the editors concluded, this wasn't appropriate.

Few Big Media people will see these kinds of community publications as competitive. But their presence has at least two positive effects. First, it shows people that they can do it themselves. Second, it expands the information pool at a time when Big Media is cutting back on staff and resources. There's also an unmistakable vitality to the Melrose Mirror and Junior Journal that is missing from much of journalism today. Maybe, said Driscoll, these kinds of operations will wake up Big Media. At the least, this style of journalism adds needed voices.

"I see it as an extension of news," Driscoll said. "We're broadening the definition of news as seen through the perspective of average people who have life experience, something to share. It's news anyway you look at it."

## ALTERNATIVE MEDIA FLOURISHES

Oddly, perhaps, America's so-called "alternative press" has not used the Net very well. Alternative newspapers in particular have been somewhat slow to expand their mission to new media. This may be due, in part, to consolidation in that industry leaving many alternative papers in the hands of just two companies, Village Voice Media and New Times Media.[193] Some, though not all, have lost their edgier qualities. So a new kind of alternative media has arisen on the Net, above and beyond blogs.

One of the best known is the Independent Media Center, also known as Indymedia.[194] The project was founded in 1999 by a group of antiglobalization activists who wanted to cover the Seattle World Trade Organization meeting in ways traditional media would not. Activists working at the center pulled together material from a variety of sources, including camera-equipped people on the streets who captured images of local police officers mistreating protesters. With a newsletter and web site, Indymedia drew a large audience—and a heavy-handed visit from the FBI that brought the group considerably more attention. Buoyed by the Seattle effort, the Independent Media Center spread its wings. By mid-2003, it had dozens of affiliates in the United States and around the world.

When the United States invaded Iraq in the spring of 2003, protesters took to the streets of San Francisco, and by many accounts just about shut down the city. Deploying digital cameras, laptops, and Wi-Fi, Indymedia reporters—a self-assembling newsroom—captured the events brilliantly. "Indymedia kicked our ass," Bob Cauthorn, former vice president for Digital Media at the *San Francisco Chronicle*, told a group of online journalists in April 2004. In particular, he said, the independent journalists revealed several cases of police brutality that the major media had missed.

Overall, the Indymedia effort has produced some admirable results. But it has an uneven track record in ways that make traditional journalists uncomfortable, in large part due to a lack of editorial supervision. The Google News site removed Indymedia stories from its listings, the search company says, because of concerns about the deliberate lack of centralized editorial control over what individual contributors to the site posted there.[195] Much of what the site publishes is solid, occasionally path-breaking journalism; but, as with all advocacy reporting, a reader is well advised to maintain a skeptical eye.

The editorial process is a key part of *Democracy Now!*,[196] a left-leaning radio and web operation sponsored by the Pacifica radio network. Amy Goodman and her colleagues are demonstrating new media's technical leaps, often with on-the-fly innovation, while producing material with real impact. Goodman, who was beaten by Indonesian government agents and deported from East Timor while covering the Timorese struggle for independence, did some of the best reporting on that conflict. Getting material out of the country wasn't simple, she said; at one point she asked passengers on Australia-bound planes to carry out CDs with compressed video programming, and the proprietor of an Australian Internet café then forwarded the programming to the organization's New York headquarters. While covering the Iraq conflict, her colleague Jeremy Scahill explained how the Iraqi government, in the run-up to the 2003 invasion by the U.S., censored outgoing media; one method was not to allow files of larger than half a megabyte to be sent from Internet cafes. So he found some software that broke 80-MB video reports into smaller chunks, which he and colleagues dispatched from different cafes back to New York.

*Democracy Now!*, while still relying on traditional forms of communication, is also becoming "an interface between the Web world and mass media," Goodman told me. The Web is chock-full of great information, she said, but most people don't have access to computers. So, for most of the world's population, the mass media still dominates. But all *Democracy Now!* programming, radio and video, is available via web "streams," which allow a user to watch or listen to the show without downloading massive files first. Like Indymedia, the organization is using open source software and offering its tools to others. Whenever possible, the programs bring people to the Web so they can find more information, such as additional video footage, extended interviews, and supporting documents, on the subject at hand. This is powerful stuff.

One of my favorite independent news sites is written and edited entirely by its readers. Kuro5hin, as noted in Chapter 1, has brought an open source style of journalism to the fore. Users vote on what they like, and the voting moves stories up or down the page. One wrinkle I especially like is the ability to comment on the advertising—talk about empowering the readers.

Another kind of self-organizing newsroom came powerfully to life during the 2003 Gulf War. It was called the "Command Post",[197] and it was a collection of people who, for the most part, had never met each other. Their goal was to gather every bit of data they could find about the conflict, including news stories, and post it all as fast as possible. The site, which became must reading for many people, later evolved into a political site covering the U.S. election cycle.

If I.F. Stone, the hero of an earlier age of independent journalism, were around today, I have no doubt that he'd be a big fan of—and maybe a contributor to—the Center for Public Integrity,[198] an organization that's finally getting the public acclaim it deserves. The nonprofit was founded in 1989 by Charles Lewis, who'd worked in network TV news. Its Washington-based reporting has become one of the best investigative journalism operations you'll find anywhere, and that includes the investigative units of the major newspapers and TV networks. Like *Democracy Now!*, the center has won some of journalism's top awards, including, in 2004, the George Polk honor for its reporting on Iraq and U.S. government contracts to politically connected corporations. The center also distributes its information in print. A book by Lewis and his colleagues, *The Buying of the President 2004*, sold well and is backed up by voluminous online data the center collected and disseminated on the various candidates starting in primary season. No mainstream journalism organization has done as good a job.

How could they? "To do something like *The Buying of the President* took hundreds of interviews, 53 researchers and editors," Lewis told me. "No traditional news organization would ever do that."

Lewis and his team may be the model for a new generation. If Big Media declines, public-spirited foundations and wealthy individuals may increasingly see organizations such as the

Center for Public Integrity as one of the only ways to empower an informed citizenry.[199]

## THE WIKI MEDIA PHENOMENON

The Wiki is a profoundly democratized form of online data gathering. In February, 2004, Wikipedia,[200] one of the world's most comprehensive online reference sites, created and operated by volunteers, published its 500,000th article. More precisely, one of the site's contributors published the article.

Wikipedia is one of the most fascinating developments of the Digital Age. In just over three years of existence it has become a valuable resource and an example of how the grassroots in today's interconnected world can do extraordinary things. It is a model of participatory media quite unlike any other, and is a natural extension of the Web's capabilities in the context of journalism.

On the surface, the notion is bizarre—and certainly will chill the typical professional journalist. Why? Because almost anyone can be a contributor to the Wikipedia. Anyone can edit any page. (Only serious misbehavior gets people banned.) Thousands of people around the world have added their expertise, voice, and passion, and new volunteers show up every day.

It defies first-glance assumptions. After all, one might imagine, if anyone can edit anything, surely cyber-vandals will wreck it. Surely flame wars over article content will stymie good intentions. And, of course, the articles will all be amateurish nonsense. Right?

Well, not necessarily. The open nature of Wikipedia has been its greatest resource, and it has emerged as a credible resource.

Wikipedia uses the Wiki software described in Chapter 2. To refresh, a Wiki allows any user to edit any page. It keeps track of every change. Anyone can follow the changes in detail.

When it works right, it engenders a community—and a community that has the right tools can take care of itself.

The Wikipedia articles tend to be neutral in tone, and when the topic is controversial, will explain the varying viewpoints in addition to offering the basic facts. When anyone can edit what you've just posted, such fairness becomes essential.

"The only way you can write something that survives is that someone who's your diametrical opposite can agree with it," Jimmy Wales, a founder of Wikipedia, explained to me.

Urban planners and criminologists talk about the "broken window" syndrome, said Ward Cunningham, who came up with the first Wiki software in the 1990s. If a neighborhood allows broken windows to stay that way, and fails to replace them, the neighborhood will deteriorate because vandals and other unsavory people will assume no one cares.

Similarly, Wikipedia draws strength from its volunteers who catch and fix every act of online vandalism. When vandals learn that someone will repair their damage within minutes, and therefore prevent the damage from being visible to the world, the bad guys tend to give up and move along to more vulnerable places.

This isn't to say that disagreements don't occur, or that Wikipedia works perfectly. The editors try to channel disputes in a way that ultimately produces a greater result. There are metapages—discussions of Wikipedia entries—where people debate, sometimes viciously, about what should go into the entry. In the end, even bitter opponents may find common ground by being inclusive and acknowledging the differences, thereby giving the encyclopedia greater breadth. But some debates are ultimately intractable. inclining to do good

Jimmy Wales is the benevolent dictator of the operation, settling the most serious disputes. But he's been working on a mediation and arbitration system that will let members of the community decide, for example, if someone should be banned from posting, a rare occurrence.

Wikipedia has about 200 hardcore contributors who show up daily, or almost daily, to work on the site, Wales says. He estimates that another 1,000 or so are regular contributors. Tens of thousands more are occasional or one-time contributors.

One upcoming project is a "Wikipedia 1.0" release—"suitable for print," he said—in which articles will go through a more organized review. This raises intriguing questions. If some articles will be singled out for quality, does that make the rest of the Wikipedia inherently untrustworthy? I don't think so. Now, I wouldn't base a major decision on what I read in this or any other encyclopedia. I'd check it out first. But my experience tells me that the Wikipedia community does its homework, at least when it comes to subjects about which I have some deeper knowledge.

I still marvel at how Wiki communities, which seem at first glance to be so fragile, are actually very resilient. They work because everyone can do their part.

One lesson, then, is deceptively simple. When you remove the barriers to changing things, you also remove the barriers to fixing what's broken. Successful Wikis are inherently fragile, Cunningham told me, but they show something important: "People are generally good."

Wikis strike me as an almost ideal journalistic tool under the right circumstances. The WikiTravel site[201] shows this potential. It's a worldwide travel guide written entirely by contributors who either live in the place they're covering or have spent enough time there to post relevant information. The site is thin in many respects, but the potential to become a superb resource is evident. I've compared the data to my real-life experience in several places and found it to be accurate.

Wikis don't have to be completely open to the outside world. They can live behind a firewall and can be protected by passwords. SocialText,[202] a California company, has been combining Wikis with weblogs. Its chief executive, Ross Mayfield, has journalistic notions as well.

Early in 2004, Mayfield was ruminating on the possibilities of creating a national political campaign Wiki called "Public Record." The project wasn't off the ground as of this writing, but Mayfield made eminent sense when he described it (on a Wiki, of course) as follows:

> Public Record is an independent self-organizing resource that tracks the issues and influencers of the 2004 presidential campaign. Accountability and trust in the democratic process is at an all time low, which weakens our civil society and democratic institutions. An opportunity exists to provide a resource for citizens, by citizens, to strengthen our civil institutions.
>
> What if the media didn't compete, but instead co-operated to develop a public record? Leads, sources and facts are only shared after going to print. But what if there was no print? Obviously, print persists and competition drives more than commerce. But as an alternative, the ability for amateurs to reason and assemble at least affords a new production model.
>
> Primarily based upon a wiki, Public Record allows any public citizen to contribute to construction of a website at any time, a tool that fosters trust by giving up control. Augmenting the wiki with weblogs allows healthy debate on issues and content to occur without degrading the content itself—in a publish/subscribe format that does not overload participants. Wikis allow a larger portion of the citizenry to participate in the open source movement by allowing contributions through horizontal information assembly (in contrast to vertical information assembly only available to programmers).

I can come up with a dozen problems such a site would face from the start, not least the matter of accuracy. But with the appropriate backing from one or more major media organizations—and an appropriate amount of editing (or policing, if you will)—this could be a serious journalistic resource.

## BUSINESS MODELS FOR TOMORROW'S PERSONAL JOURNALISM

"I have the perfect business model," an executive with BBC News' online operation once joked to me. "Pay or go to jail."

He was referring to the license fees—essentially taxes—TV owners in the United Kingdom must pay to the organization.

Only one online journalism organization in the world can spend $100 million a year based on that model. The rest of us have to find other ways to make this work pay. The gifted amateurs who abound in the personal journalism world will continue to do great work, but some people will want to make a living at it, or at least supplement their income. Some intriguing business models are emerging, as are variations on the open source method in which people scratch a journalistic itch for noncommercial reasons.

Advertising, as you'd expect, is one potentially workable model. Subscriptions may someday be another; so far, a tip-jar approach is the furthest that notion has gone.

For most blogging and other personal journalism, the return on investment—assuming the author wants some, and however it's calculated (time and/or money)—comes with an enhanced reputation. Glenn Fleishman's blog on wireless networking, noted in Chapter 2, isn't a moneymaker, but it burnishes his professional credentials as an expert. Susan Mernit, an Internet/media consultant, posts frequently to her personal blog[203] on a variety of related subjects. It's personal PR, and it's effective.

Of all the emerging business models, one of the most promising fits into the category of "nano-publishing," as some are calling the genre. Nick Denton's publications, for instance, target specific niches, and do so with style and quality. Gawker[204] is a weblog devoted to news and gossip about New York City and its gossip-heavy industries. Gizmodo,[205] also a weblog, covers electronic gadgets. Fleshbot[206] covers erotica. And a new gossip site, Wonkette,[207] covers the world capital of insider chat, Washington, D.C. More such blogs are coming.

Denton (who, of course, has a blog[208]) is a former print journalist, who worked for such publications as the *Financial Times*, where he was a well-regarded correspondent. His entrepreneurial instincts led him to the Net. Before he moved to the weblog world, he cofounded Moreover,[209] which gathers news and headlines from across the Web. Moreover was, in a sense, an early and much broader version of an RSS newsreader.

Denton and his colleagues are now pushing the boundaries of nano-journalism by making the most of the Net's simple publishing tools and low cost, as well as the advantages that accrue to those who exploit new models. Traffic doubled every two months at Gizmodo, the first of his nano-publishing sites, he told me.

Early on, Gizmodo generated revenue by sending readers to Amazon.com, where they could buy items they'd read about, causing a commission to be generated for Gizmodo.[210] But Gizmodo has become so popular that it's now drawing advertisers. This has greater potential, in my view, because gadget hounds (among whom I count myself) tend to buy magazines as much for the ads as for the articles—both are interesting information.

Denton and his team are playing a smart demographic game by exploiting niches that are too small to aim a magazine. It costs about $1,000 to launch a blog of this type,[211] a small fraction of launching a magazine. Clearly, we're looking at a major shift in publishing models. The economics have changed forever, and I suspect these kinds of sites will bedevil traditional media organizations. They won't lure all the readers or advertisers away, but they could be among the many new alternatives that carve away some of the most coveted readers and advertisers.

Another nano-publishing effort comes from Jason McCabe Calacanis, former publisher of the Silicon Alley Reporter, now part of a venture capital site. He launched Weblogs Inc.[212] in late 2003, describing it as a business-to-business publishing company for creating niche business blogs in life sciences, technology, media, and finance.

Weblogs Inc. differs from the Denton operation in a key way: though Denton owns the blogs and pays freelancers to write them, Calacanis creates more of a partnership, giving the author both ownership and a share of the revenues. There's room for both approaches, but Calacanis will probably attract a more entrepreneurial type of blogger.

The financial arrangement is simple, he told me. The blog writer takes the first $1,000 in revenue each month, splitting additional revenue 50-50 with the company. The blogger and Weblogs, Inc. jointly own the contents, and a blogger who departs can take a copy of all postings. Finally, either side can end the arrangement at any time.

The site launched in the fall of 2003. As of February 2004, it had about 20 blogs, one of which (a social-software site) had been sponsored for $2,500 a month. Calacanis said he was looking to have 100 blogs by the end of 2004, and have each of them generate $1,000 to $2,000 a month in revenue.

Many bloggers, meanwhile, have signed up with Google AdWords, a scheme offered through the Google search engine that allows Google to place ads on a web page based on the topic of the page. The revenue-sharing model has given some bloggers a small but worthwhile income.

And then there's Blogads,[213] an advertising service created by Henry Copeland, aimed solely at blogs. Copeland boasts several notable successes, including, as noted in Chapter 5, the special-election congressional campaign in Tennessee, where Democrat Ben Chandler saw a 20-1 return on ads placed on political blogs.

J.D. Lascia, who writes an excellent blog called New Media Musings,[214] has been experimenting with several advertising forms, including Google AdWords, Blogads, and plain text ads from several different online ad sales operations. He's not enamored of some of the gambling sites his advertisers are promoting. But, as he told me, the gambling ads have been "by far the most lucrative: $300 a month for text links on my blog and personal web site." Early on, he posted a notice that said he wasn't vouching for the services or products being advertised, only that they were legal. He also tells advertisers he'll kill their ads if they put spyware or other rogue code on users' computers. He explained further:

> As distasteful as it may be to see these ads in the early days of a new medium, a reader can find much more risqué, questionable advertising in the back pages of any alternative weekly. One day we'll get to a place where targeted advertising really works and mainstream advertisers find value in blogs like mine that attract a daily audience of 3,000 or more upscale, educated, leading edge technologists and media people. Until that day arrives, I'm reluctant to turn down paying advertisers out of some effete sense of propriety.

As with so many other bloggers, the more useful payback for Lasica is how his writing enhances his reputation as an expert in online media. "Freelance writing also bolsters one's credentials, but regular blogging or frequent online dispatches seem to be the best ways to validate one's authority in a chosen topic," he said.

## NEW BUSINESS MODELS: THE TIP JAR

There's nothing new about sponsorships for creative works or journalism. But bloggers and other online journalists have brought the concept into the modern age. And where sponsors in earlier times tended to be wealthy patrons, today, journalists can use the Net to raise money more widely. Probably the best-known example of this is Andrew Sullivan, a magazine writer whose blog[215] was one of the first to solicit readers' money via pledges, somewhat akin to the methods of public radio and television stations.

I'm even more impressed with Chris Allbritton, a former wire-service staff writer turned blogger, who brought the concept into the modern age in 2003. In an appeal to his Internet readership, he wrote, "Send me money, and I'll go to Iraq and cover the war." They did, and Allbritton made journalistic history. He also set a precedent that I hope will become far more common in coming years.

Allbritton's historic trip started in 2002 when he spent time in Turkey and more than a week in northern Iraq. Upon his return to the U.S. that fall, he heard the war drums beating from Washington and decided he should go back to Iraq to cover the conflict he knew was coming. That October, he launched a site called Back to Iraq[216]—a blog on which he asked readers to send money. From October through December, he raised just $500.

He got lucky in February 2003 when Wired News, the online news operation, did a story about him and his seemingly quixotic quest. Over the course of three days he raised another $2,000. Then other media organizations wrote about him and his site traffic "went through the roof," he said. In all, some 342 readers kicked in about $14,500. Allbritton flew back to Turkey, snuck back into northern Iraq and, with some distinction, covered the conflict from there.

A blogger has to pick a topic and stick to it, he told me; most blogs are too unfocused. But to raise money this way, one needs to "find something that's controversial and hopefully polarizing. The war was tailor made for that kind of thing." He had a specific project, and specific dates. People trusted him from his earlier work or were willing to take a chance, and they contributed. In late 2003, Allbritton decided to go back yet again and set up a Back to Iraq 3.0 web page. When we talked, he'd raised enough to cover immediate expenses and was planning to supplement his stay with other freelance articles.

A key to Allbritton's relative success in this venture has been his relationship with readers, not just the ones who paid and got postings by email earlier than people who simply went to the web site. The readers became his eyes on the world outside northern Iraq. "Readers were good about sending me roundups of the day's news," he said. Readers also posted voluminous comments on the blog. Sometimes the comments were downright mean and wrongly accused him of lying about what he was seeing, but other readers jumped to his defense.

Allbritton wasn't the first blogger to solicit funds from readers, though he may well have been the first to raise money for a project of this sort. He certainly wasn't the last.

In January 2004, Joshua Micah Marshall, author of the superb political blog Talking Points Memo,[217] asked his readers to help him travel to New Hampshire to cover the presidential primary. They sent him more than $4,000, and his on-the-ground reporting was some of the finest that came out of the early and perhaps pivotal presidential nominating contest. Marshall doesn't live off the blog; he's written for a variety of publications, including a column for *The Hill*, a trade journal for the Washington political elite. But if you're in the political game or even care about politics, Marshall's blog is both addictive and required reading.

I don't expect to see many wealthy bloggers or independent media operations, unless they have trust funds, rich benefactors or other sources of income. But we're on the verge of a time when people can bring serious alternatives to the public and get paid for what they do. Ultimately, the audience will make the decisions. Success will come to those operations that make themselves required reading, listening, or viewing. This is how it's always worked and how it always will.

Chapter 8

# Next Steps

In the mid-1990's, just as the World Wide Web was gaining popularity, I was sure that the Internet would become a powerful force in our lives. But I didn't have a clue that services such as Google would emerge, or that weblogs and other personal media would play such a transformative role in my chosen craft.

I didn't anticipate online experiments such as Feed, the pioneering but now defunct online magazine that had an edginess bloggers later incorporated, or group-edited sites such as Kuro5hin, where the audience writes and ranks the stories and then adds context and ideas as they discuss them. I didn't imagine that blogs and other tools would come along to make writing on the Web almost as easy as reading from it. So I won't try to predict the shape of the news business and how it will be practiced a decade from now. But even if we can't make specific predictions, we can look forward and make some safe assumptions about the architecture and technology of tomorrow's news, and then consider what they suggest.

My assumptions rest on two guiding principles. The first is a belief in basic journalistic values, including accuracy, fairness, and ethical standards. The second is rooted in the very nature of technology: it's relentless and unstoppable.

Only one thing is certain: we'll all be astounded by what's to come.

## LAWS AND OTHER CODES

As we've already established, the mass media in the latter part of the 20th century was organized, for the most part, along a fairly simple, top-down framework. Editors and reporters inside big companies decided which stories to cover. They received information from a variety—but not too big a variety—of mostly official and sometimes unofficial sources. Editors massaged what reporters wrote, and the results were printed in newspapers and magazines or broadcast on radio and television. Alternatives did exist, particularly when desktop publishing came on the scene. But the conversational aspect of the news we've been discussing in this book hadn't arrived.

Technology and an increasing dissatisfaction with mass media have created the conditions for a new framework. To understand this, we must first understand the technology and the trends underlying the collision of journalism and technology. These trends take the shape of laws, not the kind enacted by governments but the kind imagined by scientists and acute observers of society.

The first law is named after Gordon Moore, cofounder of computer chip maker Intel. More than any other, Moore's Law is the key to understanding today's reality and tomorrow's possibilities.

Moore's Law says that the density of transistors on a given piece of silicon will double every 18 to 24 months. It's been true since Moore came up with the notion in the 1960s, and the pace of improvement looks set to continue for some time to come. There's no historical equivalent for this kind of change; humans are fortunate to do anything twice as fast or as twice as well even once, much less double that improvement again and again. Moore's Law is about exponential change: it doesn't take long before you've increased power by thousands-fold.[218]

As engineers shrink millions of transistors onto tiny chips, they can embed enormous calculating power—something akin to intelligence—into almost every electronic device we use. You and I use many computers each day: the microprocessors, also called microcontrollers, are in computers, handheld devices, alarm clocks, coffee makers, home thermostats, wristwatches, and automobiles. Most of these devices contain vastly more processing power than early mainframe computers.

Not only are we embedding brains into everything we touch, but we're adding memory to everything, too. The manufacturers of computer memory chips and disk drives are improving their products at an even faster pace than Moore's Law. And now, with modern communications—wired and wireless—we're connecting devices that are more and more powerful.

Grassroots journalism feeds on all these innovations. Devices for collecting, working with, and distributing data are becoming smaller and more powerful every year. People are figuring out how to put them to work in ways professional journalists are only beginning to catch on to, such as collaborative news sites where readers do the writing and editing and posting newsy pictures from camera phones.

Moore himself has been somewhat surprised at how long Silicon Valley's engineers have kept his law not just alive, but vibrant. "It went further than I ever could have imagined," he told me in 2001.

Next, consider Metcalfe's Law, named after Bob Metcalfe, inventor of the Ethernet networking standard that is now ubiquitous in every personal computer.[219] Essentially, Metcalfe's Law says that the value of a communication network is the square of the number of nodes, or end-point connections. That is, take the number of nodes and multiply it by itself.

The canonical example of Metcalfe's Law is the growth of fax machines. If there's only one fax machine in the world, it's not good for much. But the minute someone else gets a fax machine, both can be used, and real value is created. The more people with fax machines, the more value there is in the network—a utility that greatly exceeds the raw numbers—because each individual user has many more people to whom he can send faxes.[220]

Each new Internet-connected computer is a node. So, increasingly, is each new mobile phone that can send and retrieve Internet data. And in a few years, it's probable that most of the smarter devices made possible by Moore's law—everything from refrigerators to cars to computers—will be a node. When billions or even trillions of people and things are connected, the value of the network will transcend calculation.

Finally, we have Reed's Law, named after David Reed, about whom I'll talk more in Chapter 11. Reed noticed that when people go online, they don't only conduct one-to-one communications, as they would with a telephone or fax machine. They conduct many-to-many, or few-to-few, communications.

According to Reed's Law, groups themselves are nodes. The value of networks in that context, he asserts, is the number of groups *factorial*. Here, factorial means that you take the number of groups, and every integer less than that number all the way back to one, and multiply all of those numbers together. For example, 8 factorial is 1 times 2 times 3 times 4 times 5 times 6 times 7 times 8. The number of group nodes factorial is a very, very, very big number.[221]

Obviously, Metcalfe's Law and Reed's Law are as much opinions as anything else. But they make sense intuitively, and more and more they make sense in a practical way: the more the Net grows, the more valuable and powerful it becomes.[222]

All of these trends, applied to communications in general, add up to an even more "radical democratization of access to the means of production and distribution," Howard Rheingold told me.

The people who'll invent tomorrow's media are not in my age bracket. They are just growing up now. In a decade, Rheingold observed: "The 15-year-olds today in Seoul and Helsinki, who are already adept at mobilizing media to their end, will be 25. And what they carry in their pockets will be thousands of times more powerful than what they have today."

What does this mean for news and journalism? As the technologies of creation and communication grow more powerful and become smaller, and ultimately become part of the fabric of life, we'll have vastly more raw data. And we'll need tools—and humans—to help us make sense of it all.


## CREATING THE NEWS

There's no longer any doubt that personal publishing of various stripes is becoming a major trend. The Pew Internet & American Life Project found that in mid-2003, slightly less than half of adult Internet users had used the Net to "publish their thoughts, respond to others, post pictures, share files and otherwise contribute to the explosion of content available online."[223] If you added in the under-18 population, no doubt the numbers would rise significantly. While much of what is considered publishing on the Net consisted of trading files, causing some doubters to downplay the survey, the bottom line was that there was an enormous and growing cadre of content creators, some of whom were creating news.

The tools of creation are now everywhere, and they're getting better. Musicians can get the near-equivalent of a big recording studio in a package costing only a couple of thousand dollars, or considerably less if they're willing to make some compromises. Digital video is becoming so cheap that anyone with the requisite talent can make a feature film for a fraction of what it once cost. The notion of writing on the Web is expanding to include all kinds of media, and there's little to stop it.

The Web can't compete today—and may not compete in our lifetimes—with live television for big-event coverage. The architecture just doesn't permit it. But for just about everything else, it's ideal. Adam Curry, who became prominent as a VJ on MTV and has since been exploring the blogosphere and even newer media,[224] envisions "Personal TV Networks" that use the Net in a more appropriate way to deliver video content. In an introduction to a session at a 2004 blogging conference,[225] he described it this way:

Since the invention of the video tape recorder, most content delivered via television is created offline and prepared well in advance of its broadcast slot. In many cases a program will have to be cleared through the legal department and be reviewed for network "policies." And so the program sits in a queue, waiting to be distributed. During this time the program could be distributed by bike messengers and still arrive on time when you would normally turn on your set as directed by TV Guide. Or...it could be distributed via the Internet. Since big files take a long time to download, a day's worth of downloading should be time enough. The download can take place at night, when usage of your network and pc is low and, most importantly, you aren't waiting for it. It'll "just be there" in the morning.[226]

Hundreds of millions of people in the U.S. and abroad are using camera phones (soon to be video-camera phones) and SMS to share information. Soon, said Larry Larsen, multimedia editor at the Poynter Institute, location will be one of the data points. For example, he told me that if he's house-hunting, he should be able to visit a location and ask his Treo handheld for all relevant news stories within a two-mile radius. "If the bulk of that includes violent crimes," he wrote me, "I'm out of there."[227]

But how easy will it be to use the tools of creation? Blogs set an early standard, but they're still relatively crude instruments. You still need to know some HTML to make a blog work. In the future, tools need to be drop-dead simple, or the promise of grassroots journalism won't be kept.

The reporter of the future—amateur or professional—will be equipped with an amazing toolkit. But reporting is more than collecting facts, or raw data. Rheingold's smart mobs are morphing into a news team of unparalleled reach. Is there depth to match?

In *Snow Crash*,[228] a 1991 novel of a post-apocalyptic American future, Neal Stephenson offered an image that has stuck with me.

> Gargoyles represent the embarrassing side of the Central Intelligence Corporation. Instead of using laptops, they wear their computers on their bodies, broken up into separate modules that hang on the waist, on the back, on the headset. They serve as human surveillance devices, recording everything that happens around them. Nothing looks stupider, these getups are the modern-day equivalent of the slide-rule scabbard or the calculator pouch on the belt, marking the user as belonging to a class that is at once above and far below human society.

The gargoyles in the novel aren't journalists in Stephenson's vision. They're more like human personal assistants, with a dual role: recording what's going on in the environment and then interacting with the network by looking up someone's face or biography from the Net, for example. In a sense, the gargoyles are web-cams with brains.

"Journalists are supposed to filter information, not just be web-cams," Stephenson told me. There's too little respect for the journalistic function when people see it as "a primitive substitute for having web-cams everywhere. No one has time to sift through all that crap."

The sifting process will be handled both by people and machines. The role of the journalist will surely change, but it will not go away. But the role of automated tools will grow.


## SORTING IT OUT

The ability to get the news you want is the hallmark of a networked world. People can create their own news reports from a variety of sources, not just the ones in their hometowns, which typically have been dominated by a monopoly local newspaper and television stations that would have to dig deeper to be shallow.

Creating our own news reports is still a largely haphazard affair. The sheer volume of information deters all but the most dedicated news hunters and gatherers. But the tools are improving fast, and it won't be long before people will be able to pick and choose in a far more organized way than they do today. New kinds of Big Media are emerging in this category, including Google, Microsoft, and Yahoo!. But the opportunity for small media is enormous, too.

I've been a fan of Google News[229] since it launched in "beta" form (it was still beta as I wrote this) in early 2002. The brainchild of Krishna Bharat, it has become a popular, and I'd argue essential, part of the web news infrastructure. The search engine "crawls" various news sites—designated by humans—and then machines take over to display all kinds of headlines on a variety of subjects from politics to business to sports to entertainment and so on. The display is calculated to resemble a newspaper. It's an effective glimpse into what's big news on the Web right now, or at least what editors think is big.

A user who wants to be better informed on a particular topic can use Google News to drill deeper, which may be the most important aspect of the site. One click and the user gets a list, sorted by what Google estimates is relevant or by date, of all stories on a given topic. There's a great deal of repetition, but it can be eye-opening to see how different media organizations cover the same issue, or what different angles they choose to highlight.

A useful element of Google News is called Google Alerts, a service that lets users create keyword searches, the results of which are sent by email on a regular basis. But as of early 2004, the service didn't let you read the alerts in RSS (the syndication format I discussed in Chapter 2 and will look at again below), a serious drawback.

Another Google News drawback, as of this writing, was a refusal to acknowledge news content from the sphere of grassroots journalism. For example, only a few blogs are considered worthy. This underestimates the value of the best blogs. Bharat told me the site has one basic rule: news requires editors, and Google News is displaying what editors think is important at any given moment. He saw the site as "complementary" to what newspapers do, but this seemed to understate its potential. Of course, it would not exist without the actual news reporting and editing from elsewhere. But it has the potential to turn into the virtual front page for the rest of us.

Microsoft, racing to catch Google in the search-engine wars, has long been established in the news business. MSNBC, the company's partnership with General Electric's NBC News unit, is a classic news site—big, heavy, rich with content. It's innovative in how it provides multimedia news. Now Microsoft is making Google-like experiments in news, too, with its "Newsbot,"[230] the early tests of which closely resemble Google News.

More interesting, by the sound of it, is an upcoming Microsoft product called NewsJunkie, which is due to be released later in 2004. As Kristie Heim reported in the *San Jose Mercury News* on March 24, 2004, it is being designed to keep track of what readers have already seen, but with refinements. "It reorganizes news stories to rank those with the most new information at the top and push those with repetitive information to the bottom, or filter them out entirely," she wrote.

In looking at the major web companies' moves, I've been most impressed with Yahoo!'s direction. The MyYahoo! page has been more customizable than any of the other major sites, letting the user create a highly tailored news report. In early 2004, Yahoo! folded RSS into the service, letting users select feeds from weblogs and other sites and add them to the MyYahoo! news page.[231] It's the best blend yet of old and new.

## SYNDICATION TAKES OFF

Let's revisit RSS. You'll recall that RSS is a file generated automatically by weblog and web site software, and increasingly by other applications, that describes the site's content for the purpose of syndication.

Here's an example. A typical blog consists of a homepage with several postings. Each posting consists of a headline and some text. The RSS "feed," as it's known, is a file containing a list of the headlines and some or all of the text from the postings. In other words, RSS describes the structure and some of the content of a particular page.

RSS feeds can be read by "aggregators" or "newsreaders," software that allows individuals to collect news from many different sites into one screenful of information instead of having to surf from one page to another. Today, RSS readers are fairly primitive, but that will change in coming years.

Some of the most exciting new work surrounding RSS is coming from fledgling companies such as Feedster, which mines RSS data and keeps track of bloggers' mentions of products, among other things. The inherent possibilities seem nearly endless, including the ability to follow conversations in much more detailed ways. As I was finishing this book, Microsoft quietly let it be known that it was planning "Blogbot," a search tool that sounded very much like Feedster and Technorati. Surprisingly, Google, which owns Blogger, a company that makes blogging software, hadn't done any of this.

The technologists looking at this field see rich lodes in RSS and other data created on blogs and web sites. Mountains of data are being created every day by RSS feeds and other structured information, and smart entrepreneurs and researchers are creating tools that I believe will become an integral part of tomorrow's news architecture.

## THE WORLD LIVE WEB

Dave Sifry, a serial entrepreneur, started Technorati in 2002. By April 2004, he was tracking more than two million blogs, with thousands coming online every day. Though many people abandon their blogs, the trend line is growing fast.

Technorati's tools are basically semi-canned queries that go into a giant, constantly updated database that Sifry likens to a just-in-time search engine. The service helps people search or browse for interesting or popular weblogs, breaking news, and hot topics of conversation. It also lets users rank people and their blogs and blog topics not just by popularity—the number of blogs linking to something—but by weighted popularity, determined by the popularity of the linking blogs. You can also see not just the most popular blogs, but the fastest-rising ones. My blog had about 2,100 incoming links the last time I checked. If I get 100 more, that's gratifying but not, relatively speaking, a huge change. But if someone who has a dozen incoming links today gets six more, that's an enormous relative change, and Technorati will probably flag it. Think of this as a "buzzmeter" for determining how fast a blogger—or a blogger's specific posting—is rising or cooling off.

The idea behind Technorati might be called the Google Hypothesis: link structure matters. Knowing who is linking to whom can take a seemingly random collection of weblogs and extract a highly structured set of information. This information can then be filtered in a variety of ways. The original Technorati application was the "Link Cosmos"—what Sifry called "an annotated listing of all weblog sources pointing to a site [blog] in recent time." Type in the URL of a weblog (or an individual posting), and the engine shows a list of weblogs pointing to that URL, sorted by time of linking or by "authority"—the "most popular" linking weblog is ranked first. Searching on any linking weblog will show its Cosmos as well, and so on. (Imagine what this would look like displayed graphically as a web of links. Inevitably, someone will offer such a tool.)

In addition to the Cosmos, the Technorati data can also be expressed as ordered lists. The Top 100 list, for example, shows the hundred most popular sites on the Web (whether weblogs or web sites such as Slashdot), based on the number of outgoing links from blogs. Though Technorati's algorithms are simpler than Google's, Technorati can offer the blogging community what Google offers news junkies with the Google News site: timeliness. Because the weblog world moves so fast, it's helpful to know when something was posted. Google looks at links and documents to get its Page Rank, Sifry explained, but Technorati adds two things: time of posting and the fact that with blogs, the postings are typically more personal than institutional. Combine all of this, he said, and you end up with a "World Live Web," a subset of the World Wide Web that gets at the actual conversation.

As of March 2004, Technorati's services included News-Talk ("News items people are talking about"), BookTalk ("The books people are talking about"), and Current Events ("Conversations going on around current events"). For serious news users, these were invaluable additions.

But these are only the start of something much more interesting. The Web transcends mere links. Machines are talking to each other on our behalf.

## PROBING APIS AND WEB SERVICES

Few users of Technorati know, and fewer care, about something called the Technorati API. API stands for "applications programming interface," a term used by tech people to explain how to hook one piece of software to another. In effect, APIs are standards created to help ensure that one product can interoperate with another. Think of the phone jack in your wall as an API that allows you to connect your phone to the phone network. Anyone can make an RJ-11 plug, connecting to a wire that runs between your phone and the wall.

Software development relies on APIs. Operating systems have them so that independent software programmers can create applications, such as word processors, that use the underlying features of the system. They don't have to reinvent the proverbial wheel each time they write software, and they help ensure a vibrant ecosystem on whatever programming platform they're using. Technorati is one of a growing number of web companies, including Google and Amazon, to create and publish APIs for its software. Most blogging software also has APIs.

With these and other APIs, programmers are using a technology called "web services" to further change the basic rules of the information game. According to programmer and blogger Erik Benson,[232] "A web service is basically a system that lets web sites talk to each other, sharing information between each other without the intervention of pesky humans." In a sense, humans have used the Web this way for years: type a query into Google, or buy a book on Amazon, and you're using a web service.

When Google[233] and Amazon,[234] and Technorati[235] (among others) offer APIs into their data, they're not offering us the entire database the way the U.S. government does with, for example, census data, much of which can be downloaded and massaged at will. They're offering a way to get specific information out of the databases in a structured way. But their willingness to do this means we can build, using web services, entirely new kinds of queries—and learn new things—with just a little bit of expertise. This may be beyond you and me, but programmers have already created some useful applications using APIs and web services, such as "Amazon Light,"[236] which uses the Amazon API to turn the retailer's site into something more closely resembling a search engine. Another extraordinarily interesting application is Valdis Krebs' analysis of people who buy books about politics with a right or left slant, and how little overlap there is among people who buy those books.[237]

Web services get even more interesting when you consider how we might wire them together to create new kinds of applications. Long before Technorati started watching conversations about books, Benson had created AllConsuming,[238] which combined four web services to watch and highlight the books bloggers were discussing. I'm also fascinated by GoogObits,[239] which takes newspaper obituaries and essays and then augments them with Google searches.

These technologies will be part of future news dissemination systems. They'll help us do something essential: keep better track of conversations. For example, I would like to be able to track news of innovative applications for my Treo smartphone. The news includes conversations among people I respect, not just standard journalists. If someone in the group I trust posts an item about the Treo, I want to know about it, of course. But I also want to know what others in that group—and people they designate as trustworthy or well-informed—are saying about this news. I want software that tracks not just the top-level item, which in this case could be a news story or blog posting or SMS response, but how the conversation then takes shape about the item across a variety of media. Now imagine having the same ability to track conversations about local, national, or international issues. Today, this is impossible except in a laborious and time-wasting way. Web services will eventually make it possible.[240]

## OKAY, BUT WHOSE "INFORMATION" DO YOU TRUST?

Among the missing components in this hierarchy is a way to evaluate a person's reputation beyond the crude systems in place today. A reliable reputation system would allow us to verify people and judge the veracity of the things they say based, in part, on what people we trust say about them. In a sense, Google is already a reputation system: Google my name and you'll discover a lot about me, including where I work, what I've written, and a lot about what I think about various issues—

and what some other people think of me (not all flattering by any means). Technorati is also this type of system: the more people linking to you, the more "authority" you have. But it's important to note that the majority of blogs tracked by Technorati have nobody linking to them. This doesn't mean the blogs lack value, because there are people close to the bloggers who trust them. No matter who you are, you probably know something about a topic that's worth paying attention to.[241]

Someday, a person who is interested in news about the local school system, which rarely rates more than a brief item in the newspaper except to cover some extraordinary event, will be able to get a far more detailed view of that vital public body. Any topic you can name will be more easily tracked this way. Just in the political sphere, the range will go beyond school governance to city councils to state and federal government to international affairs. Now multiply the potential throughout other fields of interest, professional and otherwise. And when audio and video become an integral part of these conversations—it's already starting to happen as developers connect disparate media applications—the conversations will only deepen.

The tools are being built now. Look on the accompanying web site for this book, where we will maintain a comprehensive list along with links to the toolmakers.

## DINOSAURS AND DANGERS

The technology tells us we're heading in one direction, but the law and cultural norms will have something to say about the process.

The media of the late 20th century was largely the province of big corporations. All else being equal, it might be headed toward extinction. But all is not equal in the halls of power and influence. If today's Big Media is a dinosaur, it won't die off quietly. It will, with government's help, try to control new media rather than see its business models eroded by it.

Meanwhile, one of the valuable artifacts of modern journalism is a commitment—however poorly kept at times—to integrity. The growth of grassroots journalism has been accompanied by serious ethical issues, including veracity and outright deception. Are traditional values compatible with this new medium? The questions of integrity and struggle for control are potentially deadly flies in the ointment of tomorrow's media. We'll look at them closely in the next several chapters.

*Chapter 9*

# Trolls, Spin, and
# the Boundaries of Trust

In the spring of 2001, almost no one was surprised to hear that several Hollywood studios had been setting up phony web sites to create buzz for new movies. The sites, supposedly run by fans, were just the latest version of some standard tricks in parts of the marketing world.

The exposure of the deception again brought to focus a reality of the modern age: for manipulators, con artists, gossips, and jokesters of all varieties, the Internet is the medium from heaven.

Technology has given us a world in which almost anyone can publish a credible-looking web page. Anyone with a computer or a cell phone can post in online forums. Anyone with a moderate amount of skill with Photoshop or other image-manipulation software can distort reality. Special effects make even videos untrustworthy.

We have a problem here.

## CUT AND PASTE, RIGHT AND WRONG

The spread of misinformation isn't always the result of malice. Consider the cut-and-paste problem.

Until recently, people would clip a news article from a paper or magazine. They'd give or mail it to someone else. Now we just copy it digitally and send it along. But when we cut and paste text, we can run into trouble. Sometimes the cutting removes relevant information. On occasion, words or sentences are changed to utterly distort the meaning. Both practices can prove harmful, but the latter is downright malicious.

In one of the most famous cut-and-paste cases, a column by *Chicago Tribune* columnist Mary Schmich made its way around the Net as a supposed MIT commencement address by novelist Kurt Vonnegut. Schmich had written a wry version of a graduation speech she'd give if asked—"Wear sunscreen," her commencement address began. But somehow, as it spread far and wide, her name came off and Vonnegut's replaced it. (I must have gotten a dozen emails quoting it.) In August 1997, commenting on the case in a subsequent column, Schmich wrote: "But out in the cyberswamp, truth is whatever you say it is, and my simple thoughts on floss and sunscreen were being passed around as Kurt Vonnegut's eternal wisdom. Poor man. He didn't deserve to have his reputation sullied in this way."[242]

Far more troubling was the case of Avi Rubin, a computer scientist and official election judge in the 2004 Maryland primary, who had been fiercely critical of electronic voting machines. He wrote a long article about his 2004 experience with the new machines, and while he maintained his strong objections to flaws in the process, he did make some positive remarks about the machines' potential.[243] His words were then taken out of context, he told me several weeks later, by supporters of the flawed machines. He forwarded me an email from a legislative aide in Ohio that confirmed the misimpression— whether it was inadvertent or deliberate wasn't clear—and he was trying hard to correct it.

I've had material misquoted or misrepresented on a number of occasions. The most telling instance took place in 1997 when I wrote a satiric column—labeled as such—"quoting" an unnamed Microsoft executive admitting to illegal business practices. In the same column, a spokesman for two software-industry trade groups was quoted as admitting his organiza tions might be making wildly inflated guesses about how much software is being illegally copied. Finally, I had a spokesman for the PC industry announce the end of the sleazy practice of showing video monitors in computer advertisements, but then, in small print, saying the monitor isn't included.

A week later, after the column had been sent out by the Knight Ridder Tribune wire service, I got a call from an earnest woman at the Business Software Alliance. She was astounded, she said, by the quotes attributed to the spokesman for her organization and the Software Publishers Association. She wanted me to know that no one there could possibly have told me that the software industry was making up its piracy estimates, as my column suggested.

"It was a joke," I said.

There was a pause on the other end of the line. "Oh," she said. It turned out that someone had sent her an email containing the offending quotes, but without the column's introductory line that said, "News stories we're unlikely to read," a missing piece that led to more than one misunderstanding. Indeed, I got a similar call later that day from a well-known public-relations person. She reported that email was flying around Microsoft and her PR firm, with various executives insisting they weren't the unnamed sources in my piece.

It had taken almost no time for the column to morph into an urban legend. Musing about this episode later, I wrote: "Actually, the worst part is that Bill Gates interrupted his speech to world leaders in Switzerland to call and offer me $10 million (plus stock options) to stop writing this column and become the editor of the column he writes for *The New York Times* syndicate. I told my boss and asked for a raise, but for some reason he didn't believe me." Happily, neither did anyone else, this time.

I learned a valuable lesson: email a copy of the entire article, or a URL to the original, and let the reader be the judge. And, as my case suggests, be careful of satire; some people are just too dense to get it.

## NEW WAYS TO MISLEAD

In early 2004, John Kerry's presidential campaign drew fire when conservative web critics—and several gullible newspapers—published a composite photograph of him and Jane Fonda, one of the right wing's favorite targets. Kerry and Fonda, in a photo that turned out to have been doctored, were shown "together" at a 1970s rally protesting the Vietnam War.[244] It was unclear who created the fake picture, but the willingness of many people to trust this picture spoke volumes about how easy it is to manipulate public opinion.

Moreover, the incident was only the latest demonstration of a truly pernicious trend of modern fakery. Photos are evidence of nothing in particular.[245] This is why publications that print these kinds of photos are subjected to withering criticism, as was *National Geographic* when it moved one of the Egyptian pyramids in a cover photo. Doctoring photos without clearly labeling them as such is a serious offense in most newspapers and news magazines.[246]

Nothing, in a journalistic sense, justifies blatant deception. But the line between improper doctoring and making an image better is less clear than we might like. For example, simple cropping can remove someone who was in the original picture or it can highlight an important element in the image. Photoshop and other image-manipulation tools give darkroom technicians, who once used various physical techniques to highlight some parts of photos and move others into the background, powerful new ways to alter images.

Even more worrisome is the increasing use of doctored video. It's now common practice for televised sporting events to feature advertising digitally inserted on, for example, stadium walls that are actually blank. The growing field of "product placement"—putting brand-name products into TV shows and movies—is moving closer to the news process, and that should disturb everyone. As the film *Forrest Gump* showed, we can put someone into a scene who wasn't there in reality; digital technology's steady improvements mean this will become trivially easy.

An element of trickery has been present for years in news programming. For example, the backdrops of urban settings behind anchor people are often inserted electronically. But CBS News, for one, took this to another level in 1999 when Dan Rather's newscast, anchored from Times Square, included digitally created billboards advertising products. At the time, CBS officials said they saw nothing wrong with the practice.[247] This isn't deception on the scale of Jayson Blair, who made up fictitious stories in *The New York Times*, but no responsible news organization should ever insert things into a report that are not really there. If viewers are getting used to this kind of trickery, we're all in trouble.

These techniques are made to order for the Internet, where lies spread quickly and can do enormous damage before the truth catches up. Some of the remedies—including digital watermarking of photos and videos so fakes can be discovered—have surface appeal. But they are not foolproof technically because hackers can consistently defeat such schemes, and they would encourage copyright restrictions even more onerous, and therefore more damaging, to grassroots media and scholarship than the ones currently in place.

## WHO'S TALKING, AND WHY?

In 2000, Mark Simeon Jakob put out a phony press release that sent the stock of a company called Emulex into a free fall after credulous news organizations took it seriously. He'd sold the stock short, in effect betting that the price would plummet, and made almost $241,000 before he was caught. He pleaded guilty to a felony and was sentenced to prison.[248]

His offense was egregious. But how much did it differ from chat rooms and discussion boards that have grown so popular in recent years? Pump-and-dump schemers have worked these discussions for years, planting information and then selling or buying accordingly. The Internet bubble was fueled, in no small way, by this kind of behavior—and not just online. Famous Wall Street "analysts" were telling the public to buy shares in companies they were calling dogs in private emails to their colleagues. I have some sympathy for small investors who lost big in the bubble, and contempt for the people who knowingly touted absurdly overpriced stocks. But greed was everywhere, and small investors who were looking for something that was too good to be true violated common sense.

Yet the investment forums can be a source of incredibly good information, too. Sometimes disgruntled employees post insider tales that can be a warning of harder times to come for shareholders. Sometimes a particularly bright amateur analyst spots something relevant the pros have missed. To dismiss all online information out of hand is as foolish as ignoring it entirely—but the failure to do one's homework before making a serious decision may be the most foolish mistake of all.

In doing homework, one of the most crucial exercises is to consider the source. Good journalists know this as a matter of practice. We don't pick a random bystander and assume he's an expert on, say, nuclear power. And we'd laugh out loud at the notion of reading some anonymous Net posting and using it as the factual basis for an article—at least I would.

Internet gossip monger Matt Drudge doesn't practice what I'd call respectable journalism (and, to be fair, he doesn't call himself a journalist), but I respect him for this much: he signs his name to everything he posts. That probably didn't come as much consolation to John Kerry, the 2004 Democratic presidential candidate. Kerry, you may recall, was dogged in early February by a rumor of an extramarital affair, a "scandal"—for which there was absolutely no evidence and which was flatly denied by everyone supposedly involved—that got its legs after Drudge published it on his web site.[249]

Unfortunate as the entire "Kerry affair" may have been, at least we knew who was largely responsible for having put it into play in the first place. And we could weigh the allegations in the context of the writer's previous work. However, we can't make such judgments about a lot of other things we read online. One of the Net's great features, the ability to remain anonymous, can also be one of its chief defects.

People I respect have told me we need to do away with anonymity on the Net. They have good reasons.

But anonymity is enshrined in our culture, even if its use can be distasteful at times. And there are excellent reasons for keeping one's identity hidden. A person with AIDS or another disease can lose a job or housing, or be persecuted in more violent ways. Someone holding unpopular political views in a small town that leans strongly in one direction may want to discuss it with others of like mind. Corporate and government whistle blowers need to be able to contact authorities and journalists without fear of being revealed. More than anyone, political dissidents in nations where such behavior can be life-threatening deserve the protection of anonymity when they need it.

Though the benefits of anonymity are clear, it also has its hazards. In one now famous example in 2004, a software glitch at Amazon.com revealed what many people suspected about the site's customer-written book reviews: authors were penning rave reviews of their own work under false names and, in some cases, slamming competing books. A *New York Times* story[250] showed a remarkable willingness on authors' part to excuse their deceptions as just another marketing tool. A more reasonable excuse was counteracting trash reviews by enemies. I worry what will happen when this book is published. I certainly have my share of adversaries. Will they trash me on Amazon? No doubt. Will that hurt sales? Probably. Can I do anything about it, assuming they don't libel me? Probably not.

In one online discussion on my blog about copyright, I challenged a commenter named "George" on his refusal to say who he was. "You're welcome to remain anonymous," I said. "I think you would enjoy even more credibility in this discussion if you said who you were. A casual reader might wonder why you want to be anonymous."

He replied: "You should judge my credibility by how my statements correspond with the facts, logic, and the law—not by who I am."[251]

He had it partly right. Debating skills are not proof of anything. In the absence of a foundation for his comments, he hadn't earned anyone's trust. Credibility stems not just from smart arguments; it also comes from a willingness to stand behind those arguments when a compelling reason to stay anonymous is absent. There was none in this case.

Another commenter, also using a false name, defended an electronic voting machine maker's use of copyright law to suppress memos that revealed flaws in its voting systems. It seemed that he or she was also posting comments, using a different name but similar (and in some cases identical) language, on a blog about intellectual property sponsored by the University of California-Berkeley journalism school. I learned this because Mary Hodder, one of the principal authors of that blog,[252] noted similarities in style in postings on our respective sites, which we believe share a number of readers due to the topics we cover. We checked the Internet addresses from which the comments had been posted; they were identical. This didn't absolutely prove that the same person was making both comments, but it helped make the case. Not only was this person refusing to be identified, but he or she was trying to make it seem as though a posse was patrolling our blogs to show us the error of our ways when, in fact, it was just one person on both.

What do these examples suggest? People reading comments on discussion boards would be wise to question the veracity of a commenter whenever they aren't absolutely sure where the posting is coming from.[253]

As we discussed in Chapter 8, advances in technology are likely to bring us better ways to gauge and, in effect, manage reputations and verify a commenter's bona fides without exposing his or her actual identity to the world.

Googling someone, to see what else he or she has said online in other places, sounds like a good way to start. But it ultimately isn't the answer. If, however, someone has been using a consistent pseudonym, at least we have the possibility of knowing if a person is reputable or has been making trouble elsewhere.

At the moment, my favorite solution is not the most practical: if everyone had a blog or other kind of web site, they could include a link as a kind of digital signature. Yes, web sites can be faked, but a hoax that uses someone else's name or hides behind a pseudonym for improper purposes, could attract unwelcome attention from the authorities—and because web site owners have to pay someone for hosting their site, the owner can be traced. Again, I would do nothing to stop anonymity on the Internet. But if we are going to have serious online discussions, I think all parties should, with few exceptions, either be willing to verify who they are, or risk having their contributions be questioned and, in some cases, ignored.

## TROLLS AND OTHER ANNOYANCES

Grassroots journalism has more problems than deciding whether anonymous posting is a good or bad idea. For starters, consider the trolls.

Rob Malda, Jeff Bates, and their colleagues at Slashdot have been dealing with trolls for years. At Slashdot, subtitled "News for Nerds: Stuff that Matters," the readers do the heavy lifting. They're constantly combing the Web for interesting information—articles, news stories, press releases, and mailing list postings—and recommend the material to Slashdot's tiny editorial staff. Each day, the editors select a dozen or so of the best items, which they highlight on the Slashdot homepage with a short summary and hyperlink, and invite readers to comment online. Then the editors sit back to watch what happens, and so do hundreds of thousands of other people.

The initial summaries and links are the beginning of the conversation on Slashdot, not the end. The average item generates about 250 comments. Some generate far more. Moderators, themselves selected on the basis of their participation in other discussions, rate the quality of the postings, and readers can adjust the results so they see everything or, as most do, a subset of the more substantive comments.

The Slashdot team has had to keep tweaking the software that runs the Slashdot site, as well as the user-based moderation system, because of the trolls and vandals who try to clog the site with irrelevant or obscene postings, ruining the experience for others. It's a constant annoyance, Bates told me, but part of the price of doing business.

How do you know if a troll is on your site? The definition on Ward Cunningham's Wiki says it best:

> A troll is deliberately crafted to provoke others with the intention of wasting their time and energy. A troll is a time thief. To troll is to steal from people. That is what makes trolling heinous.
>
> Trolls can be identified by their disengagement from a conversation or argument. They do not believe what they say, but merely say it for effect.
>
> Trolls are motivated by a desire for attention by people and can't or won't acquire it in a productive manner.
>
> Someone may be insufferable, infuriating, fanatical, and an ignorant idiot to boot without being a troll.
>
> Also note that a troll isn't necessarily insulting, snide, or even impolite. Only the crudest, most obvious, forms of trolling can be identified so easily.
>
> If you find yourself patiently explaining, at length and in great detail, some obscure point to someone who isn't even being polite to you, then you are probably being trolled.[254]

User registration on comment systems, with a name and verifiable email address, can be a deterrent to trolls. The worst thing you can do, as Netizens know, is feed the troll. Ignoring him is usually the best answer. If people become abusive, they can be banned from discussions. Not everyone has a right to speak on everyone else's site or be part of everyone else's conversation.

## SPIN PATROL

Journalists become accustomed to a process known as spinning. Wikipedia accurately describes this, in the context of public relations, as "putting events or other facts, especially of those with political or legal significance, into contexts favoring one-self or one's client or cause, at least in comparison to opponents. Newmakers and their PR legions have been spinning us since the media became a way to get information to the public, and we've been alternately falling for it or resisting it all this time."

In the physical world, I always try to ask myself what a person I'm interviewing has to gain from doing an interview. We need to recognize that motives play a part in what we're told, and we adjust our ultimate coverage accordingly.

But spin takes some insidious routes to the public. One of the worst forms is the media's lazy use of press releases as news. Some smaller newspapers are known to print them verbatim, as if a reporter had actually done some reporting and writing. Lately, video press releases have become a stain on both the PR profession and journalism. Local TV stations are handed video releases, often including fake "reporters" interviewing officials from the company or government agency that wants to get its news out, and too often stations play all or part of these mock-eries of journalism. In March 2004, the Bush administration was properly chastised for sending out video releases to promote, in a highly political way, a drug-benefits bill Congress had passed a few months earlier.[255]

Online spin varies from the relatively harmless, and even amusing, to more ethically challenged methods. On the harmless side is "Google bombing," a method of connecting a word or phrase to a specific web site through the Google search engine. After one group of Google bombers got "miserable failure" to point to George W. Bush's biography page on the White House site, his supporters retaliated by connecting John Kerry's page to the word "waffles."[256] Sooner or later, Google will either prevent this kind of thing or risk some of its own credibility.

Cyber-spin is getting more sophisticated, especially when it comes in comments or other postings by someone who's trying to make a point but doesn't identify his or her connection to the subject. The entertainment-industry copyright defender who made such a point of critiquing my blog was, in effect, spinning not just me but my audience as well. This is an unintended effect of the conversation, but one we'll have to live with.

Just before the January 2004 Consumer Electronics Show, I got an email from someone telling me, in a fairly breathless way, about a product due to be announced at the show. He was gleeful, it seemed, that the company had inadvertently given out information it intended to keep under wraps until the official announcement. He pointed me to several pages, including one that had a picture of the gadget (some gear for networking multimedia at home) and another where the company's chief executive had essentially confirmed the product's existence on a product support forum.

So I posted this information on my blog. "Consider this a small example of tomorrow's journalism today," I wrote. "A reader who knew much more than I did about something did some reporting and found information worth noting. Now you know, too."

Was I spun? After all, it wasn't a product I was likely to cover in the first place. My guess, based on some follow-up checking, is that this wasn't spin but a tip from someone who really thought he was giving me a scoop. Still, I plan to be more cautious before posting such things in the future.

Some online spin is obviously deceptive, as Adam Gaffin discovered. Gaffin runs an online forum called "Wicked Good" on the Boston Online site.[257] A 2003 forum thread talked about a fictional company in a soap opera holding a "Sexiest Man" contest. Someone named "dixie wrecked" was talking up the contest and the TV show. Gaffin got suspicious and checked the Internet address from which "dixie" was posting, and discovered it originated at a Washington-based firm, New Media Strategies, a company that offers, according to its web site, online word-of-mouth marketing to create buzz about products and brands. "We've been played," Gaffin told his forum[258] members, adding, "So, just in case Google indexes this page: New Media Strategies sucks. Let me repeat, New Media Strategies sucks."

Interestingly, by early 2004, one item on the first page of Google listings using the search term "new media strategies" was a pointer to a Boston Online page entitled, "Why New Media Strategies sucks." (The item had moved down to the second page by late April.)

I don't mean to pick on New Media Strategies here, or to suggest that its mistake in this case represents the company's general methods.[259] I do want to suggest that just one such episode, if it's caught and then stirs up any degree of irritation online, can be a lasting blemish.

Another lesson: exposure can be a reasonable counterweight to spinmeisters. Unfortunately, not everyone can catch such acts. We need better ways to sniff them out and then expose them with a variety of tools, including reputation systems. In many cases, the best solution is to ensure an open conversation among informed readers because they'll collectively inform each other.

## CITIZEN REPORTERS TO THE RESCUE

Blogger Ken Layne[260] captured one of the online world's essential characteristics in a classic posting in 2001. "We can Fact Check your ass," Layne said.[261] When there are lots of citizen reporters scrutinizing what other people say, they have a way of getting to the truth, or at least shining light on inconsistencies.

Case in point: Kaycee Nicole created a blog to talk openly about life, illness, and loss. As she grew sick and lay dying, she created a community. Thousands of people visited her blog in 2000 and 2001. They comforted her—and each other—with messages of support and offers of help. They researched her illness, looking for a way to make her better. And Kaycee did get better, at least for a while. Then she sickened again and finally succumbed to her leukemia.

But on May 18, 2001, someone named "acridrabbit" posted a simple question on MetaFilter, a collaborative blog and news site: "Is it possible that Kaycee did not exist?" The query set off a furious controversy. A relatively small but relentless group of Net denizens unraveled the tale of anguish and discovered a hoax. They investigated court records. They checked their findings with each other. They did some of the best detective work you'll ever see.

What this group accomplished was, in a sense, investigative reporting. But they weren't professional journalists. They were strangers who, for the most part, only knew each other online. But combining the power of the Internet and old-fashioned reporting, they'd come together—first in sorrow, then in dismay that morphed toward anger—to scrutinize a situation and, ultimately, solve a mystery.[262]

Fact-checking is a just one tool a community can bring to bear. As in open source projects, combining all those eyes and ideas can create a self-righting phenomenon. In the summer of 2003, David Weinberger and I discovered other community benefits. We'd launched a small, noncommercial web site called

WordPirates,[263] the purpose of which was to remind people how some good words in our language have been hijacked by corporate and political interests.

We opened the site to allow anyone to add a word plus an explanation of why it should be there. As we expected, some folks used the system to make off-point, irrelevant, or puerile postings, often with no explanation. We've had to prune heavily.

But a vandal found a security flaw in the software powering the site and exploited it by posting programming code inside a comment form—some HTML that took users to an unaffiliated web page containing one of the most disgusting photographs I've ever seen. We removed the offending post, thanks to a sharp-eyed programmer who let us know how the page had been misused so foully. Finally, the developer of the software we were using, who hadn't anticipated this kind of abuse, fixed the security breach.

We'd surely seen the downside of the Net. But we also saw the upside in the way the community helped us find, analyze, and fix the problem. As Weinberger noted after our dust up with the rogue coder: "It's as if the Internet is not only self-correcting about matters of fact but also morally self-correcting: A bad turn is corrected by several good ones."

## A FLIGHT TO QUALITY?

The flood of unreliable information on the Net could have the ironic effect of reinforcing the influence of Big Media, at least in the short term. This assumes, of course, that users of online journalism trust Big Media in the first place. Many do not.

Unlike many Americans, and in spite of some media scandals, I have substantial faith that major newspapers try hard to be accurate and fair. For example, I've been reading *The Wall Street Journal* for years, and I trust that the typical front-page news article in the *Journal* has been well reported, written, and edited. That doesn't mean I assume that everything in it is true, though I do assume the paper has done its best, and that there are institutional mechanisms in place to correct something if it's wrong. Those beliefs have carried over as, increasingly, I read the *Journal* online rather than in print. (Even after the Jayson Blair mess, I'd say the same thing about *The New York Times*.)

But Big Media, as it participates in the new conversation online, takes on risks that could hurt credibility even more. One of these days, someone is going to break through the security of a major media web site—the *Journal* or the *Times* or CNN—and post some "news" that turns out to be absolutely false. Maybe the story will announce wonderful news for some company, or terrible tidings, thereby giving the unscrupulous computer crackers, terrorists, or even politically connected malefactors a way to manipulate the stock market, cause panic, or steal an election.[264]

This act, which I consider more a certainty than a possibility, will change the news media's trust equation, at least for a time. Will it have long-lasting impact? Only if it happens repeatedly.

## PLAIN OLD COMMON SENSE

Being a reporter involves some basic practices. When I see or hear about something I think may be worth reporting to my audience, I verify it, or quote credible people who should know, or go to the source (human or document). If I link to something intriguing on my blog but don't know whether it's true, I offer that caveat. Generally, I don't just repeat an anonymous posting. If the fact in question didn't come from a source I trust, I check it out.

Users of online information need to develop similar filters. They need a hierarchy of trust.

In my own hierarchy, I trust *The New York Times* more than a supermarket tabloid. I trust what Doc Searls tells me on his blog more than what a random blogger says on a page I've never seen before.

As noted earlier, we need better recommendation and reputation tools, software that lets us traverse the Web using recommendations from trusted friends and friends of friends. We'll be figuring this out in the next few years, and I'm confident we'll get better and better at it.

But for now, people need to take information on the Internet with the proverbial grain of salt. When they see things that promise a measurable impact on their lives—such as a news story that persuades them to sell or buy something expensive—they should verify the claim before reacting.

There are limits to this, but on matters where the personal stakes are sufficiently high, it's probably worth remembering the legendary admonition given by crusty old editors to green reporters: if your mother says she loves you, check it out.

## Chapter 10

# Here Come the Judges
# (and Lawyers)

Brock Meeks was way ahead of most of us when it came to understanding the power of the Internet as a journalism tool. In 1993, then a reporter for Washington-based *Communications Daily*, a trade publication, he created a pathbreaking email news wire. He called it CyberWire Dispatch, and for the next several years, he regularly scooped the major media on story after story.[265]

But Meeks, now an MSNBC correspondent, has another claim to fame—and this is one he'd just as soon not have. He was, by most accounts, the first Internet journalist to be sued for libel. For all practical purposes, Meeks won the case; he paid nothing to the Ohio company that sued him over his critical report about the company's business practices, though he did agree to notify the company before publishing anything else about it or the man who ran it.[266] Meeks did pay his lawyers, including several noted First Amendment specialists who donated the vast majority of their time. He was lucky, in a sense, because his case drew the attention of people who wanted to protect our rights.

The Meeks case was a warning shot of sorts. It was a reminder that while the Net is a medium that grants great freedom, it doesn't exist in a vacuum. Law applies online and off, and people who intend to practice grassroots journalism need to keep that in mind.

This chapter isn't intended to scare anyone away from the Internet. Far from it. Nor should any reader consider this even remotely to be legal advice. To abuse a famous cliché, I'm not a lawyer and I don't intend to play one on these pages. If you need a professional answer to a legal question, please look elsewhere. (This book's accompanying web site, *http://wethemedia.oreilly.com*, includes links to legal sources.)

But it's important to consider some of the legal issues that have arisen in the online sphere. Libel is only one, and it applies not just to people who call themselves journalists but also to commenters in chat rooms. Other questions include copyright, linking, jurisdiction, and liability for what others say on your site.

## DEFAMATION, LIBEL, AND OTHER NASTY STUFF

I'm fairly sure I've been personally libeled. That is, people have written plenty of unflattering things about me, the kinds of things that I would never, ever write about someone else without some extraordinarily credible sources. I haven't sued anybody, though. And after almost 25 years in journalism no one has sued me, either. I may be wrong in my opinions or my interpretation of facts, but I try hard not to get basic stuff wrong, and when I learn I've made a mistake, I correct it.

Online journalists are no less required to follow the law than anyone else. A blogger who commits libel may have to face the consequences.[267]

There has been at least one defamation suit filed against a prominent online journalist. In 1997, Internet gossip maven Matt Drudge quoted unnamed sources who claimed that Democratic operative, author, and former Clinton White House aide Sidney Blumenthal had committed spousal abuse. Drudge's posting was false, and he corrected it in fairly short order. But Blumenthal sued him for defamation of character. In 2001, the case was settled. According to various press accounts, Blumenthal paid some $2,500 in travel expenses for a Drudge lawyer. In effect, Drudge prevailed, or at least didn't lose.

As noted in Chapter 9, I don't care for his style or willingness to publish rumors so readily, but I'm troubled by the fact that he was sued in the first place. After all, he did quickly retract the story and said of his source(s), "I think I've been had." Blumenthal's lawsuit may have been understandable—the charge was disgusting and could have been a disaster for his career—but anyone who cared to know learned quickly that the story was bogus. He also didn't count on conservative political groups offering to defend Drudge, thereby running up expenses on a case that was not going to be easy to win in any event, given the fast retraction and removal of the offending words from the Drudge Report site. In the end, however offensive Drudge's original posting may have been, the case advanced journalistic freedom.[268]

One of Brock Meeks's attorneys in his libel case was David L. Marburger. Marburger has been practicing First Amendment law in Ohio for more than 20 years. Though he doesn't claim to be an expert about Internet law, he offered some advice that applies to all kinds of journalists, including cyber-reporters.

First, he told me, anyone who writes regularly on the Net about other people or institutions should try to be insured against libel. "If it's affordable and you can get it," he said, "you need insurance." Second, writers "should keep in mind who most often sues: people whose livelihoods depend on the goodwill of the public, who depend on reputation." In this category, he said, are lawyers, doctors, and government officials, along with companies.

Marburger raised a common issue in one of his cautionary remarks: writers who work without editors—most bloggers, for example—typically "don't have that second and third set of eyes to look at stuff. The risk is going to be higher. You're less likely to critically analyze your own work than an editor would be."

Publishing on the Web appears to have had its advantages in this regard. After all, when your readers can let you know you've made an error, you can fix it quickly and stop the mistake from being widely disseminated. But as Marburger noted, "Sometimes your reader can be your plaintiff, too."

Glenn Reynolds is both the prolific blogger Instapundit and a teacher of Internet law in Tennessee. He's somewhat more sanguine about the prospects for bloggers, at least for most of them, because blogging tends to be more about opinion than reporting.

"Most of what bloggers do is punditry," he said. "It's hard to libel via punditry. Most blogs involve linking to someone else's work and then commenting on it."

What's more, well-known bloggers tend to write about "public figures," people who must meet a much higher standard to prove libel. You can't libel a public figure, even if the story is false, unless you publish it with what's called "malice," which in this instance means either the standard definition of the word or indifference to whether the story is true or not.

In any event, most bloggers probably don't have enough money to make it worthwhile to sue, assuming, of course, that winning monetary damages is the plaintiff's goal. However, if the goal is to shut someone up, just the threat of a lawsuit can do the trick because the cost of defense can be huge.

That's why Reynolds called himself "an insurance agent's dream"—that is, adequately insured for any trouble. "The real reason is not for fear of libeling someone," said the lawyer who is well aware of how not to defame others. "It is to guard against having someone sue me into bankruptcy out of spite or to shut me up."

Even if a blogger can libel someone else with her own comments, a blog owner is probably not liable for what someone else writes in the comments, according to Jack M. Balkin,

Knight Professor of Constitutional Law and the First Amendment and director of the Information Society Project at Yale Law School. On his Balkinization weblog,[269] commenting on an appeals court ruling, he wrote that the 1996 Telecom Act "protects people who run web sites from being sued for republishing the libels of another person."

"This does not mean that bloggers are immune from libels they themselves write," Balkin continued. "It means that they are immune from (for example) libels published in their comments section (if they have one) because these comments are written by other people and the blogger is merely providing a space for them to be published. Congress wanted to treat operators of chatrooms and other interactive computer services differently from letters to the editor columns in a local newspaper."[270]


So far, bloggers may have avoided the legal chopping block, though threats against bloggers abound. Commenters on Internet forums have had more trouble. In particular, some companies have been especially assertive in financial forums, demanding from Internet service providers the identities of people who have made allegedly defamatory postings.

Policies on how to deal with such requests vary among Internet service providers. Some will turn over subscribers' personal information without telling the customer. More honorable ones won't; they'll tell the subscriber in order to give him time to challenge a subpoena. In some cases, these "John Doe" subpoenas are granted, especially when the posting is libelous on its face.

But civil-liberties groups have asked judges, sometimes successfully, to apply a tough standard in these cases. In one, which started in 2001, a Canadian pharmaceutical company called Nymox demanded that Yahoo! hand over the names and other subscriber information regarding some "John Does" who'd been posting to the service's Nymox message board. There was no doubt that the messages were inflammatory, alleging corporate malfeasance, but the question was whether they rose to a level at which the company had a legitimate defamation case.

The Stanford Cyberlaw Clinic at Stanford Law School fought the subpoenas. In early 2003, the clinic won an important ruling from a federal judge in San Francisco. He wrote that Nymox, in order to win its motion, had to demonstrate, among other things, that the statements posted on the Yahoo! board were, in fact, "actionable"—in other words, Nymox needed to show that a judge wouldn't dismiss the case for lack of evidence should an actual defamation suit be filed. In addition, he wrote, Nymox had to show that the postings in question had actually damaged the company.

One statement was clearly defamatory, the judge said. But he noted that it was essential to consider the context of the message, not just its content:

> The statement was posted anonymously on an Internet message board. The tenor of all the submitted postings would lead the ordinary reader to regard their contents skeptically. Nymox has made no effort to trace any injury to the doorstep of this posting. Although Nymox said at the hearing, weakly and vaguely, that its stock fell after the postings were made, no investor would have relied on such manifestly unreliable information.

He granted John Doe's motion to quash the subpoena, allowing Doe to remain anonymous.[271]

I'm no fan of fishing expeditions. At the same time, the anti-Nymox poster in this case didn't rate anyone's sympathy on an ethical basis because the postings were crude at best. But preserving the value of anonymity, and robust speech, is vital. The judge, striking an appropriate balance, said there's no right to defame and damage others under a cloak of anonymity. The company just didn't make its case.

## JURISDICTION

If I call the judges of the High Court of Australia some of the most obtuse people on the planet, do I need to cancel my next trip Down Under? Possibly, because one or more of them may decide that I have defamed them by offering such an opinion. Thanks to their ruling in a 2002 lawsuit, they have created a right to sue me on their home turf, under their own restrictive defamation laws, for what I've said on my blog and column, both of which are based in the U.S.

The case in question is about an article that appeared in *Barron's*, a Dow Jones weekly newspaper published in the U.S. A corporate executive in Australia didn't like what it said about him, so he sued in Australia, effectively arguing that Internet publication was like putting out a local newspaper in every jurisdiction. Astonishingly, the High Court agreed.[272]

The ruling was a blow to the open nature of the Internet. To say that defamation occurs where something has been read, as opposed to where it was posted, is an invitation to forum-shopping—and abuse by plaintiffs.

Jurisdiction questions have bedeviled the Net for some time. In 1994, the Justice Department under President Bill Clinton hauled the owners of a Milpitas, California, adult-oriented computer bulletin board to the heart of the Bible Belt and prosecuted them on obscenity charges. The bulletin board offered pornographic images that were not in violation of California standards, but a postal inspector's downloading of them to Nashville was deemed to violate his community's local standards. The owners of the online service were convicted and sentenced to prison terms. The prosecution was an abuse of the criminal justice system and a direct attack on First Amendment rights because it suggested that standards in the nation's most repressive communities could determine what the rest of us may read, hear, or view.

Now we have to ask if the most repressive nation could set our standards. French courts told Yahoo! in 2001 to block auctions of Nazi memorabilia. Yahoo! got a U.S. court to say the order was invalid, but in the end the online service shut down its European auction sites altogether—a business decision, the company said.

Under the Australia court's logic in the Dow Jones case, every person or organization that posts something on the Internet will need to understand and comply with the libel laws of 190 nations and who knows how many subnational jurisdictions. That's absurd. It's also dangerous, because it encourages powerful and paranoid people to use local laws, some of which will be designed to stamp out unwelcome news or opinions. Does that sound paranoid? It's not, because dictators have already recognized the usefulness of restrictive laws to stifle or silence critics. In the African dictatorship of Zimbabwe, the government prosecuted a British reporter for something posted on his newspaper's United Kingdom web site. He was acquitted and deported, but at serious financial cost to his publication and to the practice of professional journalism in a nation that needs more, not less, serious reporting.

Decisions such as the one in Australia are arguments for an international treaty that establishes libel rules, preferably extremely liberal ones for publishers. The alternative is an increasingly balkanized Internet. Jonathan Zittrain, cofounder of the Berkman Center and a law professor at Harvard, anticipates increased efforts to "zone" content on the Net, for example. What an American would then see on a given web site would not be what a person from France sees even when both type in the same web address. This raises at least two questions. First, is such zoning an altogether bad idea on a multicultural planet? After all, newspapers such as *The New York Times* and *The Wall Street Journal* have national and international editions. If the alternative means the most restrictive jurisdictions can control content, maybe zoning is a better alternative. Second, is zoning simply inevitable? I hope not. To force sites to provide versions for every jurisdiction is not practical, and it's fundamentally antispeech.

## EMAIL AND FREE SPEECH

Intel Corp., the giant Silicon Valley maker of the microprocessors that serve as the central brains of most personal computers, used a novel legal theory when it sued a former employee for sending anti-Intel emails to current employees. Kourosh Kenneth Hamidi, the company argued, was trespassing on its computer servers.

Intel overreached, the California Supreme Court said in 2003. The court's decision, by only a 4-3 margin, will have important free-speech implications. The court said Ken Hamidi wasn't legally trespassing on Intel's computers by sending unsolicited email because there was no harm to the company's systems. The ruling did not endorse what he did, but said that Intel couldn't use inappropriate laws to keep out Hamidi's speech.[273]

Predictably, Intel and its supporters raised the specter of massive spamming as they denounced the ruling. But this case was never about spam, and Intel had technical ways to handle Hamidi's missives without resorting to a legal position that veered into an attack on speech itself.

What was striking about the opinions, pro and con, was the way the justices struggled, unsuccessfully for the most part, to come up with apt metaphors. "He no more invaded Intel's property than does a protester holding a sign or shouting through a bullhorn outside corporate headquarters, posting a letter through the mail, or telephoning to complain of a corporate practice," wrote Justice Kathryn Werdegar in the majority opinion. But court dissenters likened his actions to breaking into the mailroom and delivering letters to 30,000 employees. What mattered, in the end, was that the court majority couldn't be persuaded that Hamidi was doing any real harm beyond what was protected by free speech.

## MISUSING OTHER PEOPLE'S WORK

Harder to monitor, perhaps, is cheating. Yet cheating is rampant in our society. Some students see no problem with cheating in class. Corporations see cheating as a business tactic. And corporations and individuals routinely cheat on tax returns. The current attitude toward cheating seems to be: "What's acceptable is what you can get away with."

Traditional journalism has had its share of cheats recently. The infamous Jayson Blair, formerly of *The New York Times*, lied and plagiarized his way to fame, then ruin. More recently, *USA Today* revealed that star reporter Jack Kelly had fabricated some of the work that made him a Pulitzer Prize finalist.

A culture of cut-and-paste is made to order for the Net, where an almost-anything-goes attitude prevails. Cutting and pasting is not, by itself, a bad thing; quoting the work of others is a routine aspect of research, for instance. But when people routinely pass off the work of others as their own, it goes too far. Student cheating has drawn most of the attention in this category because it appears to be the most rampant violation. But web journalists have done it, too. In one case, a Canadian contributor to a technology news web site even copied material from my *Mercury News* colleague Mike Langberg; according to our coverage of the story in 2001, she was fired. In 2002, popular blogger Sean-Paul Kelley publicly apologized for lifting Iraq war–related material from other sources. In an age when some refuse to acknowledge what they've done even when caught, his willingness to take responsibility for his actions was refreshing. Even so, his credibility took a hit, at least temporarily.[274]

Cheating may abound, but the Net gives us a mechanism to catch the violators. Search tools such as Google, and more targeted tools for educators such as the "Turnitin" software[275] (which compare student papers to a vast database of published writings on and off the Web), have been effective.

People draw their bottom lines in different places. But ethical behavior and the law say roughly the following: if you use someone's work, even a small amount, you should give him credit, and you can't legally copy more than what's acceptable in a "fair use" context; that is, a short quotation. If you copy others' work and resell it, except in traditional ways, such as quoting from it for another piece, you may find yourself in court.

Wendy Selzer, an attorney with the Electronic Frontier Foundation (EFF), urges caution in comparing copyright infringement and plagiarism in the first place. She explained:

> While you might be less likely to be sued for posting a large chunk with attribution, if someone did sue, the attribution wouldn't convert infringing conduct into fair use. Quoting a large portion of "the heart" of a copyrighted work with attribution might be ethically OK but legally infringing; and vice versa, taking a short quote without attribution might be fair use but ethically questionable. One of the problems with fair use is that it doesn't always track general notions of "fairness."

We may never be able to precisely define fairness, but we all know what cheating is. Society accepts too much of it.

## COPYRIGHTS AND WRONGS

One of most pernicious trends in recent times has been the application of property rights to almost all things digital. Copyright law is the biggest problem, as we'll see later and in Chapter 11, but the issues extend to a variety of arenas.

One is trademarks: the words, phrases, logos, and other things that help define a brand. "Trademark law begins from consumer protection: trademarks, words and symbols that identify a source of goods are protected so that the public can rely on them as indicators of quality (or take warning to avoid a brand after a bad experience)," Selzer said.

According to the Chilling Effects Clearinghouse,[276] an organization sponsored by the EFF and some prominent law schools, including Harvard and Stanford, trademark complaints are fairly common today. One common complaint is the use of domain names "identical or similar to well-known marks" that are typically registered by so-called "cybersquatters" who want to capitalize on the traffic or sell back the name. U.S. law bans "bad faith intent to profit" from such activities. A second is outright copying of logos onto a site to suggest an "authorized connection" to someone else's better-known product or service.

It's hard to object when a trademark holder wants to stop someone from trying to piggyback on its brand. Few Netizens objected when *The New York Times* persuaded the World Intellectual Property Organization (WIPO),[277] one of the organizations empowered to make such decisions, to give it the newyorktimes.com domain, which had been registered by a third party.

But suppose you found yourself looking at a web site called "mercurynewssucks.com," an online attack on my newspaper, the *San Jose Mercury News*, and its contents. Barring libelous assaults or misrepresentations designed to confuse the public, such a site would be protected as a form of free speech. For the same reason, we'd most likely be laughed out of the U.S. courts if we sued to take away the domain. We'd probably have better luck, unfortunately, if we took our case to WIPO's headquarters in Switzerland. It might order the domain-name registrars to hand the offending web address over to us because WIPO's mission is not about freedom of expression. It is, in a fundamental way, the promotion of intellectual property rights.

WIPO, despite claims of neutrality in its arbitration process, has shown a strong bias toward handing over disputed domains to the holders of trademarks. As of mid-March 2004, according to statistics on the WIPO web site, the organization had granted the complaining party's request to transfer the domain in 80 percent of the cases it has decided.

Some of WIPO's decisions have stretched logic, to put it mildly. As the Washington-based Consumer Project on Technology[278] pointed out in 2000, in a number of cases WIPO ordered that anticorporate sites using "companyname-sucks.com" monikers be turned over to the trademark-holding companies that complained.

For example, in a dispute in which the London-based Dixon's electronics-store chain complained about a site called dixons-sucks.com, the case examiner noted the growth of web sites used in this way and wonders if such a domain name is "plainly disassociated" from the company that's complaining about the use of its name in this way. No, the examiner concluded:

> The first and immediately striking element in the Domain Name is the Complainant's name. Adoption of it in the Domain Name is inherently likely to lead some people to believe that the Complainant is connected with it. Some will treat the additional "sucks" as a pejorative exclamation and therefore dissociate it after all from the Complainant; but equally others may be unable to give it any very definite meaning and will be confused about the potential association with the Complainant.[279]

Confused? I suspect that the average 10-year-old could tell the difference.

I don't want to suggest that WIPO always does the bidding of trademark holders. But decisions like these are not just illogical; they're hostile to concepts that are just as deserving of protection as property rights—freedom of speech, for one. Unfortunately, cyberspace doesn't have a global First Amendment written in law, even if it exists, for the most part, in practice.

Sometimes a site will imitate the entire look and feel of another, and then try to use it for commercial gain. This is obviously improper. But when the purpose is satire, the situation is hazier.

In March 2004, the National Debate web site posted a page featuring "corrections" of *The New York Times* opinion columns, done in the style of the *Times'* own corrections page.[280] Since the *Times* wasn't running column corrections—under an evolving policy, it was leaving them to the writers to include them (or not) in their columns—the fake page was filling what the National Debate's author, Robert Cox, perceived as a hole in the Paper of Record's content. Some of the "corrections" struck me as nonsense, but many were anything but frivolous. The satiric content, while biting, was a useful exercise in media watchdogging.

The *Times* clumsily dispatched its lawyers, using the Digital Millennium Copyright Act in a remarkably inappropriate way. The Act allows copyright holders to tell Internet service providers that copyrighted works are being infringed, and the ISP must take down the allegedly offending pages unless the owner of that site says he'll fight in court (more on the DMCA in Chapter 11). This seemed more like a trademark matter than a copyright question, even if the *Times* had one legitimate point: the page used enough elements of the actual *Times* layout that it might have conceivably led some reader, somewhere, to imagine that the *Times* itself was responsible for the site.

The result of the threats was predictable. Several other web sites started mirroring the forbidden content—posting it on their own computer servers—in deliberate defiance of the *Times*. So the National Debate had more readers than ever, and the *Times* looked like a heavy, hardly the response the newspaper might have envisioned. In the end, the *Times* said it would be satisfied if the National Debate prominently labeled its page as a satire and not the real thing. And the *Times* ultimately changed its internal policy for dealing with a columnist's factual errors by requiring columnists to put corrections in subsequent columns.[281]

## FORBIDDEN LINKS AND OTHER OUTRAGES

If the Web has a central function, it's linking. Publish a page and anyone can link to it, right? Well, not always.

Sometimes it's just a bad idea. I would be very unlikely to link to a site I considered harmful, such as a site advocating violence. If the link served a specific journalistic purpose, however, it's conceivable I'd include it, but even then I'd think long and hard first. Where we draw the line on such matters tends to be a personal and professional decision. Most of all, we need to think about it in terms of ethics and news judgment.

But that assumes I'm allowed to make the link. Several corporate spats have tested that assumption. In 1997, Ticketmaster, the event-ticketing company, sued Microsoft because Microsoft's city-guide company was linking deep into the Ticketmaster site, straight to the page describing the event, rather than routing people through Ticketmaster's virtual front door (the homepage). A judge ended up ruling that deep links were legal.

What made the case strange was Ticketmaster's unwillingness to use technology better; it's not difficult to block someone from deep-linking into a site. If Ticketmaster was so upset about Microsoft's action, all it had to do was stop the referrals. Of course, this begged a question: why was Ticketmaster unhappy at having business directed its way? Ticketmaster's explanation that it had a right to control access by insisting all visitors start from their front page never washed with me.[282]

A much more serious case of "forbidden links" was the case of Universal v. Reimerdes, and it takes some explaining.

When the DVD format was first being developed, the film studios, paranoid over copyright issues, and the cartel of companies that controlled the DVD format got together to create an encryption standard. The standard was developed to prevent people from playing DVDs on devices that hadn't been authorized for playing them. Owners of DVDs could copy the files containing the digital data, but they couldn't play them. The software encryption code used to keep the files from being cracked was called CSS, which stood for Content Scrambling System.

But in September 1999, a Norwegian teenager named Jon Johansen (and other unidentified individuals) cracked the code, which by almost any account was weak protection indeed. Johansen said he wanted to play his DVDs on computers running the Linux operating system, for which there were no authorized DVD players. His work, which he called DeCSS, was posted on the Internet, where people adapted it for other operating systems. The studios panicked because their absolute control over DVD playback had been compromised.

Lawsuits followed, including one in Norway. Johansen was charged with violating copyright law and was acquitted by a Norwegian court. The prosecution appealed, and another trial was held. He was acquitted again.

Meanwhile, in a case with serious implications for journalism, several studios sued the editor of a hacker magazine called 2600. By posting the DeCSS code on the 2600 web site, and by linking to other sites containing the code, the movie companies said Eric Corley, the magazine's editor, was violating the Digital Millennium Copyright Act for making technology that could be used to circumvent copyright protections available to others. The studios won, and in the process tore down some vital First Amendment protections, as we'll see.

In a series of rulings starting in 2000, a trial court in New York, and later the Second Circuit Court of Appeals, upheld the notion that while code is speech entitled to First Amendment protection, "functional" code has a second-class status, and therefore can be banned because of unlawful uses it might enable, even if there are lawful uses. In response to these rulings, cyber-activists have put the DeCSS code on T-shirts.

They've posted it in the haiku form of poetry and a variety of other formats that, no doubt, could be ruled illegal but which demonstrate the essential illogic of the ruling. But such satiric reactions don't diminish the club now in the hands of the copyright holders and governments, should they choose to wield it selectively against individuals.

Second, and even more alarming, the courts agreed that even linking to the offending code—that is, posting a hyperlink to a web page containing the code, even one outside U.S. jurisdiction, was also violating the law. The trial judge, supported by the appeals court, said hyperlinking under these circumstances could be proscribed.[283]

The potential stifling effect of this ruling is obvious should copyright holders choose to pursue it. Neither my employer nor I were sued by the movie studios when I also linked to DeCSS code from my blog. Was I a more "legitimate" journalist than Corley? The court effectively made that distinction, but it was a frightening one. As Mark Lemley, a University of California-Berkeley law professor, told the online magazine Salon:

> The court clearly tries to limit the circumstances in which linking leads to liability, but nonetheless, the fact that [the court is] saying it's illegal to make reference to information that resides somewhere else—well, that's got some troubling implications for, among other things, the news media; if Salon, for example, wants to show its readers what all the fuss is about [with DeCSS], reporters could be pulled into court and asked why they decided to link to the information. I can imagine that there will be a lot of litigation over the intent of the press, and a lot [of] reporters in court.[284]

The good news is that, as far as I know, this scenario hasn't come to pass. But the potential remains, with another danger lurking. If judges can say that one kind of journalist is legitimate and another kind of journalist is not, the entire concept of grassroots media is threatened. We are creating a division that

a) doesn't exist and b) should chill all so-called "legitimate" journalists. Does this mean journalists will be licensed someday?

The DVD-CSS case raised another free-speech issue when the movie industry sued a Texas man in a California court, alleging his posting of the DeCSS code amounted to stealing trade secrets. His lawyers, including attorneys from the EFF, pointed out that, given the widespread dissemination of the code, it was hardly a trade secret anymore. The court agreed.[285] Score one for common sense.

The copyright debate goes far, far beyond attacks on speech and linking. It goes to the heart of the Internet and technology. We'll explore this further in the next chapter.

*Chapter 11*

# The Empires Strike Back

The promise was freedom. And, for a time, freedom was the reality.

The Internet, some of us believed early on, would be a largely unregulated sphere where boundaries would not matter—where, for good and bad, individual freedom would be the paramount condition. After all, the Internet was a robust communications system; it could, in theory, withstand a nuclear attack. So early Netizens can be forgiven for assuming that different rules applied because, for a time, they did.

Cyber-liberty, we saw, would extend to culture and information in powerful, even unprecedented, ways. The Internet—the first many-to-many medium—was going to liberate us from the tyranny of centralized media and the rancid consumerism that says we are merely receptacles for what Big Business, including Big Media, wants us to buy. We were going to turn the world of "take it or leave it" into an informed global conversation. Consumers would become true customers. The governed would become "we, the people" participants in the political process.

But the clampdown has begun. Everywhere we look, the forces of centralization and authority are finding ways to slow—and perhaps halt altogether—the advances we've made.

They include the usual suspects, namely government, big telecommunications companies, and what I call the copyright cartel of entertainment companies. But, sadly, they also include some of the technology pioneers who once promised so much in the way of digital liberty.

Could these increasing restrictions impinge on grassroots journalism? They could indeed, and we will have to fight to keep our freedoms. The alternative could be a news regime that is dictated almost entirely by governments and mega-corporations—a situation worse than what we have today when Big Media already controls so much.

What follows is a description of the most serious threats, and what we might do, individually and collectively, to counter them.

## GOVERNMENTS GET NERVOUS; BIG BUSINESS GETS NOSY

So far, state intervention has tended to be more blunt than subtle when applied to grassroots journalism. For example, several times during 2003, the government of China flipped a switch, figuratively speaking, and indiscriminately turned off access to thousands of weblogs. The Great Firewall, already in use to block specific news and information sites the government didn't want its people to see (including my own newspaper's), was now preventing all manner of sites created on Blogspot.com (a leading blog-hosting site) from being read by web users inside the country.[286]

China is far from alone in censoring political content. Saudi Arabia has pervasive controls, according to a study by Jonathan Zittrain and Ben Edelman of the Berkman Center for Internet and Society at Harvard Law School. But government interference—such as stopping data traffic at arbitrary borders on the whim of a government or a company—is growing more common in general, not less, and it's not just in repressive regimes such as China and Saudi Arabia, but also in France and Singapore. Nor is filtering the only infringement. Law enforcement officials in the Western democracies, including the United States, are pushing for surveillance capabilities that would surely have a chilling effect on politically off-center speech.[287]

Truly free access to information—the word "free" is used here in the context of "freedom," not cost—implies an ability to send and receive information without being tracked. We're losing that ability swiftly, and the supreme irony is that American businesses, not governments, have been the prime privacy invaders when it comes to applying technology for everyday surveillance.[288]

Under the Web's original architecture there was no way for anyone to know you'd visited a web site or what you'd done there. But in the mid-1990s, Netscape developed "cookies," little files placed on users' computers that allowed the owner of a web site to track where visitors went, and when. Stanford law professor Lawrence Lessig, concerned about the privacy implication of cookies, said that rather than naming the technology something "sweet and happy like 'cookies,'" they should have named it what it was: "Network Spy."

Cookies had, and have, big privacy implications. But like all such technologies, they have their good points. They can save time for the user, storing one's preferences for a particular site. Without cookies, my personalized Yahoo! page would not exist. But fears about cookies led some Net users to set their web browsers to refuse their placement on their computers so their movements couldn't be tracked. Site developers, meanwhile, found them invaluable for marketing and ease-of-use purposes. Cookies became a staple on the Internet, and they aren't going away.

Cookies become a more serious privacy problem when you consider a real-world situation. When you go to a shopping mall, no one follows you around with a video camera, recording everything you look at. (Hidden cameras, becoming more ubiquitous, may change this equation.) But that's exactly what cookies allow: a view of everything a computer user does on the Web. As a result, people's private data has become a commodity to be bartered to the highest bidder, or to anyone wielding a subpoena.

Computers can also track the movement of information around the Internet. Lessig related the time he set up a Morpheus peer-to-peer server so people could freely download copies of his lectures. He got a frantic call from the Stanford "network police"—the university's systems administrators— saying there had been illegal activity detected on a machine in his office—and as a result, the machine had been disconnected. Fearing the wrath of the entertainment industry, the administrators had assumed illegal acts because of the presence of the technology, even though they were actually thwarting an entirely legal use of the software.[289]

Filtering of spam and other so-called objectionable content, meanwhile, has led to an ad hoc system of content blocking. Spam blacklists run by volunteer organizations have been adopted widely, causing the mail of innocent users—who happen to be using an Internet service provider that also has a spammer using the same system—to disappear into a black hole. This isn't censorship, legally, because governments aren't doing the blocking. But it's a disturbing trend when good intentions lead to the widespread blocking of content that is objectionable only to a narrow subset of those who'd receive it.

Filtering can include what technologists call "IP Mapping," in which a server checks the Internet address from which some data is being requested. The inevitable result will be Internet zoning. As noted in Chapter 10, someday soon, when people from different countries visit the same page, they'll see different information.

## THE COPYRIGHT CARTEL

Article I, Section 8 of the Constitution gives Congress the power to "promote the progress of science and useful arts, by securing for limited times to authors and inventors the exclusive right to their respective writings and discoveries."

I won't go into the historical details of copyright law (Lessig's writings, in particular his book *Free Culture: How Big Media Uses Technology and the Law to Lock Down Culture and Control Creativity*,[290] are a good place to learn more.) But, it's safe to say that today's situation has perverted the Founders' intent, and it looks as though the situation could get much worse.

What's important to understand is how the very notion of copyright has changed since the Founders first enshrined it in the Constitution. Originally intended as a bargain between creators and the rest of us, it has become an instrument of harsh, absolute control. Balance has disappeared.

By law and tradition, copyright laws gave rights to users of a copyrighted work, not just to the work's creator. For example, scholars could quote from copyrighted works in order to create new works. This is the notion of "fair use"—to use a small portion of another's work as part of a new work. Fair use has expanded in recent times to include, among other things, making personal backups of software and time-shifting television programs (recording a show to watch it later). But the forces of control have moved the line. They believe fair use is something that can be granted only by the copyright holder if he or she (or it, in the case of a corporate holder) is willing to grant fair use—and the law, when new technology comes into use, increasingly supports their position.

But the whole point of fair use is to define a zone of use that copyright holders don't specifically authorize, and may even oppose, but which is legal anyway. Siva Vaidhyanathan, director of the undergraduate program in communication studies in New York University's Department of Culture and Communication, tells the story of the author who wrote a scholarly book about country music but didn't quote any lyrics. The author's skittish publisher, fearing lawsuits from copyright holders even though use of such quotes would plainly have fallen under fair-use guidelines, decided it wasn't worth the trouble to get permission; hence, the book was published without all the lyrics she wanted to use.[291] To turn fair use into the exclusive realm of authorized uses is to remove fair use almost entirely. We'll come back to this crucial point later in this chapter.

One of the keystones of "intellectual property" is that a work goes into the public domain after what the Founders defined as "limited times," which allowed a copyrighted work to pass into the public domain so others might freely build upon it. "Limited times" were first defined as 14 years but have been progressively extended by Congress at the behest of copyright holders such as Disney. What were once 14-year terms have now been extended to the life of the author plus 75 years, or 95 years when a copyright is held by a corporation. By amazing coincidence, copyright terms seem to get extended every time Mickey Mouse comes close to entering the public domain, which means that nothing is going into the public domain anymore. This is a double-barreled heist by the copyright holders. They're stealing from our common heritage in order to protect a few valuable works. And they're thwarting innovation.

If the rules and enforcement regimes that apply today had been applied in the 1930s, Walt Disney might never have been able to create Mickey Mouse, which was a derivative work based on other people's creations. And Victor Hugo is surely spinning in his grave at the way the Disney empire of today took *The Hunchback of Notre Dame* and turned that story into a children's cartoon. But his work had entered the public domain, and new art was the result.

What does this mean for modern grassroots journalism, which relies on people's freedom to use all manner of digital content in all manner of ways? Nothing good.

## EYE OF THE BEHOLDER

There are many ironies in the current copyright debate. None is more notable than the fact that the industries now pushing for such absolute control got their start doing what they'd call "piracy" today. But it's also a shame to see an industry that has fought so honorably to maintain First Amendment protections, without which it could not itself survive, now leading a charge that threatens other people's speech.

Technological advances always threaten established business models. And the people whose businesses are threatened always try to stop progress. Cory Doctorow is an online civil libertarian and science fiction author who published two novels and also made them freely downloadable online the day they were in bookstores. "The Vaudeville performers who sued Marconi for inventing the radio had to go from a regime where they had *one hundred percent* control over who could get into the theater and hear them perform to a regime where they had *zero* percent control over who could build or acquire a radio and tune into a recording of them performing," he told me. The performers, in other words, wanted to prevent new technology from disrupting a successful old business model.

It wasn't the only time. In one of the most important recent examples, Hollywood tried to kill off the home video recorder. Only by the narrowest margin in the Supreme Court, in a crucial 1984 decision, did Americans preserve the right to tape a TV show and play it back later.[292]

The advent of digital technology terrified the entertainment industry, and for apparently good reasons. After all, a digital copy of something doesn't degrade the way analog copies, such as a copy of a videotape, do in just a couple of generations. And cyberspace threatened to be the world's biggest enabler of infringement because of how easy it is to copy and distribute materials over it.

But the industry has cleverly, though wrongly, framed the argument as "stealing" versus "property rights." In fact, the issue is nothing of the kind. Ideas are different than physical property, and they have been treated distinctly through our history. If I take your car, you can't use it. If I have a copy of your song, you still have the song. Infringement is wrong, and I don't

The next problem Valenti identified was what the entertainment companies call the "analog hole." Humans can't read the zeroes and ones that make up digital media. Machines translate digital content into what our eyes and ears see and hear as video and audio. So even if you can lock down the zeroes and ones, all someone has to do is play the video on a TV, then use a video camera to make a copy of what's on the screen, redigitize that copy and, boom, the problem starts again. The industry is looking for technology—and laws—to make it impossible and illegal to do this.

The third area of worry was the biggest: peer-to-peer online file sharing. The movie industry watched what happened in the music business and got scared.[298] The movies now available on the Net have escaped control forever, but something needs to be done to prevent theft of movies through file-sharing networks, he said.

The entertainment companies are now demanding that technology companies restrict the capabilities of devices at the outset. They want to cripple PCs and other devices so they can't make copies the copyright holders don't explicitly allow. The Broadcast Flag is one such step in a dangerous direction. Even more brazenly, the entertainment industry also wants permission to hack into networks and machines it believes are being used to violate copyrights. In 2002, a California congressman proposed legislation that would legalize this corporate intrusion; so far, thankfully, it hasn't gone very far.[299]

Give copyright holders the ability to "fix" all of their perceived infringement problems, and you give them unprecedented control over tomorrow's information, over culture itself. Here's an example: it is currently illegal to copy a snippet of video directly from a DVD to use as part of another work. But you can do this with a piece of text, though the e-book industry is working to prevent even a small cut and paste unless authorized by the copyright holder. If we need permission or have to pay, simply to quote from other works, scholarship will be only one casualty.

There is also a serious privacy question in the copyright debate. The only possible way for entertainment companies to enforce their copyrights will be to track what individuals purchase and how they use it. Someday, sooner than you may like, big corporations and governments will know every copyrighted work you read, listen to, and watch. Anyone with a sense of history should fear such a system.[300]

This kind of future would doom much, though not all, of the participatory journalism I've been promoting in this book. For example, if every amateur journalist had to ask permission before quoting from a copyrighted work or was forced to pay for each quotation, most wouldn't bother. The ever-present threat of the copyright police who interpret fair use through Congress' latest restrictive laws, would be as chilling as anything we could imagine.

Sadly, it isn't just the movie and music companies that are taking this stance. Book publishers have increasingly looked at online distribution with fear, when they should see it as a practical step beyond antiquated printing and distribution systems, and an opportunity to win new customers. They are supporting a system that mocks the First Amendment, on which they rely for their very existence; publishing, after all, is built on a foundation of free speech. Lending libraries in particular are in jeopardy if publishers take the same hard line that the music and movie companies have taken, because in a pay-per-view copyright regime, lending becomes impossible.[301]

Then again, intellectual consistency rarely survives financial threats, perceived or real. Again, I can understand the worries. Publishers are worrying more about the effect illegal distribution might have on the bottom line than they are considering the incredible possibilities in exploiting (in the best sense of the word) the potential. I like the idea of being able to annotate an electronic book and go to other resources via, say, hyperlinks; but if the cost is an inability to make a backup copy to use on another electronic device, or even a restriction prohibiting me from giving the book away, that's too high.

Here's one more way the entertainment industry's goals could put a severe crimp on tomorrow's journalism. In Chapter 2, I explained the value of peer-to-peer technology for inexpensively distributing large audio and video files created, for example, by a blogger. Internet service providers charge based on the amount of traffic your site receives and the amount of bandwidth it takes to serve your content to the people who want to see it. In other words, the more popular your content becomes, the more it costs you—a painfully opposite situation then the one you face in the physical world where economies of scale work in your favor.

Now remember that the entertainment industry hates peer-to-peer technology because it doesn't control it. Also recall that it has launched a blizzard of lawsuits that killed innovative companies such as Napster and ReplayTV, a company that created home video systems for recording and storing programs, as well as for skipping commercials. The entertainment industry has also launched a platoon of lobbyists to persuade Congress and regulators to put the clamps on other peer-to-peer technologies, and it's going after people who use them.[302]

If it succeeds in its clampdown, it will foreclose the single most effective method of distribution for grassroots audio and video. Even if all it accomplishes is to force peer-to-peer services to individually track what is sent and where, it will send a chill over the kind of grassroots journalism that has been so vital to freedom in authoritarian nations. The future of media doesn't just belong to people who can depend on a First Amendment; it also belongs to the rest of the world, or it should.

## THE TECH INDUSTRY SELLOUT

A few years ago, policy watchers talked about the war being waged between copyright protection and innovation. The lines were drawn: Silicon Valley was inventing new technology, and Hollywood wanted to control its use. The news from the front is not good for the people who depend on technology to produce tomorrow's news.

Slowly but surely, key members of the tech elite have evolved from being fiercely independent to being a lackey for the entertainment companies on some key issues. Intel, the giant maker of computer chips, has its fingers all over the Broadcast Flag technology that the FCC has mandated. This wasn't the first time Intel betrayed its own customers. It did so during the DVD negotiations years earlier, when Hollywood demanded a Content Scrambling System that led to severely restricted uses for DVDs—a system that an Intel insider later acknowledged had caused PC users real problems.

But no technology company has done more to curry favor with the copyright cartel than Microsoft, a company that (like many technology firms) repeatedly ignored copyright law in building its own powerful business. Here's how Cory Doctorow put it:

> When Microsoft shipped its first search-engine (which makes a copy of every page it searches), it violated the letter of copyright law. When Microsoft made its first proxy server (which makes a copy of every page it caches), it broke copyright law. When Microsoft shipped its first CD-ripping technology, it broke copyright law.
>
> It broke copyright law because copyright law was broken. Copyright law changes all the time to reflect the new tools that companies like Microsoft invent. If Microsoft wants to deliver a compelling service to its customers, let it make general-purpose tools that have the side-effect of breaking Sony and Apple's DRM [Digital Rights Management], giving its customers more choice in the players they use. Microsoft has shown its willingness to go head-to-head with antitrust people to defend its bottom line: next to them, the copyright courts and lawmakers are pantywaists, Microsoft could eat those guys for lunch, exactly the way Sony kicked their asses in 1984 when they defended their right to build and sell VCRs, even though some people might do bad things with them. Just like the early MP3 player makers did when they ate Sony's lunch by shipping product when Sony wouldn't.[303]

Unfortunately, Microsoft's answer has been to build Digital Rights Management—the more appropriate term is "Digital Restrictions Management"—into just about everything it makes. Restrictions range widely. You might be allowed to view something on multiple devices, or just one. You might be permitted to copy a section, or all, or none. You might not be able to print a text document, and so on. These restrictions are notably part of the "Windows Media Center" system that connects PCs with TVs and other devices. The mantra of DRM-believers is that they are enhancing security and protecting intellectual property. The effect, however, is to deny people fair use and other non-controversial uses of what they have bought, or even own.

Even Apple has jumped aboard the DRM train, though not with the same zeal Microsoft has shown. Apple's iTunes Music Store, which sells songs, encodes them in a format that can't easily be converted to the wide-open MP3 or OGG formats. The DRM scheme, instituted because the music industry demanded it, gives Apple users more freedom to copy songs among different devices than we saw in prior DRM schemes. But it tends to penalize some of Apple's best customers—people who repeatedly buy new Macs. An iTunes Music Store customer can listen to the songs on five computers, but managing authorizations can be a hassle. It's also important to remember that what freedoms Apple gives today can disappear tomorrow.[304]

Microsoft, Intel, and several other major technology companies are now working on a "Trusted Computing" initiative, putatively designed to prevent viruses and worms from taking hold of people's PCs and to keep documents secure from prying eyes. Sounds good, but the effect may be devastating to information freedom. The premise of these systems is not trust; it's mistrust. In effect, security expert Ross Anderson wrote in 2003, trusted computing "will transfer the ultimate control of your PC from you to whoever wrote the software it happens to be running." He went on:

[Trusted Computing] provides a computing platform on which you can't tamper with the application software, and where these applications can communicate securely with their authors and with each other. The original motivation was digital rights management (DRM): Disney will be able to sell you DVDs that will decrypt and run on a TC platform, but which you won't be able to copy. The music industry will be able to sell you music downloads that you won't be able to swap. They will be able to sell you CDs that you'll only be able to play three times, or only on your birthday. All sorts of new marketing possibilities will open up.

But now consider the ways it could be used, beyond simple tracking by copyright holders of what they sell. Anderson wrote:

The potential for abuse extends far beyond commercial bullying and economic warfare into political censorship. I expect that it will proceed a step at a time. First, some well-intentioned police force will get an order against a pornographic picture of a child, or a manual on how to sabotage railroad signals. All TC-compliant PCs will delete, or perhaps report, these bad documents. Then a litigant in a libel or copyright case will get a civil court order against an offending document; perhaps the Scientologists will seek to blacklist the famous Fishman Affidavit. A dictator's secret police could punish the author of a dissident leaflet by deleting everything she ever created using that system—her new book, her tax return, even her kids' birthday cards—wherever it had ended up. In the West, a court might use a confiscation doctrine to "blackhole" a machine that had been used to make a pornographic picture of a child. Once lawyers, policemen and judges realise the potential, the trickle will become a flood.[305]

The Trusted Computing moves bring to mind a conversation in early 2000 with Andy Grove, longtime chief executive at Intel and one of the real pioneers in the tech industry. He was talking about how easy it would soon be to send videos back and forth with his grandchildren. If trends continued, I suggested, he'd someday need Hollywood's permission. The man who wrote the best seller, *Only the Paranoid Survive*,[306] then called me paranoid. Several years later, amid the copyright industry's increasing clampdown and Intel's unfortunate leadership in helping the copyright holders lock everything down, I asked him if I'd really been all that paranoid. I never got a direct reply.

## THE END OF END-TO-END?

A key design goal of the original Internet was called the "end-to-end principle." Essentially, it states that we want to keep the intelligence out at the edges of the network and make the transportation of data as simple as possible in between. In other words, use the network to get the zeros and ones back and forth with as little interference as possible, and let people using PCs, servers, and other devices do everything else. In an email, David P. Reed, one of the people credited with the notion, described it this way:

> Communications systems should not implement functions that can be implemented by their users. In particular, systems designers should work very hard to find or invent system designs that avoid putting specific user-oriented functions into inflexible infrastructure, by moving the implementation of those functions to the edges of the network where they are implemented as part of the user-controlled applications.
>
> It's been the experience in the Internet design community that many functions that are thought to be "network" functions or capabilities are possible to implement in the form of protocols among users or user applications. For example, security can be implemented by end-to-end encryption and end-to-end credentials [that can't be forged], so that the network need not be secure at all.
>
> Similarly, when you are forced to think about problems such as spam in an end-to-end way, you start to realize that

the problem with spam cannot be solved in the "network"—
instead it is a problem among users of the network, and must
be solved there. It's still difficult, of course, but its difficulty is
inherent in the conflict between the desire to allow anyone to
contact us freely and the desire to be left alone. The network
cannot understand the details of our individual desires; the
end-to-end principle says it should not even try.

The positive value of the end-to-end argument is that it preserves the flexibility of the network to adapt to both new
unanticipated uses, and new unanticipated implementation
technology.

In a world where we may end up with one, two, or at most
three broadband telecommunications providers in any given
community, the end-to-end principle is in serious jeopardy.
Should giant telecommunications companies—namely cable and
local phone providers—have vertical control over everything
from the data transport to the content itself? For example, as I
was writing this book, Comcast, the cable monopoly in my area,
was trying to buy Disney. The attempt failed. If this happened,
Comcast could have decided to deliver Disney's content online
more quickly than someone else's, discriminating on the basis of
financial considerations. Such a regime would have been a
disaster for the unimpeded flow of information. We should
insist on a more horizontal system, in which the owner of the
pipe is obliged to provide interconnections to competing services. Unfortunately, today's regulatory and political power bro-
kers lean in the wrong direction.

In 2003, the cable and phone companies insisted that they
needed vertical control. Otherwise, they threatened, they
wouldn't provide broadband data connections to U.S. households. They persuaded the Federal Communications Commission's chairman, Michael Powell, and a majority of his colleagues, that their stand was correct. The FCC gave U.S.
regional phone companies the right to control access to any new
high-speed data pipes they built, even though they were told
they had to keep sharing, for the time being, their copper lines.

This policy essentially mirrored earlier rules allowing the cable companies, which also created networks by getting government-granted monopolies, to refuse to share access to their lines.[307]

The cable and phone companies have shown again and again that they abuse their power. They are historical monopolies with control over vast territories given to them by governments. But they used to be regulated monopolies. Increasingly, they are freeing themselves of regulation.

The big telecom carriers, which have been too slow to actually build out their own broadband infrastructures, don't like it when others use their tactics. State and local governments can and should be building their own fiber networks, as some already have done, such as in Ashland, Oregon. Unsurprisingly, the phone and cable companies have been lobbying state legislatures to forbid this practice, and in several states it's now illegal for municipalities to be Internet service providers.

In a few years, barring major inroads by wireless competition, U.S. high-speed data access could be largely under the thumb of two of the most anticompetitive industries around: the cable and phone monopolies. I doubt they'd dare to stamp out speech they don't like. But they could turn their systems into what industry people call "walled gardens," where the content they provide receives preferential treatment and where they discriminate against material they don't control; my Comcast-Disney example hasn't occurred yet, but the concept isn't idle speculation.

Cisco Systems, the company that sells the equipment used to direct Internet traffic around the Internet, is happily offering telecommunications companies the tools to create these walled gardens. Shamefully, the earliest use of this technology has been by dictatorships, with which Cisco and a host of other big tech firms, including Nortel and Microsoft, have cooperated. According to Amnesty International, the technology is used to firewall their citizens from certain content. The companies denied the implications, saying they weren't responsible for how customers used what they sold.[308]

Even without overt discrimination, market power distorts choices. SBC Communications, one of America's biggest telecommunications companies, has a partnership with Yahoo! for customers who sign up for DSL connections. Yahoo! content receives preferred placement on subscribers' homepages. Subscribers can change the homepage, but most customers of any product stick with the default.

"It's not an on-off thing," Yale Braunstein, professor in the School of Information Management and Systems at the University of California-Berkeley, told me. "Yes, you'll be able to get to *The New York Times*, but it may be harder to get there."

News-article text will always be a relatively quick download. But when it comes to more advanced information content, video in particular, the telecom providers' opportunities for turning a system to its own advantage are far greater.

This is why Walt Disney Co. signed a little-noticed letter in late 2002 to the FCC, urging the FCC to insist on equal treatment for all Internet services on these increasingly concentrated pipelines.[309] Disney's co-signers included Microsoft and several public-interest groups that are normally not on the side of either of those companies. I've been critical of Disney's intentions in some areas, but here the company is standing for freedom.

The cable-TV industry responded to the letter by noting, accurately, that Microsoft was hypocritical to be decrying the kind of anti-competitive tactics for which it had become notorious over the years. Even hypocrites, however, can be right.

At the moment, the cable giants have an even greater incentive to rig their systems than SBC does. The cable giants own much of the TV programming that flows on their systems and they want to keep it that way. Comcast, now by far the biggest American cable operator, has many ownership interests in content.

Worrying about explicit cross-ownership misses the bigger issue, Braunstein said. If you replace ownership with exclusive contracts such as SBC's deal with Yahoo!, you've achieved the same result.

Big Media's inattention to this issue is at least somewhat understandable. The threat is still more theoretical than real, at least in the United States. People in China, where the government censors Internet content, know firsthand the danger of centralized choke points.

Of course, the mass media, buried in a conflict of interest, is also ignoring the current threat posed by growing ownership concentration. Witness the recent scandalous failure to cover the FCC's media-ownership rules until after the fact. The TV network news shows all but ignored their corporate parents' lobbying to extend media consolidation while the rules were pending. This wouldn't be such a problem if there were lots of data conduits, but there aren't. The answer is to separate content from delivery in such concentrated markets.

The Internet is an infinitely diverse medium. But if you can't find it, or if there are artificial barriers to seeing content on it, diversity means nothing.[310]


## RETURN OF THE JEDI USERS

At the annual Consumer Electronics Show in January 2004, Carly Fiorina, the chief executive of Hewlett-Packard, surrounded herself on a Las Vegas stage with some popular entertainers. She, the head of a technology company, then declared an oath of fealty to the copyright industry.

In coming years, HP will be selling consumer electronics such as PC-based home media centers, music players, digital TVs, and more. Fiorina vowed that HP will use every method at its disposal to help copyright holders block unauthorized use of their content. If HP also restricts customers' "fair use" rights—the ability to make personal copies and quote from others' works—I guess that's someone else's problem.

Well, here's my oath: the HP laptop I bought a couple of months ago is the last product I'll buy from the company until it

remembers some of the other principles of its founding and success, such as customer empowerment.

What I'm getting at here is the power of the customer. The
problem is that the Microsofts and Intels and HPs think first of
their customers in the entertainment industry, and second of
their customers in the real world.

I'm also getting at the power of the customer to become
politically active. How? Here are three things anyone can and
should do:

- Write and call your elected officials, not just in Washington
  but also in state capitals, because Hollywood and its allies are
  working at all levels of government to control information.

- Contribute to organizations that defend your rights. The
  Electronic Frontier Foundation[311] is just one of many that
  hire lawyers and lobbyists to counter the armies of professionals doing the copyright industry's bidding. Check this
  book's accompanying web site for a list of organizations
  and what they do.

- Use your power as a customer. Don't buy from companies
  that cheat artists and abuse fair use. When you attend a
  concert of an independent artist, buy her CD there. Again,
  there are more tips on the web site.

Hackers are coming to the rescue in some respects. I'm not
advocating civil disobedience, though I am occasionally in technical violation of the copyright laws (such as when I "rip" a
DVD I've just purchased to my computer's hard drive to watch
it on a plane).

Technologists are now building "overlay networks"—systems of running encrypted (scrambled) and anonymized data
over other networks and then making the data look like normal
communications. If they succeed, there will be several effects
beyond the obvious threats to copyright holders, a serious issue
that I don't deny. But the positive impact would be real, too.
Telecommunications carriers won't be able to look inside the
data stream and discriminate against certain content. If all

traffic is indistinguishable, notes Doctorow, then the only answer is to pull the plug and shut everything down.

I do encourage people who are creating content to license it under a "Creative Commons" license,[312] which lets you reserve some rights while giving people more freedom to use your material in ways that honor our traditions. This book, for example, is being published under a Creative Commons license that permits people to download it freely from the Internet, but not to sell it (more on this in Chapter 12).

How can we preserve the end-to-endness of the Net in the face of the new monopolists? We could embark on a crash program, funded by taxpayers, to bring broadband to every home and business in America in the same way we built the interstate highways at taxpayer expense.[313] Maybe it should be a build-out of networks using fiber and wireless technologies. Maybe it should be subsidies that allow end users to buy what they want, spurring industry innovation along the way.

We could also build fiber-optic lines (or systems combining fiber and wireless) to everyone, filling in the "last mile"—connecting our homes to the high-speed "backbone" lines linking geographic regions—that has been so underserved. Then let the marketplace provide the content and management of the networks.

At the very least, we must have rules—and yes, that means hard-nosed regulation and enforcement—ensuring that the cable and phone companies cannot discriminate against any content.

## A DEREGULATORY RESCUE?

Another wildcard has appeared, and it's the most exciting of all, because we might be able to give the monopolists what they're demanding and still have genuine competition. Why? Because the FCC may truly be moving toward a rational policy on how to regulate—or, in this case, deregulate—the airwaves.

The FCC Spectrum Policy Task Force[314] is looking for ways to update the regulation of this vital public resource. Since the 1930s, the United States has licensed specific parts of the spectrum—the airwaves that carry radio, TV, cellular calls, police and emergency communications, and more—to government agencies and private companies, based on the principle that spectrum was scarce and we had to apportion a dwindling resource.

This principle is based on old science, according to some of the best thinkers in the field. They say, persuasively, that spectrum is essentially limitless if we use it right—that is, with modern radios and transmitting devices that make yesterday's interference problems go away.

These thinkers may well have persuaded FCC Chairman Michael Powell, who has been disturbingly willing to give the media, cable, and phone companies what they want. What he said in a speech in 2003 shows that he grasps the spectrum issue and the opportunity it may present to spur genuine competition in broadband.

"Modern technology has fundamentally changed the nature and extent of spectrum use," Powell said. "I believe the commission should continuously examine whether there are market or technological solutions that can—in the long run—replace or supplement pure regulatory solutions to interference."[315]

If Powell and his colleagues—and a Congress that tends to bow to the interests of well-financed corporations that have power and want to keep it—enact smart spectrum policy, all the sleazy machinations of the cable and phone monopolies won't matter.

There's plenty of evidence that innovation would explode if the FCC frees up more unlicensed spectrum. Look at what has happened with Wi-Fi, a brand-new technology and resultant industry that went from nothing to widespread deployment in just a few years using unlicensed spectrum. Or maybe, as I'll discuss shortly, the spectrum is even more open for innovation than most people suspect.

Some in the tech industry understand this well. Even as they hold their noses and support the cable/phone broadband duopoly in the short term, they're also pushing for the emergence of competition from other sources including innovative new wireless technologies. A senior Intel executive told me he loathed the phone and cable companies, but hoped to bypass them entirely in the end.

If the FCC does the right thing with spectrum, while local governments deploy lots of fiber, the phone and cable companies can have their wires because then the monopolists won't have the power to abuse what they own, not when competition has arrived to provide an alternative.

In the long run, we might restore the end-to-end principle through sheer physics.


## THE END OF SCARCITY?


What if the scarcity of the airwaves turns out to be an artifact of history and outmoded technology? If scarcity can be overcome, the implications are both exciting and disruptive—we will see a cornucopia of communications that foreshadows woes and opportunities for some of our biggest telecommunications companies. David P. Reed told me that the FCC's fundamental mission is flawed, maybe obsolete.

Reed is no newcomer to the tech scene. He holds a Ph.D. from the Massachusetts Institute of Technology, where he taught computer science and headed the Laboratory for Computer Science's Computer Systems Structure Group. He was chief scientist at Lotus Development and Software Arts, two pioneering software companies, and worked at the now closed Interval Research, the Paul Allen–funded think tank in Palo

Alto. He's been involved in the technical details of the Internet for several decades, and lately has been a consultant, entrepreneur, and researcher.[316]

Simply put, he said, we have to start looking at spectrum as an almost limitless commodity, not a scarce one.

The current regulatory regime that allocates spectrum "is a legal metaphor that does not correspond to physical reality," he told me. Why not? First, he said, the notion of interference has more to do with the equipment we use to send and receive signals than with the physics of radio waves. "Radio waves pass through each other," Reed said. "They do not damage each other."

In the early days of radio, the equipment could easily be confused by overlapping signals. But we can now make devices that can sort out the traffic.

The second way that reality defies the old logic is what happens when you add wireless devices to networks. I won't go into the details of Reed's argument, which you can find on his site, but he contends that you end up with more capacity—the ability to move bits of data around—than when you started.

"In principle, the capacity of a certain bandwidth in a certain physical space increases with the number of transceivers in a given space," he said. Yet the FCC regulates the airwaves as if the capacity was a fixed amount.[317]

Yes, he said, this is counter-intuitive. And, to be sure, there are experts who disagree with him.

But if he and others in his camp are right, we have a lot of work ahead to fix a hopelessly broken regulatory system. And if that happens, the sky is literally the limit for future communications. At the same time, the consequences for some of the most powerful companies in our economy may be grim because they are based on economic scarcity. The value of the big broadcasting companies, for example, has much to do with their government-granted licenses to control specific parts of the airwaves.

Reed wants the FCC to open up some spectrum for the new, more open wireless networks, giving entrepreneurs a new public space in which to innovate and create value for the rest of us. He's not sure who'll make money in this space, but surely, equipment manufacturers and other companies, especially software companies, will be in the middle of a wave of innovation.

Software is a key, perhaps the key, to the future Reed envisions. Most radio-like devices using today's spectrum—radios, televisions, mobile phones, and the like—are based on the old way of doing things, constrained by hardware to receive and transmit signals in specific ways and in specific places.

To get the full multiplier effect, he said, we need devices with fairly generic but powerful hardware components. "Software defined radios" will be vastly more adaptable and useful than their old-fashioned cousins, according to Reed and others who are promoting the concept. The military has been using these devices, called "agile radio," for some time; civilian availability is getting closer as costs come down.

Imagining this new world conjures a boost for a civil liberty we take for granted in America but which has been dampened under the current regulatory scheme. I'm talking about free speech. Regulation of the airwaves has specifically included curbs on speech, such as the FCC's commands to the nation's TV and radio broadcasters about what may or may not be said on the air. That regulation took an ugly turn in the spring of 2004 as the FCC, egged on by an election-year Congress, slammed huge fines on broadcasters in what was surely the most direct attack in years on free speech.

Such restrictions on speech have been justified, in part, under the idea that the spectrum is a public and limited resource. If that is not true, there's no reason to regulate speech in this way. Someday, perhaps, the First Amendment will mean something when people broadcast their views, not just when they put them on paper or on the Internet.

The worst direction for the FCC to move right now, Reed said, is to keep giving or auctioning spectrum to "monopoly owners" that won't use it efficiently. A new kind of open space is all about the public good, he said, and there's a fine analogy in recent history.

"We need to do for spectrum," he said, "what the Internet did for the network."

*Chapter 12*

# Making Our Own News

We tend to be bound by our past, even when we can imagine the future. Yet sometimes we are transformed, and media can be at the center of how we see these changes.

The Italian Renaissance gave Western civilization several crucial transformations. None, for our purposes, matters more than perspective. Painters such as Giotto di Bondone in the 1300s and Tommaso Masaccio a century later gave depth to what had been a mostly two-dimensional world of European art. Boccaccio's *Decameron*, published in 1353, was among the earliest works of literature to propose that a point of view was crucial to understanding.

Gutenberg's printing press brought forth a revolution that no one could have anticipated at the time. The Vatican's monks, who controlled publishing, were helpless with the onslaught of this new technology. After Gutenberg, the word of God was liberated from the Pope's doctrine.

The Internet is the most important medium since the printing press. It subsumes all that has come before and is, in the most fundamental way, transformative. When anyone can be a writer, in the largest sense and for a global audience, many of us will be. The Net is overturning so many of the things we've assumed about media and business models that we can scarcely keep up with the changes; it's difficult to maintain perspective amid the shift from a top-down hierarchy to something vastly more democratic and, yes, messy. But we have to try, and nowhere is that more essential than in that oldest form of information: the news. We will be blessed with new kinds of perspective in this emergent system, and we will learn how to make it work for everyone.

Blogs and other modern media are feedback systems. They work in something close to real time and capture—in the best sense of the word—the multitude of ideas and realities each of us can offer. On the Internet, we are defined by what we know and share. Now, for the first time in history, the feedback system can be global and nearly instantaneous.

My goal in this book has been to persuade you that the collision of journalism and technology is having major consequences for three constituencies: journalists, newsmakers, and the audience. The evidence seems persuasive that something big is happening.

Journalists are beginning to get it. For the first three years of its existence, my blog was one of a few lonely outposts in newspaper journalism. No longer. High-profile blogs have appeared at some of the biggest news organizations.

However, I'm still not convinced that Big Media is doing the most important thing: listening. We are still in a top-down mode and don't realize that the conversation is more important than our pronouncements. I see progress, but not enough.

Newsmakers are not much further along in understanding what's happening to them in this new world of communications. Nor have they used the tools that would help them deal with the public, including the news media, more effectively. Some executives, mostly from the technology industry, have shown they do get it. A few politicians have tapped the power of the grassroots, and more are doing it all the time. Some public-relations people have also caught on, but the industry is woefully behind the times in most respects. They've grasped the dangers, such as the fact that everyone can have a very public say about what newsmakers do; it's hard to keep secrets and harder to stonewall effectively. And they've seen the potential; more transparency is almost always better.

Yet I'm most gratified at how the "former audience," as I call it, has taken these tools and turned its endless ideas into such unexpected, and in some cases superb, forms of journalism. Yes, this new media has created, or at least exacerbated, difficult issues of credibility and fairness. We'll be wrestling with these issues for decades, but I'm confident that the community, with the assistance of professional journalists and others who care, can sort it all out.

The former audience has the most important role in this new era: they must be active users of news, and not mere consumers. The Net should be the ally of thought and nuance, not a booster shot for knee-jerk reaction. An informed citizenry cannot sit still for more of the same. It must demand more, and be part of the larger conversation. We will lose a great deal if this does not occur.

Sometimes, I fear that it won't be allowed to occur. We are vastly better informed today because of mail lists, web sites, blogs, SMS, and RSS. These tools have roots in networks that encourage innovation.

Open systems are central to any future of a free (as in freedom) flow of information. Yet the forces of central control—governments and big businesses, especially the copyright cartel—are pushing harder and harder to clamp down on our networks. To preserve their business models, which are increasingly outmoded in a digital age, they would restrict innovation and, ultimately, the kinds of creativity on which they founded their own businesses. The danger in this is massive, but the public remains all too oblivious, in part because Big Media has failed to cover the story properly. I don't think that's a coincidence.

I've no doubt that technology will eventually win because it is becoming more and more ubiquitous. I also have faith, perhaps misguided, that public officials will ultimately pay proper attention to the interests of their constituents, and not just to the industries that pad their campaign war chests.

## A CREATIVE COMMONS

More than once during this project, I've been asked if my passion for openness includes the contents of this book. It does.

Despite ample evidence to the contrary, some people believe I am against copyright. I think highly of copyright as it was originally conceived. I believe it should be a sensible bargain that gives creators of new works the fruits of their labor, while providing society with the more important fruits of a robust debate, the ability to innovate and create new works based on old ones, and, ultimately, the benefits of the public domain itself.

I value copyright. I loathe its abuse.

Luckily, I have a way to express my views that both endorses copyright and uses it appropriately. Equally luckily, I have a publisher that gets the point and is willing to be part of an exercise most other publishers would flatly reject.

That vehicle, as I mentioned in Chapter 11, is called Creative Commons Copyright, an alternative copyright licensing system that allows the creator of a work to decide which rights he wants to reserve for himself, while allowing the public to build on his ideas. You've seen the standard copyright notice, which says, "All Rights Reserved." Creative Commons is a system of "Some Rights Reserved."[318]

So here's what my publisher and I have done with this book. First, we are explicitly setting the term of the copyright to be 14 years, which was the term when America's Founders first wrote a copyright law. As noted in Chapter 11, the current copyright term is the life of the author plus 75 years, an outrageously long period that doesn't give authors any serious additional incentives even as it denudes our vital public domain.

Second, we will publish the book on the Web and offer it for free from the day it's in the stores. Free in this case does not mean the right to reprint it for resale. It does mean the right to download and read it without buying the book. Naturally, I'd prefer that you buy it. My publisher and I believe we won't lose sales overall, that free downloading will create more, not less, demand. But even if we're wrong and suffer financially because of it, we're willing to take the chance.

Why am I doing this? Two reasons. First, I believe in copyright and want to support it—but in the right way. In the process of creation, we stand on the shoulders of those who have gone before. Locking down heritage means locking out vital innovation, and I don't want to be one of the people who turns reasonable protections into absolute control.

Second, I'm wondering what people will do with this book. Consider what happened with Lawrence Lessig's latest, which he and his publisher put under a Creative Commons license. One group of people created an audio version. Someone else turned it into a Wiki. Since one of my goals in writing this book is to encourage experimentation, I'm hoping that people will—within the boundaries of a "some rights reserved" license—use this book to expand the conversation in ways I hadn't imagined. We'll have a web site, of course, but I'm hoping that's just the beginning.

## DAY-TO-DAY CHANGES

One of the challenges—and joys—in writing this book has been watching the velocity of technical change. Every day, it seems, there's been a new web site or news event that shows how quickly the shift is occurring. By the time this book is in stores, the map will look different. This is one reason why we're creating a living, breathing web site (*http://wethemedia.oreilly.com*) that keeps a close eye on the changes, with constant updates about innovative new tools and major events. And please remember to participate in the ongoing development of the site. This may be the end of the book, but the conversation continues—and it's as much about your interests as mine.

I hope that I've helped you understand how this media shift—this explosion of conversations—is taking place and where it's headed. Most of all, I hope I've persuaded you to take up the challenge yourself.

Your voice matters. Now, if you have something worth saying, you can be heard.

You can make your own news. We all can.

Let's get started.

# Epilogue and Acknowledgments

On the afternoon of March 10, 2004, I posted a draft of the Introduction and Chapter 1 of this book on my weblog. I asked readers to let me know, preferably by email, if they noticed any factual errors. I also asked whether I'd missed any crucial topics, or whether they knew of some perfect anecdote that absolutely had to be included.

They responded. One of the first emails alerted me to an incorrect web address, which I fixed immediately. Another pointed out a mistake in a section about open source software.

Others suggested I amplify certain points, or asked why I discussed a particular topic, or that I slow down the narrative. The comments section of my weblog became a discussion about the book.

The ideas I've been discussing in *We the Media* became integral to the reporting and writing of the book itself. When I started, I didn't really know what to expect. But I can say now, without any fear of contradiction, that this process has worked.

Thank you, all.

## OUTLINE AND IDEAS

My version of open source journalism got off to a rocky start. In the early spring of 2003, I posted an outline of the book and invited comments by email. My inbox overflowed.

Then a small disaster hit. I'd moved all the suggestions into a separate folder in my mailbox, but several months later, when I looked for them, they were gone. Vanished. Disappeared. I still don't know if this was my doing or my Internet service provider's. Either way, I was horrified; I'd not only lost some of the excellent ideas, but I also hadn't thanked everyone who made a suggestion. Needless to say, I didn't have a current, local backup on my hard disk.

I was able to reconstruct some of the messages from an older backup and some saved replies I'd sent. But many were gone forever. Consider this my apology to all of you who are in the latter category.

But the comments I did manage to save, which arrived from all over the world, helped me firm up my ideas for this book.

One of the most thoughtful early notes was from Tom Stites, an old friend, and an editor who once hired me and later became one of my touchstones in journalism. He said, among other things:

> If what you are describing is truly tomorrow's journalism, I fear that democracy is doomed. I lead with this alarmist statement because as I understand what you're describing only a tiny elite engages with political/news blogs; democracy needs a *tomorrow's journalism* that reaches and activates a broad audience. The blog elite I'm describing is not the business/government power elite but a highly educated, deeply curious insider group centered among the technologically proficient. The sad truth is, most people are passive consumers of news who, because of the insider jargon blogs tend to be written in, couldn't decipher most blogs even if they signed on; the segment of the citizenry that are savvy and proactive news-seekers is very small, and I don't expect that to change much.

Several readers wished I'd published the outline in a way that let them comment directly on it, in a Wiki or with comments enabled. I wish I had, too, because it would have simplified matters.

Elwin Jenkins, who writes the always interesting Microdoc News, posted a cautionary suggestion saying I was looking too much at journalism. In a blog posting of his own he concluded: "Bloggers are not journalists, we are information seekers, information builders and knowledge makers. We are more like teachers than journalists."[319] Fair enough, I thought, but then again, this book is about journalism, not the overall blogosphere. Still, the reminder of the wider context was useful.

I received suggestions on books to read, people to interview, paths to follow. One correspondent, Chris Gulker,[320] wrote about "self-assembling newsrooms," a concept that delighted me. I've used it in presentations and in this book.

As 2003 progressed, I used my weblog to discuss many of the concepts about which I was writing. When I saw relevant news stories I pointed at them, and posted my own observations about these micro examples of macro trends. I'd turned on the comment system by then, and readers chimed in with useful observations of their own.

## DRAFTS AND OTHER POSTINGS

Before embarking on this project, I chatted with David Weinberger. I'd enjoyed his second book, *Small Pieces Loosely Joined: A Unified Theory of the Web*,[321] a thoughtful exploration of this medium. He'd done it in an entirely open way by posting chapter drafts on which his audience could comment.

Software developers have an expression called the "nightly build," which is the latest update of a program. Weinberger was, in effect, posting nightly builds of his book. I asked him how the process worked.

"Don't do that," he warned me. It was more trouble than it was worth. Posting chapter drafts was a fine idea, he thought, but not every single change he was making. Good advice, and we took it.

A couple of days after posting drafts of the Introduction and Chapter 1 of my book, an email arrived from Stephen B. Waters, publisher of the *Rome Sentinel* in upstate New York. "If you're interested," he wrote, "I made the effort to comment." Attached was a file containing Chapter 1 in Microsoft Word format, with the "Track Changes" feature turned on so I could see what changes and suggestions he'd made.[322]

Waters hadn't just made an effort. He'd torn the thing apart, picking at small and large problems he saw. In his summary at the end, he wrote: "The time is right. The subject is right. But your book deserves to be better than this."

After retrieving my ego from the trash, I thought about what he'd said. I called him up. In our conversation and subsequent emails, I learned something about him. He's a computer geek who came back to his family's newspaper business. He studied history. He loves the blogosphere and what it can do. He's a thoughtful man with good ideas, and on some important issues, he knew more than I did. Waters took his virtual blue pencil to every chapter I posted. I carefully looked at his suggestions and incorporated many of them.

I also heard from some people whose work I'd mentioned in the book. Several offered corrections or clarifications. This was exactly what I'd hoped for, and I was thrilled with the result.

Did mistakes creep into the book as published? As I write this, I assume some did, and we'll correct them online and in future printings. But are there fewer errors than there might have been? Unquestionably. And did more thought and nuance make its way into the book? I'm convinced it did.

My experience was, in a sense, a test of the next version of journalism. It proved workable, which was not surprising to me. I believe it can work for almost anyone.

## ACKNOWLEDGMENTS

First, thanks to the many folks who posted comments on my blog, called, or wrote in with suggestions, comments, and corrections. Because I lost some mail, as noted earlier, I can't thank everyone individually. (If you were among that group, please let me know and I'll add your name to the list when it goes online and in future printings and/or editions.) But those whose messages I didn't lose (including several who offered only pseudonyms) include: Paul Andrews, Nick Arnett, Alfredo Ascanio, Jerry Asher, Kevin Aylward, Phil Baker, Alessio Balbi, Peter Basofin, Bill Baur, Morten Bay, Andrew Beach, Michael Bean, Tim Bishop, Charles Brownstein, Buzz Bruggeman, C.R. Bryan III, Scott Burki, Kevin Burton, Brian W. Carver, Frank Catalano, David Cassel, Gilbert Cattoire, Guillermo Cerceau, Brian Clark, Joe Clark, Michael O'Connor Clarke, Michael Collins, Joyce Conklin, Jeff Danziger, Tom Dolembo, Dave Donohue, John Dougan, Stephen Downes, Amy Eisman, Greg Elin, Mark Federman, Sean Fitzpatrick, John Fleck, Dave Fletcher, Trip Foster, Bjorn Freeman-Benson, Rhonda Geraci, Ward Gerlach, John Gilmore, Bernie Goldbach, Phil Gomes, greep, Chris Gulker, Steve Harmon, Tim Harding, Eszter Hargittai, Rodney Hoffman, Denise Howell, Ryan Irelan, Terri Irving, Joanne Jacobs, Elwin Jenkins, Nicholas Jenkins, Dennis Jerz, Morrie Johnston, Gordon Joseloff, Chris Kaminski, Rohit Khare, Susan Kitchens, Brian Krause, Tony Lacey, Geoff Langhorne, Larry Larsen, Leonard Lin, Hetty Litjens, Scott Love, Tristan Louis, Richard Lundquist, Zack Lynch, Mark McBride, Mike McCallister, Wayne Mercier, Jim Miller, Bill Mitchell, Neal Moore, Andrea Moro, Robert Niles, Maureen S. O'Brien, Mike Owens, Evan Orensky, Andrew Orlowski, Olav A Øvrebø, Nigel Parry, Angela Penny, Ralph Poole, Matt Prescott, J.P. Rangaswami, Wayne Rasanen, Celia Redmore, William Riski, Cormac Russell, Jason Salzman, Rob Salzman, Gary D. Sanders, Gary Santoro, Dan Scherlis, Trudy Schuett, Pam Schwartz, professor rat,

Janet S. Scott, Linda Seebach, Bill Seitz, Ben Silverman, Some Random Humanoid, Kathleen Spracklen, Steve Stroh, Glenn Thomas, Fons Tuinstra, Manolis Tzagarakis, Mike Banks Valentine, Ed Vielmetti, Taylor Walsh, Jonathan Weaver, Joshua Weinberg, Dan Weintraub, Alex Williams, Phil Wolff, Jay Woods, Jim Zellmer and Ethan Zuckerman.

I tended to ignore remarks that said, "Don't quit your day job"—except when they explained why they thought so. I tend to learn more (or at least as much) from people who think I'm wrong than people who think I'm right, and when they offer reasons I pay close attention, even if we continue to disagree. Thanks to those of you (you know who you are) who challenged my assumptions, even harshly.

So many people were generous with their time. (One of the dilemmas in writing this book was whether to use first names when talking about or quoting the many friends and friendly acquaintances whose work has informed mine and therefore made it into the text; I used last names for consistency.) Among the people who have helped me understand this process, through conversations, formal interviews, and/or correspondence, are: Marko Ahtisaari, Chris Allbritton, Chris Anderson, Azeem Azhar, Jeff Bates, John Perry Barlow, Cameron Barrett, Yochai Benkler, Krishna Bharat, Shayne Bowman, Wes Boyd, Nick Bradbury, Yale Braunstein, Dan Bricklin, John Brockman, Buzz Bruggeman, Thomas N. Burg, Kevin Burton, Jason McCabe Calacanis, Mark Canter, Jerry Ceppos, Ying Chan, Joe Clark, Ed Cone, Robert Cox, David Crossen, Mark Cuban, Ward Cunningham, Rob Curley, Anil Dash, Nick Denton, Hossein Derakhshan, Betsy Devine, Samanthi Dissanayake, Cory Doctorow, Jack Driscoll, Esther Dyson, Ben Edelman, Renee Edelman, Charles Eisendrath, Dave Farber, Ed Felten, Rusty Foster, Karl Frisch, Glenn Fleishman, Adam Gaffin, Jock Gill, Steve Gillmor, Wiley Gillmor, Mark Glaser, Vindu Goel, Phil Gomes, Amy Goodman, Rich Gordon, Jennifer Granick, Matt Gross, Tara Sue Grubb, Justin Hall, Jay Harris, Peter Harter, Matt Haughey, Scott Hieferman, Mary Hodder, Meg

Hourihan, Michael Hoyt, Jeong Woon Hyeon, David Isenberg, Joi Ito, Jeff Jarvis, Scott Johnson, Matt Jones, Mitch Kapor, Dennis Kneale, Lance Knobel, Bruce Koon, Howard Kurtz, J.D. Lasica, Lee Pong Ryul, Jon Lebkowski, Lawrence Lessig, Tim Levell, Charles Lewis, Andrew Lih, Karlin Lillington, Chris Locke, Kevin Lynch, Rob Malda, David L. Marburger, John Markoff, Kevin Marks, Cameron Marlow, Joshua Micah Marshall, Katinka Matson, Ross Mayfield, Brock Meeks, Nicco Mele, Jerry Michalski, Bill Mitchell, Bryan Monroe, Craig Newmark, Chris Nolan, Andrew Odlyzko, Oh Yeon Ho, Steve Outing, Ray Ozzie, John Paczkowski, Dale Peskin, Chris Pirillo, Lee Raine, Mitch Ratcliffe, David P. Reed, Greg Reinacker, Glenn Reynolds, Howard Rheingold, John Robb, Pete Rojas, Jim Romenesko, Jay Rosen, Zack Rosen, Scott Rosenberg, Steve Rubel, Avi Rubin, Sam Ruby, Paul Saffo, Ken Sakamura, Chris Schroeder, Robert Scoble, Doc Searls, Wendy Selzer, Frank Shaw, Jason Shellen, Clay Shirky, Dave Sifry, Brent Simmons, Marc Smith, Neal Stephenson, Tom Stites, Halley Suitt, Ernie Svenson, Zephyr Teachout, Brad Templeton, Joe Trippi, Ben Trott, Mena Trott, Siva Vaidhyanathan, Jack Valenti, Yossi Vardi, Alex Vieux, Martin Vogel, Eric Von Hippel, Jimmy Wales, Chris Warner, Milverton Wallace, Stephen B. Waters, David Weinberger, Mike Wendland, Kevin Werbach, Wil Wheaton, Evan Williams, Chris Willis, Phil Windley, Dave Winer, Leonard Witt, Zayed, Jim Zellmer, Jonathan Zittrain, Markos Moulitsas Zúniga, and several who chose to be anonymous. I thank them all, and apologize to anyone I have inadvertently left out.

I interviewed some of these people first for columns that ran in the *San Jose Mercury News* (some material from which appears in this book) and at SiliconValley.com, an online affiliate of the newspaper and our parent company, Knight Ridder. If my good and talented colleagues thought I was crazy to try this, they were kind enough not to say so. Special thanks to my *Mercury News* editors, who let me go on a part-time schedule while I worked on this project.

Thanks to Esther Dyson, Daphne Kis, Christina Koukkos and their colleagues at Release 1.0, for whom I wrote an issue of their newsletter on blogs and RSS. Some of the material from that article is in this book.

Cory Doctorow, J.D. Lasica, Larry Lessig, Wendy Seltzer, Dan Shafer, Leonard Witt and Jeff Jarvis read draft chapters— sometimes very early drafts—and helped me understand where I was going astray and where I was making sense. As noted, Stephen Waters (the newspaper editor in New York state) pushed me to work even harder. Jay Rosen went far beyond the call of duty in reading chapters and in several long discussions. Howard Rheingold's insights and encouragement have been immeasurably helpful. Doc Searls is amazing, period.

Tim O'Reilly, the founder and chief executive of O'Reilly Media, publisher of this book, constantly impresses me with his rare combination of intellect and generosity of spirit. When I described the idea to him in 2002, he immediately said he'd like to publish the book but thought I'd do better financially with an East Coast house. I struck out in New York despite the efforts of a fine literary agency. I'm glad, in retrospect, because working with Tim and his team—including Rael Dornfest, Betsy Waliszewski, Sara Winge and their colleagues—has been an absolute pleasure.

Allen Noren, an editor at O'Reilly and accomplished author in his own right, shepherded and edited this book. I'm in awe of his patience, thoughtfulness and good sense. He constantly challenged me to make this a better book, and if it is, he deserves much of the credit. Allen, thank you.

Noriko Takiguchi is a never-ending well of calm and joy. She put up with my absurdly long hours—including months of an alarm clock buzzing at absurdly early hours—and pushed me to get my butt in gear when I got lazy. She makes me sane. She lights my life.

# Web Site Directory

20six: *http://www.20six.co.uk/*

50 Minute Hour: *http://www.50minutehour.net/*

ActiveWords: *http://www.activewords.com/*

AllConsuming: *http://www.allconsuming.com/*

Amazon Light: *http://www.kokogiak.com/amazon/*

Amazon's Web Services:
   *http://www.amazon.com/gp/aws/landing.html/102-2039287-6152169*

American Journalism Review: *http://www.ajr.org/*

Back to Iraq: *http://www.back-to-iraq.com/*

Jack Balkin: *http://balkin.blogspot.com/*

BBC iCan project: *http://www.bbc.co.uk/ican/*

Yochai Benkler: *http://www.benkler.org/*

Erik Benson: *http://erikbenson.com/*

Berkeley Intellectual Property Blog:
   *http://journalism.berkeley.edu/projects/biplog/*

BitTorrent: *http://bitconjurer.org/BitTorrent/*

Blogads: *http://www.blogads.com/*

Blogger: *http://www.blogger.com/*

Blogging of the President: *http://www.bopnews.com/*

BoingBoing: *http://www.boingboing.net/*

Boston Online: *http://www.boston-online.com/*

Bush in 30 Seconds: *http://www.bushin30seconds.org/*

Center for Public Integrity: *http://www.publicintegrity.org/*

Chilling Effects Clearinghouse: *http://www.chillingeffects.org/*

Cluetrain Manifesto: *http://www.cluetrain.com/*

Columbia Journalism Review: *http://www.cjr.org/*

Columbia Journalism Review's "Campaign Desk":
*http://www.campaigndesk.org/*

Command Post: *http://www.command-post.org/*

Consumer Project on Technology: *http://www.cptech.org/*

Creative Commons: *http://www.creativecommons.org/*

Adam Curry: *http://live.curry.com/*

CyberJournalist: *http://www.cyberjournalist.net/*

Daily Kos: *http://www.dailykos.com/*

Howard Dean blog: *http://blog.deanforamerica.com/*

Dean Defense Forces: *http://www.deandefense.org/*

DeanSpace: *http://www.deanspace.org/*

DefenseLink: *http://www.defenselink.mil/*

Democracy Now: *http://www.democracynow.org/*

Nick Denton: *http://www.nickdenton.org/*

John Dowell's MX Blog: *http://www.markme.com/jd/*

Matt Drudge: *http://www.drudgereport.com/*

Earth911: *http://www.earth911.com/*

Edventure Holdings: *http://www.edventure.com/*

Electronic Frontier Foundation: *http://www.eff.org/*

Engadget: *http://www.engadget.com/*

Fair and Accuracy in Reporting: *http://www.fair.org/*

FCC Spectrum Policy Task Force: *http://www.fcc.gov/sptf/*

FeedDemon: *http://www.bradsoft.com/feeddemon/index.asp*

Feedster: *http://www.feedster.com/*

Fleshbot: *http://www.fleshbot.com/*

Free Software Foundation: *http://www.fsf.org/*

Gawker: *http://www.gawker.com/*

Dan Gillmor's blog:
 *http://weblog.siliconvalley.com/column/dangillmor/*

Gizmodo: *http://www.gizmodo.com/*

GNU Project: *http://www.gnu.org/*

Go Skokie: *http://goskokie.com/*

Phil Gomes: *http://www.philgomes.com/blog/*

GoogObits: *http://www.googobits.com/*

Google's API: *http://www.google.com/apis/*

Google Groups: *http://groups.google.com/*

Google News: *http://news.google.com/*

Groklaw: *http://www.groklaw.net/*

Chris Gulker: *http://www.gulker.com/*

Justin Hall: *http://www.links.net/*

Rex Hammock: *http://www.rexblog.com/*

Healing Iraq: *http://healingiraq.blogspot.com/*

Hoder's "Editor:Myself" blog: *http://hoder.com/weblog/*

Dennis Horgan: *http://denishorgan.com/*

Meg Hourihan: *http://www.megnut.com/*

Indymedia: *http://www.indymedia.org/*

Interesting People Mail List: *http://www.interesting-people.org/*

Ipoding: *http://www.ipoding.com/*

IT Conversations: *http://www.itconversations.com/*

Joi Ito: *http://joi.ito.com/*

Junior Journal: *http://journal.jrsummit.net/*

Kataweb: *http://www.kataweb.it/*

Valdis Krebs' political book-buying analysis:
*http://www.orgnet.com/divided.html*

Kristof Responds:
*http://forums.nytimes.com/top/opinion/readersopinions/forums/*
*editorialsoped/opedcolumnists/kristofresponds/*

Kuro5hin: *http://www.kuro5hin.org/*

Lawrence Journal-World: *http://www.ljworld.com/*

Ken Layne: *http://www.kenlayne.com/*

Sheila Lennon blog: *http://www.projo.com/blogs/shenews/*

Lawrence Lessig: *http://www.lessig.org/blog/*

LiveJournal: *http://www.livejournal.com/*

LockerGnome: *http://www.lockergnome.com/*

Donald Luskin: *http://www.poorandstupid.com/*

Macromedia: *http://www.markme.com/mxna/index.cfm*

Tom Mangan: *http://tommangan.net/*

Janet "StrollerQueen" McLaughlin: *http://www.strollerqueen.com/*

McSpotlight: *http://www.mcspotlight.org/*

Meetup: *http://www.meetup.com/*

Melrose Mirror: *http://toy-story.media.mit.edu:9000*

Memory Hole: *http://www.thememoryhole.org/*

Susan Mernit: *http://susanmernit.blogspot.com/*

Microsoft Channel 9: *http://channel9.msdn.com/*

Microsoft Newsbot: *http://newsbot.msn.com/*

Moreover: *http://www.moreover.com/*

MoveOn: *http://www.moveon.org/*

Tom Murphy blog: *http://www.natterjackpr.com/*

MyYahoo RSS: *http://add.my.yahoo.com/rss/*

National Debate: *http://www.thenationaldebate.com/*

NetNewsWire: *http://www.ranchero.com/*

News.com: *http://www.news.com/*

NewsIsFree: *http://www.newsisfree.com/*

New Media Musings: *http://www.newmediamusings.com/*

New York Times forums:
  *http://www.nytimes.com/pages/readersopinions/*

Kaycee Nicole FAQ: *http://www.rootnode.org/article.php?sid=26*

Nieman Reports: *http://www.nieman.harvard.edu/*

Nublog: *http://www.contenu.nu/*

OhmyNews: *http://ohmynews.com/*

Online Journalism Review: *http://www.ojr.org/*

Ray Ozzie: *http://www.ozzie.net/blog/*

Pacific News Service *http://news.pacificnews.org/news/*

Patterico: *http://patterico.com/*

Pets911: *http://www.pets911.com/*

Pew Internet Project: *http://www.pewinternet.org/*

Tim Porter: *http://www.timporter.com/*

Public Journalism Network: *http://www.pjnet.org/*

David Reed: *http://www.reed.com/*

The Register: *http://www.theregister.co.uk/*

Alan Reiter's wireless blog: *http://reiter.weblogger.com/*

Glenn Reynolds (Instapundit): *http://www.instapundit.com/*

John Robb: *http://jrobb.mindplex.org/*

Jim Romenesko: *http://poynter.org/Romenesko/*

Jay Rosen's PressThink:
  *http://journalism.nyu.edu/pubzone/weblogs/pressthink/*

Salon Blogs: *http://www.salon.com/blogs/*

**Doc Searls:** *http://doc.weblogs.com/*

**Robert Scoble:** *http://scoble.weblogs.com/*

**Clay Shirky:** *http://www.shirky.com/*

**Sign On San Diego:** *http://www.signonsandiego.com/*

**SilverStringer:** *http://silverstringer.media.mit.edu/*

**Six Apart:** *http://www.sixapart.com/*

**Slate Fraywatch:** *http://fray.slate.msn.com/id/2099475/*

**Smart Mobs:** *http://www.smartmobs.com/*

**Marc Smith:** *http://research.microsoft.com/~masmith/*

**SocialText:** *http://www.socialtext.com/*

**Spokane Spokesman-Review:** *http://www.spokesmanreview.com/*

**Sreenath Sreenivasan:** *http://sree.net/*

**Ernest Svenson:** *http://www.ernietheattorney.net/*

**Tom Standage site:** *http://www.tomstandage.com/*

**Stanford Cyberlaw Clinic:** *http://cyberlaw.stanford.edu/*

**Andrew Sullivan:** *http://www.andrewsullivan.com/*

**Syndic8:** *http://www.syndic8.com/*

**Talking Points Memo:** *http://www.talkingpointsmemo.com/*

**Technorati:** *http://www.technorati.com/*

**Technorati Developers Center:**
*http://www.technorati.com/developers/index.html*

**Times on the Trail:** *http://www.nytimes.com/pages/politics/trail/*

**Tobacco Control Archives:** *http://www.library.ucsf.edu/tobacco/*

**Tron Project:** *http://tron.um.u-tokyo.ac.jp/*

**Turnitin:** *http://www.turnitin.com/*

**Jon Udell:** *http://weblog.infoworld.com/udell/*

**Urban Legends:** *http://www.snopes.com/*

**UserLand Software:** *http://www.userland.com/*

Siva Vaidhyanathan: *http://www.nyu.edu/classes/siva/*

Erich Von Hippel: *http://web.mit.edu/evhippel/www/cv.htm*

Wall Street Journal "Best of the Web":
*http://www.opinionjournal.com/best/*

Washington Post Live Online:
*http://www.washingtonpost.com/wp-srv/liveonline/*

Washington Post White House Briefing:
*http://www.washingtonpost.com/wp-dyn/politics/administration/
whbriefing/*

We Media: *http://www.hypergene.net/wemedia/weblog.php*

Weblogs Inc.: *http://www.weblogsinc.com/*

Dan Weintraub blog: *http://www.sacbee.com/insider/*

We the Media: *http://wethemedia.oreilly.com/*

Wil Wheaton: *http://www.wilwheaton.net/*

Wiki: *http://c2.com/cgi/wiki/*

WikiTravel: *http://www.wikitravel.org/*

Phil Windley: *http://www.windley.com/*

Dave Winer's Scripting News: *http://www.scripting.com/*

Wonkette: *http://www.wonkette.com/*

WordPirates: *http://www.wordpirates.com/*

World Intellectual Property Organization: *http://www.wipo.org/*

Yahoo Groups: *http://groups.yahoo.com/*

# Glossary

### Client
A computing device, such as a PC, handheld organizer, or mobile phone that requests documents from a server. For example, someone is browsing the Web with a client PC, retrieving information from servers hosting web pages.

### Database
A collection of data, usually in a structured form, that can be searched, updated, and queried. Databases can include text, numbers, pictures, and even multimedia such as video. For example, the listings on Amazon.com are in a database.

### Free software
Software in which the programming instructions, or source code, is openly available and free for downloading and modification. Examples of free software (also known as Open Source Software), include the Linux operating system.

### Hacking
Delving into the innards of a program or a network, sometimes to explore and other times to make improvements. Some hackers are malevolent and cause damage, and have given the word "hacker" a bad name. Examples of "good" hacking include updating or improving hardware devices, such as cars or PCs, in ways not specifically authorized by the manufacturer.

### HTML (Hypertext Markup Language)
A text-based markup language web browsers read to display web pages. To see the HTML of any web page, select the View ▸ Source menu of any browser.

### Linux
A Unix-like open source operating system that runs a majority of the servers on the Internet. Linux was designed as a free alternative to costly operating systems such as Unix and Windows.

### Mailing list
A topic-oriented email list people subscribe to. Every member who has subscribed to the list receives all messages sent to the list. An example from this book is Dave Farber's Interesting People mailing list.

### Open source software
Software that is collectively developed, maintained, and distributed, typically by many people throughout the world. Examples of open source software include the Linux operating system, Apache server software, and MySQL database software. Open source software is freely available and "open," so the source code can be modified.

### Operating system
The base software that regulates and controls all programs and processes on a computer. Examples of operating systems include Linux, OS X, Unix, and Windows.

### Peer-to-peer
A communications system that allows for the sharing of files, such as text, audio, and video, across networks. The most widely known example of a peer-to-peer system is the original Napster music-sharing system.

### RSS (Really Simple Syndication)
A protocol for describing news and other information on web sites for syndication to other web sites and communications devices, such as mobile phones. RSS files are read by software called aggregators or newsreaders that display the information.

### Server
A computer that serves text, audio, and video files to other computers. Any time you click a link on a web page, a server then serves the requested files for display on a browser.

### SMS (Short Message System)
A text-based communications system widely used on mobile phones. Using SMS, owners of mobile devices can send short text messages to each other.

### Weblog
An online journal of short web postings, usually posted in reverse chronological order (most recent item first). Examples include my own blog at *http://weblog.siliconvalley.com/column/dangillmor/*.

### Wiki
Wiki is software that allows anyone to freely create and edit web pages using a web browser. Wikipedia (*http://www.wikipedia.org*), an online encyclopedia, is an example of a Wiki.

# Notes

## INTRODUCTION

1. Esther Dyson's column about Nacchio incident can be found at *http://www.edventure.com/conversation/article.cfm?Counter=8648145.*

2. I'm convinced Nacchio was perfectly capable of annoying the audience all by himself. Clay Shirky, also in the room that day, felt the mood shifting, and wondered why until someone pointed out the blogging on a nearby computer screen. He told me:

   > "Now, normally, a blog entry like this would take a day or so to ripple outwards, but because this was such a wired crowd and, frankly, because Nacchio's talk was so dull, a lot of people were catching up on their blog reading during the talk, and even people not reading were near people who were. So the whole thing, from discovery to publication to spread, got really compressed, and basically happened during the time he was onstage.

## CHAPTER I, FROM TOM PAINE TO BLOGS AND BEYOND

3. Cambridge University Press, 2003

4. Bimber also observes that the Founders based their new nation essentially on information. An informed electorate was necessary to self-government. The Federalist papers, newspapers, and other writings were the beginnings of the world's first information-based society.

5. Tom Standage's *The Victorian Internet* (1998) observes the remarkable similarities in rise of 19th-century telegraph networks and the modern Internet, including stock market bubbles, absurd predictions, and, in the end, the rise of an enormously powerful tool for communications (*http://www.tomstandage.com*).

6. *Nation* magazine, July 21, 2003.

7. In the early 1970s, big newspaper companies persuaded Congress to pass a "newspaper preservation" law that limited antitrust enforcement. The law let competing newspapers merge their advertising, printing, and circulation staffs while maintaining separate newsrooms and publishing two papers. My company, Knight Ridder, enjoys the fruits of several such Joint Operating Agreements, as they're called. If there was ever a justification for this law, which is doubtful, the Net makes it less justifiable now. The nation would be better off if the law was repealed.

8. Direct mail has also pulled advertisers away in large numbers, notes Stephen B. Waters, publisher of the *Rome Sentinel* in upstate New York. "In 1979 they rejiggered the rates to begin to suck up advertising to keep postponing until the next elections a day of reckoning because of a bloated, expensive labor force," he wrote me. "The advertising dollar has gone to Direct Marketing, not radio and television. It still is the case."

9. I rely on somewhat fading memory, not archives, for the details of my XyWrite programming-assistance story.

10. Usenet newsgroups live on today in many forms, including "Google Groups" (*http://groups.google.com*).

11. Left-wing groups were also using these systems to organize, but from my observations at the time, not as effectively.

12. The MIDI standard (*http://www.midi.org*) revolutionized music, and continues to do so.

13. For example, see the Pacific News Service (*http://news.pacificnews.org/news/*).

14. Howard Kurtz column: *http://www.washingtonpost.com/wp-dyn/nation/columns/kurtzhoward/*.

15. Justin Hall: *http://www.links.net*.

16. Being available worldwide isn't the same as being seen worldwide. In his essay, "Power Laws, Weblogs, and Inequality" (*http://www.shirky.com/writings/powerlaw_weblog.html*), Clay Shirky observes that in a system such as the blog arena, "where many people are free to choose between many options, a small subset of the whole will get a disproportionate amount of traffic (or attention, or income), even if no members of the system actively work towards such an outcome. This has nothing to do with moral weakness, selling out, or any other psychological explanation. The very act of choosing, spread widely enough and freely enough, creates a power law distribution." But he adds that newcomers can gain significant audiences nonetheless.

17. McGraw-Hill, 1964.

18. Bantam Books/Random House, 1967.

19. William Morrow, 1980.

20. Cluetrain Manifesto: *http://www.cluetrain.com*.

21. Dave Winer's "Scripting News" blog: *http://www.scripting.com*.

22. UserLand Software: *http://www.userland.com*.

23. GNU Project: *http://www.gnu.org.*

24. In the early 1990s, after many of the core pieces of Stallman's software project had been created, Torvalds, then a Finnish college student, wrote a "kernel," the core element of what became Linux. It's important to recognize, as Torvalds gladly does, that Linux derived from Stallman's original vision.

25. Stallman and others in the free software movement strongly object to the "open source" terminology. For more on why, visit the Free Software Foundation's site (*http://www.fsf.org*).

26. Proprietary software makers and some security experts dispute this, saying open code is not inherently safer. But "security through obscurity" is plainly not a workable answer, either.

27. Coase's Penguin: *http://www.benkler.org/CoasesPenguin.html.*

28. Kuro5hin: *http://www.kuro5hin.org.*

29. Leonard Witt , professor of communications at Kennesaw State University in Georgia (*http://www.kennesaw.edu/communication/witt.shtml*), persuasively argues that blogs and other bottom-up journalism are doing what advocates of "public journalism"—the idea that journalists have an obligation to further civic discourse and improvement—have been pushing for years, with limited interest from professional journalists. Witt says "intermediaries are no longer needed as public journalism morphs into the public's journalism." See the essay by blogger Tim Porter, who delves deeply into these subjects, for more on this notion (*http://www.timporter.com/firstdraft/archives/000246.html*).

30. Interesting People Mail List: *http://www.interesting-people.org.*

31. 50 Minute Hour: *http://www.50minutehour.net/archive/2001_09_01_index.htm.*

32. Gus," the Brooklyn blogger: *http://www.spies.com/~gus/ran/0109/010911.htm.*

33. Meg Hourihan blog: *http://www.megnut.com/archive.asp?which=2001_09_01_archive.inc.*

34. Tamim Ansary: "An Afghan-American speaks": *http://dir.salon.com/news/feature/2001/09/14/afghanistan/index.html.*

CHAPTER 2, THE READ-WRITE WEB

35. *The Guardian*, one of the most prominent national newspapers in the United Kingdom, offers thoughtful, hard-hitting journalism from a slightly left-of-center perspective. In the weeks before the 2003 Iraq war, the site saw a big increase in visitors. This happened to most serious newspapers, but *The Guardian*'s traffic boost came in large part from Americans. What were they looking for? No one is absolutely certain, but Simon Waldman, who runs *The Guardian*'s online operations, told me he believed many of the American visitors were looking for something they couldn't find in the U.S. press: a different perspective from the relentlessly pro-war coverage

they were seeing at home. I leaned in favor of the war, but I was appalled at the lack of nuance in American journalism during a time when about half the population opposed the war.

36. Scribner, 2002

37. Steven Johnson interview: *http://www.oreillynet.com/pub/a/network/2002/02/22/johnson.html*.

38. David Isenberg's "Rise of the Stupid Network": *http://www.hyperorg.com/misc/stupidnet.html*.

39. Yahoo Groups: *http://groups.yahoo.com*.

40. Gizmodo: *http://www.gizmodo.com*.

41. Wi-Fi Networking: *http://wifinetnews.com*.

42. Jay Rosen's PressThink: *http://journalism.nyu.edu/pubzone/weblogs/pressthink/*.

43. Six Apart: *http://www.sixapart.com*.

44. Radio UserLand: *http://radio.userland.com*.

45. LiveJournal: *http://www.livejournal.com*.

46. Blogger: *http://www.blogger.com*.

47. 20six: *http://www.20six.co.uk*.

48. Wiki: *http://c2.com/cgi/wiki*.

49. Cunningham's Wiki categories: *http://c2.com/cgi/wiki?CategoryCategory*.

50. WikiTravel: *http://www.wikitravel.org*.

51. Instant messaging is also one way people spread news, mostly in the U.S., but SMS is much more global and destined, as devices become more mobile, to be *the* headline service of the Digital Age.

52. Perseus, 2002

53. Rheingold's Smart Mobs web site continues to follow this evolution: *http://www.smartmobs.com*.

54. See *The Washington Post*'s coverage of banned camera phones at *http://www.washingtonpost.com/ac2/wp-dyn/A49274-2003Sep22*.

55. Blogging of the President: *http://www.bopnews.com*.

56. Full disclosure: I've been a guest several times on the program.

57. IT Conversations: *http://www.itconversations.com*.

58. BitTorrent: *http://bitconjurer.org/BitTorrent/*.

59. LockerGnome: *http://www.lockergnome.com*.

60. NetNewsWire: *http://www.ranchero.com*.

61. FeedDemon: *http://www.bradsoft.com/feeddemon/index.asp*.

62. NewsIsFree: *http://www.newsisfree.com*.

63. Syndic8: *http://www.syndic8.com*.

64. Feedster: *http://www.feedster.com.*

65. Technorati: *http://www.technorati.com.*

## CHAPTER 3, THE GATES COME DOWN

66. For considerably more detail on the Lott incident, see the case study from the Shorenstein Center at Harvard University's Kennedy School of Government (*http://blogs.law.harvard.edu/2004/03/08*). Blogger Mickey Kaus (*http://slate.msn.com/id/2075444&#darkmatter*) says some well-timed emails from a Democratic political operative played a role, though this is less clear.

67. Talking Points Memo: *http://www.talkingpointsmemo.com.*

68. CNET quotes Intel executive on Pentium bug: *http://news.com.com/2009-1001_3-224567.html.*

69. MacMerc on how to win the Pepsi iTunes giveaway: *http://www.macmerc.com/news/archives/1270.*

70. The primary source for this section is a translation from a book by Chinese journalist Zhang Shumei, who played a key role in these events.

71. Hong Kong government's use of SMS: *The Guardian*, April 3, 2003. *http://www.guardian.co.uk/online/news/0,12597,928906,00.html?=rss*

72. Camera phone abduction story: *http://www.cnn.com/2003/TECH/ptech/08/01/camphone.abduction/.*

73. Slashdot: *http://slashdot.org*

74. Slashdot user exposes Microsoft PR trick: *http://apple.slashdot.org/apple/02/10/14/1232229.shtml?tid=109.*

75. McSpotlight: *http://www.mcspotlight.org.*

76. Tobacco Control Archives: *http://www.library.ucsf.edu/tobacco/.*

77. Memory Hole: *http://www.thememoryhole.org.*

78. Greenwood Pub Group, 1914.

79. One site's instructions on upgrading digital video recorder: *http://echostaruser.manilasites.com/dpclone.*

80. iPoding: *http://www.ipoding.com.*

81. EDN Access story on auto codes: *http://www.e-insite.net/ednmag/index.asp?layout=article&articleid=CA46067.*

82. A company called Dinan (*http://www.dinancars.com*) sells software upgrades for the BMW line, removing a governor that limits top speed in the U.S. Although I can't see why this is needed—and can imagine many improper uses—BMW's Big-Brotherish settings are also annoying.

83. Erich Von Hippel: *http://web.mit.edu/evhippel/www/cv.htm.*

84. Tron Project: *http://tron.um.u-tokyo.ac.jp.*

85. Marc Smith: *http://research.microsoft.com/~masmith*.

86. CNETAsia: *http://asia.cnet.com/newstech/communications/ 0,39001141,39127700,00.htm*.

87. *The New York Times Magazine*: *http://www.nytimes.com/2001/02/25/ magazine25STOCKTRADER.html?ei=5070&en=84cb0288bed4667a&ex =1083211200&pagewanted=print*.

88. Doc Searls on the Segway: *http://doc.weblogs.com/2001/12/ 05#theSecrecyGame*.

89. The Marketing of the President, 2004," *Baseline Magazine*: *http:// www.baselinemag.com/article2/0,3959,1410983,00.asp*.

90. Perseus Books, 1998.

91. Matt Smith column on Poindexter: *http://www.sfweekly.com/issues/2002- 12-24/smith.html/1/index.html*.

92. Cryptome: *http://cryptome.org/tia-eyeball.htm*.

93. Information Awareness Office: *http://www.darpa.mil/iao/*.

94. Jim Romenesko's Poynter Institute media blog: *http://poynter.org/ Romenesko*.

95. *The New York Times* report on Blair incident: *http://www.nytco.com/ committeereport.pdf*.

96. Donald Luskin blog: *http://www.poorandstupid.com*.

CHAPTER 4, NEWSMAKERS TURN THE TABLES

97. *The Washington Post* interview with Donald Rumsfeld: *http:// www.defenselink.mil/news/Feb2002/t02052002_t0109wp.html*.

98. The assumption of accuracy is not automatic, and the Pentagon severely compromised its credibility in April 2004 in a similar circumstance. According to *The Washington Post* (*http://www.washingtonpost.com/wp- dyn/articles/A28729-2004Apr20.html*), the Defense Department "deleted from a public transcript a statement Defense Secretary Donald H. Rums- feld made to author Bob Woodward suggesting that the administration gave Saudi Arabia a two-month heads-up that President Bush had decided to invade Iraq." Woodward provided his own transcript. Will journalists and sources be posting dueling transcripts in the future?

99. Phil Gomes blog: *blog: http://www.philgomes.com/blog*.

100. ActiveWords: *http://www.activewords.com*.

101. Tom Murphy blog: *http://www.natterjackpr.com*.

102. Ray Ozzie blog: *http://www.ozzie.net/blog/*.

103. Mark Cuban's Blog Maverick: *http://www.blogmaverick.com*.

104. John Dowdell's MX Blog: *http://www.markme.com/jd/*.

105. Macromedia aggregated blogs: *http://www.markme.com/mxna/index.cfm.*

106. Microsoft Channel 9: *http://channel9.msdn.com.*

107. Windley is now a consultant on enterprise computing (*http:// www.windley.com).*

108. Robert Scoble's Scobleizer blog: *http://scoble.weblogs.com.*

109. Scoble's "Corporate Weblog Manifesto" list: *http://radio.weblogs.com/ 0001011/2003/02/26.html#a2357.*

110. Ernest Svenson's Ernie the Attorney blog: *http://www.ernietheattorney.net.*

111. Wil Wheaton blog: *http://www.wilwheaton.net.*

112. O'Reilly, 2004.

113. Cisco's RSS feeds: *http://tools.cisco.com/newsroom/contactSearch/jsp/ syndicationSearch.jsp.*

114. Jon Udell's PR instructions: *http://weblog.infoworld.com/udell/2002/08/ 14.html#a383.*

115. NUblog: *http://www.contenu.nu.*

116. Alan Reiter's wireless blog: *http://reiter.weblogger.com.*

117. Janet "Stroller Queen" McLaughlin: *http://www.strollerqueen.com.*

118. *The Wall Street Journal,* Sept. 8, 2003, page one article.

119. Engadget: *http://www.engadget.com.*


CHAPTER 5, THE CONSENT OF THE GOVERNED

120. Daily Kos: *http://www.dailykos.com.*

121. Blogads: *http://www.blogads.com.*

122. *Wired News* story by Chris Ulbrich on Chandler and blog advertising: *http://www.wired.com/news/politics/0,1283,62325,00.html.*

123. Perseus, 2002.

124. Meetup: *http://www.meetup.com.*

125. At a dinner in Vermont while I was visiting the campaign, an old friend of Dean's (and mine; I lived in Vermont for almost 15 years until the mid-1980s) turned to me as I was describing my positive impressions of the Dean Internet activities and said, "But Howard's such a Luddite." Vermonters, I discovered, were amused by the former governor's Net savvy, because he'd been reluctant, at best, to bring the most advanced technology into state government until well into his latter terms. Another person at the table offered, "But he learns fast."

126. Dean's official blog site: *http://blog.deanforamerica.com.*

127. Dean Defense Forces: *http://www.deandefense.org.*

128. Dean campaign spam story by Declan McCullagh: *http://news.com.com/ 2100-1028_3-5065141.html.*

129. MoveOn: *http://www.moveon.org.*

130. Bush in 30 Seconds: *http://www.bushin30seconds.org.*

131. DeanSpace: *http://www.deanspace.org.*

132. Command Post: *http://www.command-post.org.*

133. The Schwarzenegger campaign was an exception. Local TV covered the recall and the candidates' positions with surprising fervor, perhaps due to the actor's star power.

134. Joi Ito's "Emergent Democracy" paper: *http://joi.ito.com/static/ emergentdemocracy.html.*

135. Cameron Barrett quote: *http://weblog.siliconvalley.com/column/ dangillmor/archives/010238.shtml.*

136. Earth 911: *http://www.earth911.com.*

137. Pets 911: *http://www.pets911.com.*

138. DefenseLink: *http://www.defenselink.mil.*

139. Note some parallels here with journalism (and other institutions being affected by the Internet)—threats to all kinds of centralized power structures from the edges, where technology gives disproportionate capabilities to individuals.

140. John Robb: *http://jrobb.mindplex.org.*

141. Maney column in *USA Today: http://www.usatoday.com/tech/columnist/ 2001/10/24/maney.htm.*

CHAPTER 6, PROFESSIONAL JOURNALISTS JOIN THE CONVERSATION

142. *Jane's Intelligence Review* thanks Slashdot readers: *http://slashdot.org/ features/99/10/07/120249.shtml.*

143. OhmyNews: *http://ohmynews.com/articleview/article_ view.asp?menu=04219&no=153109&rel_no=1.*

144. *The New York Times* forums: *http://www.nytimes.com/pages/ readersopinions/.*

145. Kristof Responds: *http://forums.nytimes.com/top/opinion/readersopinions/ forums/editorialsoped/opedcolumnists/kristofresponds/index.html.*

146. Slate Fraywatch: *fray.slate.msn.com/id/2099475/.*

147. *The Washington Post* live chats: *http://www.washingtonpost.com/wp-srv/ liveonline/.*

148. As we'll discuss in Chapter 9, blogs and other discussion sites are constantly fighting a battle against trolls and spammers; it's an arms race, but I'm hopeful that we'll be able to keep far enough ahead of the bad guys to hold onto the value of the conversation.

149. CyberJournalist.net blog list: *http://www.cyberjournalist.net/cyber- journalists.php.*

150. Dan Weintraub blog: *http://www.sacbee.com/insider/*.

151. The *Wall Street Journal* "Best of the Web": *http://www.opinionjournal.com/best/*,

152. Sheila Lennon blog: *http://www.projo.com/blogs/shenews/*,

153. Like so many journalism organizations, the *Charlotte Observer*'s excellent work has disappeared behind a pay-per-view firewall. You can find the hurricane coverage, or some of it, in the nonprofit Web Archive: *http://web.archive.org/web/20010307020840/http:/www.charlotte.com/special/bonnie/0828dispatches.htm*.

154. Tom Mangan blog: *http://tommangan.net/printsthechaff*,

155. CNN to Online Journalism Review: *http://www.ojr.org/ojr/workplace/1049381758.php*,

156. Olafson fired: *http://www.houstonpress.com/issues/2002-08-08/hostage.html/1/index.html*,

157. Dennis Horgan blog: *http://denishorgan.com*,

158. The *Nieman Reports* back issues are, perversely, available only as PDFs: *http://www.nieman.harvard.edu/reports/03-3NRfall/V57N3.pdf*,

159. So are some broadcasters. Minnesota Public Radio (*http://www.mpr.org*) looks like it will lead the way, with a variety of programs designed to bring listeners into the process.

160. Spokane *Spokesman-Review*: *http://www.spokesmanreview.com*.

161. Lawrence *Journal-World*: *http://www.ljworld.com*.

162. White House Briefing: *http://www.washingtonpost.com/wp-dyn/politics/administration/whbriefing/*.

163. Times on the Trail: *http://www.nytimes.com/pages/politics/trail/*.

164. *Columbia Journalism Review*: *http://www.cjr.org*.

165. *American Journalism Review*: *http://www.ajr.org*.

166. Patterico: *http://patterico.com*.

167. In May, Patterico, whose real name is Patrick Frey, told Online Journalism Review's Mark Glaser that he'd contacted the *Times* not as a blogger but as an interested reader. His impact was no less real in any event. See *http://patterico.com/archives/002026.php*.

168. Minnesota Public Radio's Michael Skoler put it well in an interview on Leonard Witt's Public Journalism blog (*http://pjnet.org/weblogs/pjnettoday/archives/000172.html*) when he said: "If 'establishment' media organizations can plug into the energy and wisdom of the collective brain of the public, we'll bring the strength of traditional journalism—editorial judgment, fact-checking, truth-seeking—into a new age of better, more trusted news coverage. If we don't do this, I think the unfiltered, weblog-type model of journalism will overtake traditional media with its sheer energy and we will lose a powerful way of informing the public about critical issues in our democracy."

169. NASA asks public for shuttle photos: *http://www.jsc.nasa.gov/ instructions.html.*

170. BBC call for people's photos: *http://news.bbc.co.uk/2/hi/talking_point/ 2732695.stm.*

171. Sign On San Diego Fire Coverage: *http://www.signonsandiego.com/news/ fires/weekoffire/index.html.*

172. Salon Blogs: *http://www.salon.com/blogs.*

173. *http://www.hypergene.net/wemedia/weblog.php.*

174. BBC iCan: *http://www.bbc.co.uk/ican.*

175. What's not unlimited is people's patience for reading long articles; invariably, when I encounter a lengthy piece that I want to read carefully, I print it out first.

176. Could an OhmyNews-like operation work in the United States and other countries? It's difficult to know, in part because there are different legal issues. But the indications are that the potential is there. One of the best U.S. community news sites I've seen is called iBrattleboro (*http:// www.ibrattleboro.com*), based in Brattleboro, Vermont, where the daily quasi-monopoly newspaper is owned by one of the more rapacious chains. From my distant perspective, iBrattleboro consistently covers important events and issues that the newspaper all but ignores.

177. BBC uses 3G phones: *http://www.cyberjournalist.net/news/000793.php.*

178. I started requiring my Hong Kong students to create blogs in 1999, when the software I used was still in "beta" form, and the concept itself was virtually unknown.

179. New York University student portfolios: *http://journalism.nyu.edu/ portfolio/.*

180. Do bloggers need editors? I was part of a panel on blogging and journalism where that topic was discussed at length. J.D. Lasica reported on it in Online Journalism Review: *http://www.ojr.org/ojr/lasica/1032910520.php.*

## CHAPTER 7, THE FORMER AUDIENCE JOINS THE PARTY

181. Healing Iraq blog: *http://healingiraq.blogspot.com.*

182. Rex Hammock blog: *http://www.rexblog.com.*

183. Blog postings from *The Wall Street Journal* "D" conference: *http:// weblog.siliconvalley.com/column/dangillmor/archives/001058.shtml.*

184. Rheingold's comment came at the PopTech (*http://www.poptech.org*) gathering in Camden, Maine.

185. Groklaw: *http://www.groklaw.net.*

186. Jones interview: *http://www.linux.org/people/pj_groklaw.html.*

187. Hoder's Editor:Myself blog: *http://hoder.com/weblog.*

188. See "Iranian Journalist Credits Blogs for Playing Key Role in His Release From Prison," in Online Journalism Review: *http://www.ojr.org/ojr/glaser/1073610866.php.*

189. Melrose Mirror: *http://toy-story.media.mit.edu:9000.*

190. SilverStringer: *http://silverstringer.media.mit.edu/.*

191. Kataweb: *http://www.kataweb.it.*

192. Junior Journal: *http://journal.jrsummit.net.*

193. See *The New York Times* coverage at *http://www.nytimes.com/2003/01/27/business/media/27PAPE.html.*

194. Indymedia: *http://www.indymedia.org.*

195. Google News does post some flagrantly biased stories from other sources, however.

196. Democracy Now: *http://www.democracynow.org.*

197. Command Post: *http://www.command-post.org.*

198. Center for Public Integrity: *http://www.publicintegrity.org.*

199. In focusing more on public affairs–oriented sites in this section, I don't want to slight any of the more topical online journalism being done. Technology has been a prime example of how cyberspace, where speed is of the essence, can beat paper. CNET's News.com service (*http://www.news.com*) has been a stalwart of excellent tech coverage, as has The Register (*http://www.theregister.co.uk*), a British-based site that is both smart and sassy in its coverage. Both sites are essential reading for tech journalists.

200. Wikipedia: *http://www.wikipedia.org.*

201. WikiTravel: *http://www.wikitravel.org.*

202. SocialText: *http://www.socialtext.com.*

203. Susan Mernit blog: *http://susanmernit.blogspot.com.*

204. Gawker: *http://www.gawker.com.*

205. Gizmodo: *http://www.gizmodo.com.*

206. Fleshbot: *http://www.fleshbot.com.*

207. Wonkette: *http://www.wonkette.com.*

208. Nick Denton blog: *http://www.nickdenton.org.*

209. Moreover: *http://www.moreover.com.*

210. I'm squeamish about this kind of thing because it raises ethical questions. The connection was clearly stated on the Gizmodo site, however, so at least there was full disclosure. Ultimately, Denton said, readers will decide on the credibility: "If you're pitching bad stuff, readership will decline."

211. The cost of launching a personal blog is much lower, ranging from free to a few dollars a month plus the cost of the computer and Internet access.

212. Weblogs Inc.: *http://www.weblogsinc.com.*

213. Blogads: *http://www.blogads.com.*

214. New Media Musings: *http://www.newmediamusings.com.*

215. Andrew Sullivan blog: *http://www.andrewsullivan.com.*

216. Chris Allbritton's Back to Iraq: *http://www.back-to-iraq.com.*

217. Talking Points Memo: *http://www.talkingpointsmemo.com.*


CHAPTER 8, NEXT STEPS

218. Moore's original paper on the subject is on Intel's web site at: *ftp:// download.intel.com/research/silicon/moorespaper.pdf.*

219. In this 2003 CNET interview, Metcalfe talks about the genesis and future of Ethernet: *http://news.com.com/2008-1082-1008450.html.*

220. As Hal Varian and Carl Shapiro noted in their important 1999 book, *Information Rules* (Harvard Business School Press), Metcalfe's Law relies on what economists call "network externalities." This is the notion that the larger the network, the more attractive it will be to users in most cases— and the harder it will be for a new entrant in the market to get people to switch.

221. David Reed's own explanation of his "law" is on his site: *http:// www.reed.com/Papers/GFN/reedslaw.html.*

222. I'm particularly indebted to Howard Rheingold for his observations, in conversations and his writing, which have helped clarify my own understanding of the power of these various laws.

223. Pew report on online content production: *http://www.pewinternet.org/ reports/toc.asp?Report=113.*

224. Adam Curry: *http://live.curry.com.*

225. Curry's BloggerCon session introduction: *http://blogs.law.harvard.edu/ bloggerCon/2004/04/09#a1119.*

226. Andrew Grumet has been experimenting with video as RSS "enclosures," delivered to a desktop (or other device) as needed. See *http:// blogs.law.harvard.edu/tech/bitTorrent* for more information.

227. Advertisers saw this potential long ago. In Hong Kong in 2000, a friend showed me a mobile phone that let him know if a nearby store was having a sale.

228. Bantam, 1991.

229. Google News: *http://news.google.com.*

230. Microsoft Newsbot: *http://newsbot.msn.com.*

231. MyYahoo! RSS: *http://add.my.yahoo.com/rss/.*

232. Erik Benson blog: *http://erikbenson.com.*

233. Google's API: *http://www.google.com/apis/.*

234. Amazon's Web Services: *http://www.amazon.com/gp/aws/landing.html/ 102-2039287-6152169.*

235. Technorati Developers Center: *http://www.technorati.com/developers/index.html.*

236. Amazon Light: *http://www.kokogiak.com/amazon.*

237. Valdis Krebs' political book-buying analysis: *http://www.orgnet.com/divided.html.*

238. AllConsuming: *http://www.allconsuming.com.*

239. GoogObits: *http://www.googobits.com.*

240. In April 2004, Technorati launched a preliminary version of a service that went part of the way toward making the conversation visible. It let a weblogger automatically show a link to Technorati's index of all the blogs that had linked to a specific posting. It was launched first on BoingBoing and became an instant hit.

241. As David Weinberger says, updating the Andy Warhol aporism: "In the future everyone will be famous for fifteen people."

## CHAPTER 9, TROLLS, SPIN, AND THE BOUNDARIES OF TRUST

242. Schmich column about the Vonnegut episode: *http://www.chicagotribune.com/news/columnists/chi-970803cyperspace.column.*

243. Avi Rubin article describing experience as polling judge: *http://avirubin.com/judge.html.*

244. The photo was debunked by the urban legends site Snopes.com: *http://www.snopes.com/photos/politics/kerry2.asp.*

   Ken Light, who took the original Kerry picture used for the composite, discussed the incident on the DigitalJournalist site: *http://www.digitaljournalist.org/issue0403/dis_light.html.*

245. This is not a new phenomenon. As Paul Martin Lester, communications professor at California State University at Fullerton, observes (*http://commfaculty.fullerton.edu/lester/writings/faking.html*):

   Photojournalism, photography that accompanies stories intended for newspaper and magazine readers, has a long and cherished tradition of truthfulness. The faking of photographs, either through stage direction by the photographer or through darkroom manipulation, unfortunately, also has a long tradition. As a result, Pulitzer Prize-winning images, photographs that have moved people to action, and pictures that have been hailed as beautiful humanistic documents filled with hope mud joy, have been questioned. Consequently, their impact has been diminished by charges of photographic faking. Such accusations are usually easily proven unsubstantiated and are the exception rather than the rule for photojournalism images. However, computer technology puts photographic faking on a new level of concern as images can be digitized and manipulated without the slightest indication of such trickery.

246. Columbia University journalism professor Sreenath Sreenivasan has compiled a page of doctored photos: *http://sree.net/teaching/photoethics.html.*

247. Fairness and Accuracy in Reporting report: *http://www.fair.org/activism/cbs-digital.html.*

248. See Securities and Exchange Commission documents at *http://www.sec.gov/litigation/litreleases/lr17094.htm.*

249. Matt Drudge: *http://www.drudgereport.com.*

250. *The New York Times,* February 14, 2004: "Amazon Glitch Unmasks War of Reviewers."

251. For the full exchange between me and "George," visit the posting: *http://weblog.siliconvalley.com/column/dangillmor/archives/001675.shtml.*

252. Berkeley Intellectual Property Blog: *http://journalism.berkeley.edu/projects/biplog.*

253. Some people who comment on my blog have said they choose to use phony email addresses so that spammers can't scrape their email addresses off their postings. This is a valid concern. Spammers are always looking for new email addresses and regularly spider forums and blogs for email addresses. Forum and blogging software is improving, however, and it'll soon be more difficult for a spammer's software to effectively scrape email addresses off comment postings.

254. Ward Cunningham goes far beyond simply defining trolls. He offers distinctions and good advice on what to do about them: *http://c2.com/cgi/wiki?TrollDefinition.*

255. The *Columbia Journalism Review*'s Campaign Desk site covered the drug-benefits controversy in some depth: *http://www.campaigndesk.org/archives/000446.asp.*

256. See Mark Memmott's *USA Today* story on Google bombing: *http://www.usatoday.com/news/politicselections/nation/president/2004-04-11-kerry-waffles_x.htm.*

257. Boston Online: *http://www.boston-online.com.*

258. Adam Gaffin's recounting of the "dixie wrecked" situation: *http://www.wickedgood.info/cgi-bin/forum/gforum.cgi?post=12703;#12703.*

259. For example, as another commenter observed in the "Wicked Good" discussion of New Media Strategies, the firm worked with the Burger King fast-food chain to get the word out about a potentially harmful toy being given to small children: "NMS' innovative one-on-one corporate communications strategy instantly reached millions of concerned parents and earned Burger King praise from both customers and the Consumer Products Safety Commission."

260. Ken Layne blog: *http://www.kenlayne.com.*

261. In 2002, an article in *The Guardian* attributed the Lane quote to Glenn Reynolds, who posted this funny but relevant item on his blog: "While I do say 'fact check your ass' from time to time, it's Ken Layne who coined the term. This article from *The Guardian* gives the impression that the term is

uniquely mine, which it isn't—either by origination or by frequency of use. Hey, I just 'fact-checked the ass' of an article over the phrase 'fact-checking your ass.' I think that should get me the recursive metablogging medal of the day. Or at least a good seed in the recursive metablogging tournament."

262. For more on the Kaycee Nicole case, see the "Kaycee Nicole (Swenson) FAQ": *http://www.rootnode.org/article.php?sid=26*.

263. WordPirates: *http://www.wordpirates.com*.

264. In 1998, *The New York Times'* public site was hacked, and the front page changed, but the changes were blatantly the work of people who were making an anti-*Times* point, not trying to pull off another, more serious kind of stunt.


CHAPTER 10, HERE COME THE JUDGES (AND LAWYERS)

265. CyberWire Dispatch archives: *http://cyberwerks.com:70/1/cyberwire/*.

266. Meeks told me: "There was NO requirement on me to show him anything I was going to publish prior to publishing it. That was a no brainer to accept in the settlement, as any story I would write about him he would know of well before 42 hours because I'd be calling him to ask him questions." In addition, the agreement lasted 18 months, and in any event Meeks didn't write about the company again.

267. Blogger and law professor Glenn Reynolds says: "To be libelous, a statement must be (1) a statement of fact, not opinion; (2) false; and (3) such as to materially injure someone's reputation." The standard is higher for public figures, who have to show that the writer had reckless disregard for whether the statement was true.

268. Anthony York wrote a detailed summary of the Drudge-Blumenthal case in Salon: *http://dir.salon.com/politics/red/2001/05/02/blue/index.html*.

269. Jack Balkin: *http://balkin.blogspot.com*.

270. See *http://balkin.blogspot.com/2003_06_29_balkin_archive.html#105723343690170641* for Balkin's entire analysis.

271. The Stanford Cyberlaw Clinic's files in the Nymox case: *http://cyberlaw.stanford.edu/about/cases/nymox.shtml*.

272. See the *Economist* story on this case: *http://www.economist.com/agenda/displayStory.cfm?story_id=1489053*.

273. The Electronic Frontier Foundation, which helped Hamidi, archived many of the relevant documents: *http://www.eff.org/Spam_cybersquatting_abuse/Spam/Intel_v_Hamidi/*.

274. See Mark Glaser's Online Journalism Review coverage of plagiarism on the Net: *http://www.ojr.org/ojr/glaser/1050584240.php*.

275. Turnitin software: *http://www.turnitin.com*.

276. Chilling Effects Clearinghouse: *http://www.chillingeffects.org.*

277. World Intellectual Property Organization: *http://www.wipo.org.*

278. Consumer Project on Technology: *http://www.cptech.org.*

279. Full WIPO examiner's holding: *http://arbiter.wipo.int/domains/decisions/ html/2000/d2000-0584.html.*

280. National Debate's *The New York Times* "corrections" page: *http:// www.thenationaldebate.com/other/NYTCorrections.htm.*

281. See *The New York Times,* "The Privileges of Opinion, the Obligations of Fact," March 28, 2004.

282. For other examples of antilinking threats, visit the Chilling Effects Clearinghouse web site. You'll also find some unintentionally hilarious "linking policies" by corporate sites.

283. The EFF archived this and related cases: *http://www.eff.org/IP/Video/ MPAA_DVD_cases/.*

284. Mark Lemley comment in Salon: *http://dir.salon.com/tech/log/2000/08/18/ decss_trial/index.html.*

285. Appeals Court ruling in DVD-CSS case: *http://www.eff.org/IP/Video/ DVDCCA_case/20011101_bunner_appellate_decision.html.*

CHAPTER 11, THE EMPIRES STRIKE BACK

286. *New Scientist* story on China's blocking of blogs: *http:// www.newscientist.com/news/news.jsp?id=ns99993260.*

287. Zittrain/Edelman study of Net-filtering by nations: *http:// cyber.law.harvard.edu/filtering/.*

288. Europe's data privacy laws are much stricter. Asia is relatively lax.

289. Lessig on Stanford's network police, from interview in *Reason* magazine: *http://www.findarticles.com/cf_dls/m1568/2_34/85701100/print.jhtml.*

290. Penguin Press, 2004.

291. See Siva Vaidhyanathan's blog: *http://www.nyu.edu/classes/siva/.* His 2004 book, *The Anarchist in the Library: How the Clash Between Freedom and Control is Hacking the Real World and Crashing the System* (Basic Books), is essential reading for anyone who wants to understand how the forces of central control are creating such havoc with creativity, innovation, and even freedom.

292. Supreme Court's ruling in 1984's Sony v. Universal ("Betamax") case: *http://www.eff.org/Legal/Cases/sony_v_universal_decision.php.*

293. Full text of the DMCA: *http://www.copyright.gov/legislation/dmca.pdf.*

294. Ed Felten, a Princeton University computer science professor, was threatened with legal action if he gave a talk about how easy it would be to break open an experimental music industry file format. See *http:// www.cs.princeton.edu/sip/sdmi/.*

295. Russian software company acquitted (CNET): *http://news.com.com/2100-1023-978176.html.*

296. Lexmark printer company sues ink cartridge maker (CNET): *http://news.com.com/2100-1023-978176.html.*

297. FCC broadcast flag ruling: *http://hraunfoss.fcc.gov/edocs_public/attachmatch/FCC-03-273A1.pdf.*

298. The music industry's difficulties are not due to MP3 file sharing, contrary to the propaganda. It's due at least as much to a reduction in the number of releases and the overall lower quality of music being promoted today, as well as incredibly high prices. Moreover, a deeply researched study (*http://www.unc.edu/~cigar/papers/FileSharing_March2004.pdf*) by professors at Harvard Business School and the University of North Carolina concluded that file sharing has no obvious impact on sales—and that it may actually help promote the music.

299. *Wired News'* coverage of Berman's legislation: *http://www.wired.com/news/politics/0,1283,54153,00.html.*

300. I recommend two superbly researched papers that explain the dangerous confluence of privacy and digital rights management: "DRM and Privacy" (*http://www.law.berkeley.edu/institutes/bclt/drm/papers/cohen-drmandprivacy-btlj2003.html*) by Julie E. Cohen, professor of law at Georgetown University Law Center; and the more recent "The New Surveillance" (*http://papers.ssrn.com/sol3/papers.cfm?abstract_id=527003*) by Sonia Katyal, associate professor at Fordham University School of Law.

301. Patricia Schroeder, a former member of Congress who went on to head the publishing industry's main lobbying organization, famously told *The Washington Post* in 2001 (*http://www.washingtonpost.com/ac2/wp-dyn/A36584-2001Feb7*), "We have a very serious issue with librarians." I've shown this quote to people on many occasions, and the universal response has been sheer disbelief at Schroeder's statement.

302. Congress is moving closer to outlawing peer-to-peer outright, and the entertainment industry keeps suing everyone in sight. In one case, a record company sued a Silicon Valley investor in Napster, alleging contributory infringement; that case has yet to go to trial.

303. Doctorow quote in full: *http://boingboing.net/2004/01/27/protect_your_investm.html*

304. And indeed, Apple has taken things away. In late April 2004, it released an iTunes "update" that, when installed, removed functionality from the software while adding new features. I fully expect that Apple will continue to do this.

305. Full Ross Anderson analysis of trusted computing: *http://www.cl.cam.ac.uk/~rja14/tcpa-faq.html.*

306. Currency, 1999.

307. See *http://www.siliconvalley.com/mld/siliconvalley/5231643.htm.*

308. See *Infoworld*'s coverage: *http://www.infoworld.com/article/04/02/02/ HNchinacensor_1.html.* It's more acceptable to use the Napster defense if you're a big company, apparently.

309. *http://cyberlaw.stanford.edu/lessig/blog/archives/121002%2002-52%2000-185.pdf.*

310. Throughout this section, I've used the word "content" in the broadest sense—that which is created by anyone, not just the entertainment industry. Indeed, it's crucial to recognize that the content users create is more important than what Hollywood creates, especially as we contemplate the architecture of future networks. See Andrew Odlyzko's paper, "Content is Not King," for more on this: *http://www.firstmonday.dk/issues/issue6_2/ odlyzko/#o9.*

311. Electronic Frontier Foundation: *http://www.eff.org.*

312. Creative Commons: *http://www.creativecommons.org.*

313. The interstates are an intriguing mirror image of what's required with data. In the 1950s, America's state and local highways were well-developed. What we needed, and what corporate America couldn't provide, was a system of long-distance roads. Today, the reverse is true: the long-distance data highways, the "backbone" networks, exist in abundance. It's the local roads we need, right up to our homes. Big telecom carriers say they'll provide these connections only if we allow them to control the content that flows on those lines. Imagine if we'd given the interstates to corporations that could decide what kinds of vehicular traffic could use them.

314. FCC Spectrum Policy Task Force: *http://www.fcc.gov/sptf/.*

315. Full text of Powell's 2003 speech on spectrum: *http://www.fcc.gov/ Speeches/Powell/2002/spmkp212.html.*

316. David Reed's home page: *http://www.reed.com/dpr.html.*

317. To get a fuller understanding of Reed's "open spectrum" thinking, start with this essay: *http://www.reed.com/Papers/openspec.html.*

CHAPTER 12, MAKING OUR OWN NEWS

318. A growing body of work is now available under Creative Commons licenses. See *http://creativecommons.org* for more details.

EPILOGUE AND ACKNOWLEDGMENTS

319. Elwin Jenkins' posting: *http://microdoc-news.info/home/BloggerNews/ 2003/04/11.html/1.*

320. Chris Gulker blog: *http://www.gulker.com.*

321. Perseus Books, 2002.

322. Microsoft Word was both useful and infuriating. The Mac version seems to have a severe bug that caused me and my editor no end of trouble. If there was a serious alternative, I'd use it. I note this because I posted a blog comment about the problems I was having, and related what Microsoft's technical support people had told me. (Amazingly, they advised against saving the files in Microsoft's own format.) My blog posting generated an email from one of the programmers at Microsoft who works on the Mac applications. He asked for samples of the corrupted files and said he'd try to figure out what was wrong. I sent the files but didn't hear back from him. Nonetheless, his query was another example of how the new world of information works: he, at least, was paying attention to what was going on in the online world, because it affected his product. I give Microsoft an A for this, even if I give its software a C-minus for its flaws.

# Index

# W

# ABOUT THE AUTHOR

Dan Gillmor is a nationally known columnist for the *San Jose Mercury News*. His column runs in many other U.S. newspapers, and he also writes a daily weblog for SiliconValley.com, an online affiliate of the *Mercury News*. Gillmor has been consistently listed by industry publications as among the most influential journalists in his field and has won or shared in several regional and national journalism awards. *We the Media* is his first book.

# COLOPHON

Mary Brady was the production editor, and Matt Hutchinson was the copyeditor for *We the Media*. Mary Brady was the proofreader. Reg Aubry and Claire Cloutier provided quality control. Ellen Troutman-Zaig wrote the index.

Emma Colby designed the cover of this book and produced the cover layout with Quark Express 4.1.1 and Adobe Photoshop 5.5 using Emigre's Base Twelve font. The image of a woman's gaze is copyrighted by PhotoAlto.

Melanie Wang designed the interior layout. This book was converted by Joe Wizda to FrameMaker 5.5.6. The text font is Adobe's Sabon, which was designed by Jan Tschichold in 1964.